The History of Psychology
and the Behavioral Sciences

ROBERT I. WATSON, SR., Adjunct Professor of Psychology, University of Florida, and Professor of Psychology Emeritus, University of New Hampshire, received his A.B. from Dana College and his A.M. and Ph.D. degrees from Columbia University. Dr. Watson, editor of the *Journal of the History of the Behavioral Sciences* from 1965 to 1974, has also served as Professor of Psychology at Northwestern University and as Associate Professor and Assistant Dean at Washington University School of Medicine. He is Charter President of the Division of the History of Psychology, American Psychological Association, and the author/editor of many books, including *Eminent Contributors to Psychology* (Springer), *Psychology of the Child,* 4th ed., *The Clinical Method in Psychology,* and *The Great Psychologists.* His *Selected Papers on the History of Psychology* was edited by Josef Brozek and Rand B. Evans.

The History of Psychology and the Behavioral Sciences

A Bibliographic Guide

ROBERT I. WATSON, Sr.

University of Florida, Gainesville

SPRINGER PUBLISHING COMPANY
NEW YORK

Springer Publishing Company, Inc.
200 Park Avenue South
New York, N.Y. 10003

78 79 80 81 82 / 10 9 8 7 6 5 4 3 2 1

Library of Congress Cataloging in Publication Data

Watson, Robert Irving, 1909-
    The history of psychology and the behavioral sciences.

    1. Psychology—History—Bibliography. 2. Biology—History—
Bibliography. 3. Psychiatry—History—Bibliography. 4. Social
Sciences—History—Bibliography.
I. Title.
Z7201.W373   [BF81]   016.15'09   77-17371
ISBN 0-8261-2080-6
ISBN 0-8261-2081-4 pbk.

Printed in the United States of America

CONTENTS

PREFACE

The Introduction describes the relationship of this book to two earlier bibliographic volumes; work on the preparation of the latter led me to see the need for a bibliographic guide such as this volume. Another factor leading to its preparation was a desire to make future historical work by behavioral scientists, trained in their disciplines but not in history, a little easier to carry out.

This book profited considerably from the friendly but acute criticism offered by graduate students in a seminar on historical methodology at the University of New Hampshire. They received approximately half of the first version of the manuscript in bits and pieces as it was being prepared. Among their contributions was the preparation of annotations, which, along with those of the writer, were then discussed in the seminar. I owe a debt of gratitude to these participants: Dina Anselmi, Mark Macher, Ronald Michaud, Paul Pinette, Angelyn Spignesi, and Leon Swartzendruber. Richard High, one of my graduate assistants, also prepared a considerable number of these annotations. In many instances, after minor editorial changes, their annotations appear as they were written. Stephanie Bradley-Swift was not only a student in the seminar but, since she also served as my secretary and editorial assistant, prepared annotations, kept track of the manuscript as it began to fall into place, zealously searched out details when omissions became noticeable, and in many unobtrusive ways improved the finished product. On my taking up appointment at the University of Florida, this work was very ably carried on by Cheryl Phillips. To all these individuals go my heartfelt thanks.

R.I.W., Sr.

The History of Psychology
and the Behavioral Sciences

INTRODUCTION

If lengthy titles in rolling Victorian fashion were still in vogue, the title for the present volume might have been *A Guide to the History of Modern Psychology Taking into Consideration the Relevant Aspects of the Histories of the Other Behavioral Sciences: the Influence of Philosophy, Medicine, the Social Sciences, and Literature as They Reciprocally Interpenetrate with Psychology: and the Significance for It of History in General and the History of Science in Particular.*

To open discussion in this fashion is not mere whimsy. The crucial general assumption guiding selection of references to be cited and annotated given in this more detailed title is that the history of psychology is, in fact, interdisciplinary—a crucial point not conveyed by what appears on the title page. Psychology is embedded both in the other behavioral sciences and in other disciplines. So, too, is its history. In becoming a separate discipline, psychology emerged from the matrix of philosophy and continues to have tacit relationships with it. In its early history, at least, it found physiology and physics scientific fields to emulate. Reciprocal interpenetration with medicine, especially with psychiatry, and with the social sciences is an integral aspect of its history.

The very expression, "Behavioral Sciences," mentioned in the extended title was coined to emphasize the interdependence of the empirical aspects of the social sciences—those aspects that attempt to secure data on and to analyze actual behavior of human beings. This emerging field—or fields—embraces a considerable portion of psychology, somewhat less of sociology and cultural anthropology, and some aspects of history, political science, economics, and literature in the more general sense. Although starting from a biological base, physiology and medicine, especially psychiatry, also contribute to and become part of the behavioral sciences.

A study made some years ago in collaboration with Edwin G. Boring[1] supports not only this contention about extension of psychology throughout the behavioral sciences but also can be used to explain something about the background for this volume. The first phase of our study was the selection of over 1,000 individuals

1

(living in the modern period, beginning in the seventeenth century and deceased in 1967 or before) who, in our judgment, had made some sort of contribution to psychology. The cooperation of a panel of psychologists was then secured. Nine judges from various countries were asked to rate each individual against a scale of eminence.

The nine ratings on each name were summed. They ranged from 27 (which occurred when all nine judges gave the highest score of three, indicating that unanimously they considered the individual in question as among the 500 most important) down to the two or three given zero (indicating that no one even recognized the name of the individual). It had been decided in advance that we would report on about the top 500 individuals. With a cut-off score of eleven, 538 names were isolated.

Subsequent studies[2,5] cleared up various uncertainties and omissions about dates of birth and death and added for each of them the important dimensions of major field of endeavor and of nationality.

These eminent contributors to psychology were found to come from extremely diverse fields of endeavor. Only 42 percent were psychologists in the strict sense. Despite efforts to reduce them, 22 more categories were necessary to account for the remaining 58 percent. Philosophers made up 17 percent; physiologists, 10 percent; psychiatrists, 6 percent; biologists, 4 percent; psychoanalysts, 3 percent; and sociologists, physicists, anatomists, anthropologists and neurologists, each 2 percent. But this was still not enough. Nine percent, or nearly one in ten, were found to be most aptly characterized as hypnotist, astronomer-mathematician, mathematician as such, statistician, opthalmologist, educator, chemist, geneticist, layman, theologian, or logician. Absent from these categories is any field of endeavor specifically suggesting a humanistic influence. In part this is accounted for by the decision that the contributions made to the behavioral sciences by literary figures, such as Goethe or Coleridge, could best be expressed by placing them under the rubric of philosopher.

As contended earlier, the history of psychology is inextricably related to the history of many other fields. It would seem to follow that there is an obligation to have the contents of this book reflect this diversity.

The study of eminence that has been described led, in turn, to the preparation of two bibliographic source volumes: *Eminent Contributors to Psychology,* Vol. 1, *A Bibliography of Primary References,*[3] which cites 12,000 selected references to the work of the 538 individuals; and *Eminent Contributors to Psychology,* Vol. 2, *A Bibliography of Secondary References,*[4] which presents over 55,000 references by others to their work.

The eight years of experience in the preparation of these two bibliographic source volumes was a major impetus for writing this book. This experience was also furthered by teaching a graduate historical methodology course each of these years. Students, it might be added, participated in all phases of the work.

The experience in searching out these references now served as guidance in preparing this volume. To try to limit contentually-oriented citations only to those referring to the 538 *Contributors* would, of course, result in a severe bias. Nevertheless, collectively they do give some indication of the inclusion I hoped to encompass. Methodologically, the previous work rendered present selection more expeditious and sound. If a particular bibliographic list, biographic collection, journal source, historical book, or other source cited supplied relevant secondary sources for many of these individuals, it follows that it may be of general significance. Advantage was also taken of a procedure that had been followed before. Fully half of the 55,000 secondary references in Volume 2 had been cited by "short title." The very criteria for inclusion by this means was that six or more of the *Eminent Contributors* were meaningfully discussed in that particular reference. Some of these references would seem worth citing here as of general historical interest.

It was relatively easy to "reverse" the process of reporting for the present work. In the volume of secondary references, report was by individual; now reporting from the most useful books becomes central. Ideas and organization vary in complicated ways, but points of commonality are sufficiently resident in individuals to allow them to serve as indicative of the contents of the book or article. Not only is there value in knowing just who is discussed in a particular book, but there is something more in the way of guidance in selection configuration that is akin to citation analysis. It is a rule of citation analysis that articles that cite the same publication may be suspected of having subject relationship with each other. Provided that one has some background, knowledge collectively of those individuals who are stressed in a particular book tells something more about the book than the mere names. To illustrate, let me quote from a partial annotation of one of the books in one of the sections devoted to substantive history:

Major attention is given to Adler, Bernheim, Bleuler, Breuer,

Charcot, Flournoy, Forel, Jung, Nietzsche, Schopenhauer, and, above all, to Freud and Janet.

From this one sentence alone certain inferences become plausible. Moving from the more to less obvious, it is a book in the history of psychiatry; however, it is not exclusively psychoanalytic in emphasis, since it is concerned with Janet as roughly on a par with Freud, and, as far as the complete list of individuals is concerned, they are all prominently involved with the dynamics of the unconscious. By now I suspect that some readers have inferred that I am quoting from the annotation to Ellenberger's *The Discovery of the Unconscious* (B128)—and they would be right.

This transfer value from previous work does not apply equally throughout all sections of the book. In the main, it occurred in those devoted to "General Resources" and "Historical Accounts," while the three other sections required extensive searching of the literature.

A guide such as this involves a potential paradox. Books and articles devoted primarily to a particular individual are not cited. For example, in connection with schools or systems, it is very hard to resist the temptation to cite papers and books by protagonists themselves: to cite as primary sources William James' *Principles* as a source for understanding his functionalism or to cite Freud's *The Interpretation of Dreams* for his psychoanalysis. And yet, to do so would open up an impossible task—to go back to the primary sources, not only for systems, but also for each historic figure and for every theory and research problem of the modern period. A Guide to the literature cannot be a list of that literature.

Of the 1500 books and articles referred to as being cited by short title in the earlier volume, fewer than 200 are cited and annotated here. It is obvious that severe selectivity has been exercised. On turning back and reviewing these titles once the writing was nearly completed, it became apparent that at least four kinds of references had *not* been selected: those contemporary surveys of the current status of some problem that more or less incidentally referred to historical figures; those works that, at the time of writing, dealt with the topic at hand in a then contemporaneous fashion but are now historical landmarks, such as James' *Principles of Psychology* or Freud's *Introductory Lectures*; those that centered on one individual and yet managed to bring within this context at least several other contributors, such as most biographies and those books and articles whose time span was confined to a century or two, as, for example, Leyden's *Seventeenth Century Metaphysics,* Sabra's *Theories of Light from Descartes to Newton,* or Stephen's *History of English Thought in the Eighteenth Century.*

Sources of information for the historian of psychology and the behavioral sciences are annotated as incisively as possible and, when pertinent, in terms of the period or area, the emphases given, any unique features, and, in many instances, the major historical figures considered. The absence of an annotation is not an indication of lesser significance. Sometimes the topic is so adequately reflected in the title, for example, that comment is unnecessary.

I have tried to be as catholic as possible in selecting a diversity of references. It is almost, but not quite, needless to say that inclusion is not to be construed as personal endorsement on my part. I have tried to include only literature respected in some academic quarters, but inclusion should not be interpreted as supporting with enthusiasm and with a sense of essential rightness each and every reference included. I do allow my enthusiasm to show occasionally; I try to hide my distastes. Probably the three most controversial areas are those sections labeled quantitative methods, historiographic theory, and a specific section of the narrative concerning *Verstehen.* Some historians with invidious intent may translate the first as the literature of the "quantifiers," the second as that of "philosophers," and the third as that of "intuitionists." Some historians will view any or all of these sections as representing a literature that in many instances is so irrelevant to their own practice as to be a waste of time. My hope is that a particular user of this guide will find some references valuable and then grant that another user might find a quite different array of references also of use.

Brevity is the soul of annotation. Its goal is a modest one—to identify contents in such fashion as to allow the reader to see whether he wishes to go further. This admonition was followed despite at least occasionally having to interpret an issue rich in complexity in the baldest possible terms. Only one annotation is as long as a printed page; most of them are but a few lines.

There are five major sections in this Guide: Section A: "General Resources," with subsections exemplified by bibliographies and biographical collections; Section B: "Historical Accounts," subdivided into various fields—psychology, science, philosophy, and the like; Section C: "Methods of Historical Research," with major division into the analytical-narrative and quantitative methods; Section D: "Historiographic Fields," with literature concerning the way the historical fields are interpreted by historians and others; and Section E: "Historiographic Theories," with subsections exemplified by speculative theories of history, the nature of explanation, and the dynamic theories of historical change.

There are nearly 800 titles cited and almost as many annotations supplied. These titles generated over 350 cross-citations.

REFERENCES

1. Annin, Edith L., Boring, E. G., & Watson, R. I. Important psychologists, 1600-1967. *J. Hist. behav. Sci.,* 1968, *4,* 303-315.
2. Merrifield, Marilyn R., & Watson, R. I. Eminent psychologists: Corrections and additions. *J. Hist. behav. Sci.,* 1970, *6,* 261-262.
3. Watson, R. I., Sr. *Eminent contributors to psychology.* Vol. 1. *A bibliography of primary references.* New York: Springer, 1974.
4. Watson, R. I., Sr. *Eminent contributors to psychology.* Vol. 2. *A bibliography of secondary references.* New York: Springer, 1976.
5. Watson, R. I., & Merrifield, Marilyn R. Characteristics of individuals eminent in psychology in temporal perspective: Part I. *J. Hist. behav. Sci.,* 1973, *9,* 339-359.

A. GENERAL RESOURCES

General resources available to historians of psychology and of the behavioral sciences are grouped under the headings, "Guides to the Literature," "Encyclopedias," "Bibliographies," "Biographical Collections," "Dictionaries," "Archives and Manuscript Collections," and "Journal Bibliographies." Resources in each of these categories are, in turn, cited and annotated.

GUIDES TO THE LITERATURE

The guides that are available are not often specifically directed to the historian. They are apt to be of a more general nature and embrace the literature for a particular subject field, be it philosophy, psychology, the social sciences, or whatever. However, there are guides for history in general, the history of medicine, the history of education, and the history of science.

As might be expected, general guides tend to contain some material relevant to later, more specific resource categories. For example, guides may include a chapter on bibliography, or give a list of relevant journals, or annotate some dictionaries. When a separate section of a guide is considered especially valuable, it is cited again in a relevant, more specific category.

Many other so-called "guides," prepared by historians, use the term in another sense. These guides, while perhaps giving some incidental attention to general resources, are devoted primarily either to the techniques of critical appraisal of historical document sources or to ways of presenting findings in articles or books in the usual narrative form. These kinds of guides are discussed under the subheading, "Critical Analysis–Narrative Methods," in Section C: "Historical Methods."

A1   Borchardt, D. H. *How to find out in philosophy and psychology*. Oxford: Pergamon Press, 1968.

A succinct guide to pertinent materials in philosophy and psychology that includes accounts of biographical dictionaries, encyclopedias, general retrospective bibliographies, current bibliographies and reviewing journals, national bibliographies, bibliographies of specialized fields, and, an unusual feature, the pertinent societies and organizations. The interesting narrative style with chapter headings and organization makes it possible to read it through rather than referring to it to meet a particular need. By the same token, one unfamiliar with its contents would find it relatively more difficult to use for specific reference search.

A2   Brickman, W. W. *Guide to research in educational history.* New York: New York University Bookstore, 1949.

The author lists relevant general works, bibliographies, periodicals, and sources of collections. He also discusses the application of historical research methods to educational problems, with attention paid to various problems of historical analysis, and he offers practical advice on note taking, documentation, and the organization of written reports.

A3   Chandler, G. *How to find out: A guide to sources of information for all fields; arranged by the Dewey Decimal Classification.* (3rd ed.) Oxford: Pergamon Press, 1967. (1963)

A worthwhile introductory guide is provided that is particularly useful when one is required to make an excursion into a scholarly field in which one is not a professional.

A4   Clarke, E. (Ed.), *Modern methods in the history of medicine.* London: Athlone Press, 1971.

This collection includes papers devoted to the historiography of persons, the social relations of medicine, the relation of the histories of science to those of medicine, a critique of medical biography, the application of statistical and graphical methodology, automation of bibliographies, the uses of and problems encountered in oral histories, and ways of developing collections of primary source material.

A5   Daniel, R. S., & Louttit, C. M. *Professional problems in psychology.* New York: Prentice-Hall, 1953.

In part this is a revision and expansion of Louttit's *Handbook of Psychological Literature* (A9). Introductory and final sections deal with development of, orientation within, and professional problems of psychology (the latter specifically dealing with fields, organizations, responsibilities, and the academic psychologist). The main sections of the book offer surveys of the literature in psychology, bibliographic problems (sources and construction), library usage, and reporting research (planning, writing and formal preparation of manuscripts, theses, etc.). Several very useful appendices (e.g., a bibliography of journals in psychology) are included, as well as indices.

A6   De George, R. T. *A guide to philosophical bibliography and research.* New York: Appleton-Century-Crofts, 1971.

The title reflects the contents. Relevant dictionaries, encyclopedias, bibliographies, serials, and biographies are annotated. The subdivisions in each category have been worked out in some detail. In addition to division by temporal period (ancient, medieval, and so on), categorization is also by country, by particular branches of philosophy, and by names of individual philosophers. Bibliographies of standard texts are annotated within each of these major categories. Relatively unusual annotated sections on philosophical research, publishing problems, sources of doctoral dissertations, and philosophical life (e.g., organizations) are noteworthy. Subject and name indices are supplied.

A7   Elliott, C. K. *A guide to the documentation of psychology.* London: Bingley, 1971.

Despite a disclaimer that the historian will find it of little value, this is one of the better introductory guides for psychology. The first three chapters consider the nature of psychology, the use of the library as a bibliographic tool, and the various functions of information considered to be conceptual, empirical, and procedural. The sequence of search method—preliminaries, retrieval systems, evaluation, final reporting, etc.—is specifically dealt with in one chapter. The final chapter offers advice on keeping up with current materials. The text includes several appendices: lists of organizations, journals, and newsletters; and selected bibliographies for handbooks, dictionaries, similar sources, and guides. The one short index, by subject only, would have been more useful if expanded; even more useful would have been the inclusion of an author index.

A8   Ennis, Bernice. *Guide to the literature in psychiatry.* Los
Angeles, Calif.: Partridge Press, 1971.

This *Guide* serves the purpose for which it was prepared. It discusses the relevant journals in some detail;
under the heading of "Information Sources," it annotates
indexes, abstracts, dictionaries, obituary sources, and the
like; it describes books, catalogs, book review sources,
bibliographies, and monographs listed by titles within each
list; it provides a section on nonbook material such as pamphlets, audiovisual aids, and descriptions of various archive
collections and government documents; it considers con-
trolled circulation publication, e.g., publications of various
pharmaceutical houses; it provides a directory of trans-
lators and a partial list of translated works, and it gives a
description of selected psychiatric libraries; it lists publishers; and it closes with an unannotated list of about 350
book titles catagorized under headings such as adolescence,
aesthetics, child psychiatry, and history.

A9   Louttit, C. M. *Handbook of psychological literature.*
Bloomington, Ind.: Principia Press, 1932.

As a guide to the literature circa 1930, Louttit is still
useful for the historian despite a related, more modern
volume (A5). In a thorough, accurate manner it describes
journals (their history, distribution, and, in an appendix,
their source, original date, etc.), institutional publications,
general reference works, indexes, bibliographies, abstracts,
and library services. A subject and an author index are
provided.

A10   Poulton, Helen J. *The historian's handbook: A descriptive
guide to reference works.* Assist. Marguerite S. Howland.
Foreword W. S. Shepperson. Norman, Okla.: University of
Oklahoma Press, 1972.

This is a guide to reference works useful for the historian. It is divided by categories, into catalogs (national,
trade, and world); guides (general, U.S., ancient, modern,
and by country and region); encyclopedias and dictionaries;
almanacs, statistical guides and current surveys, serials and
newspapers; geographical aids; biographical materials;
manuscript collections, diaries and dissertations; legal
sources; and government publications.

A11   Sarton, G. *Horus: A guide to the history of science: A first guide for the study of the history of science with introductory essays on science and tradition.* New York: Ronald Press, 1952.

A major guide in its field, despite a higher level of sophistication achieved since its publication in 1952. It provides a broad, general overview of resources available for research in the history of science. It includes annotations on works concerned with historical methods, encyclopedias, biographical collections, articles and books on scientific methods and the philosophy of science, works on the mutual impact of society and science, catalogues of scientific literature, scientific journals classified by century of original appearance, abstracting and review journals, academic and scientific societies, and then books on the general history of science classified as reference handbooks and instruments, and, listed by country and by temporal period, histories of the special sciences, journals on the history of the philosophy of science, and organization of the study and teaching of the history of science in terms of societies, teaching institutes, international congresses, and prizes for work in the field. Before the portion of the book serving as guide, the author presents three lectures on the purpose and meaning of the history of science.

A12   White, C. M., & associates. *Sources of information in the social sciences: A guide to the literature.* (2nd ed.) Chicago: American Library Association, 1973. (1964)

The first, or general, section of the book considers social science literature that cuts across the various disciplines (reviews, abstracts, bibliography of bibliographies, general bibliographies) and contains discussion of the development of bibliographic expertise and the influence of electronic retrieval upon bibliographic problems. This is followed by other major sections devoted respectively to history, psychology, sociology, anthropology, political science, and education, each one prepared by a subject-matter specialist. Each specialist presents an exposition of the literature of his field and its various subdivisions while evaluating the selected references. For each specific field, a library specialist also presents a related section on guides, monographs, review abstracts, bibliographic and biographical sources, dictionaries, handbooks, encyclopedias, films etc., systematic works, histories, theoretical statements, assessments of the field, organizations, and sources of current information. An excellent index—by subject, author, and title—permits rapid identification of discussions throughout the text that apply to more than the specializations under which they are grouped.

ENCYCLOPEDIAS

The references that follow are selected as meeting the criteria of being reasonably complete compendia of knowledge of whatever area they purport to cover and of being pertinent to the goals of this guide. The alphabetical order followed is of title, since most are better known than are the names of their editors.

A13 *Dictionary of American history.* (2nd rev. ed.) (5 vols + index) Ed. J. T. Adams. New York: Scribner's, 1942-1961. (1940) Vol. 6. *Supplement One.* Ed. J. G. Hopkins & W. Andrews. New York: Scribner's, 1961.

　　The original five-volume set consisted of over 6000 entries concerned with all aspects (except biographical) of the history of United States, from 1600 to 1940. Articles are arranged alphabetically; most of them are brief, but some are longer summary articles of successions of events. Usually each has a short bibliography. The index is useful for finding a particular aspect of American history with which one is concerned.

A14 *Dictionary of the history of ideas: Studies of selected pivotal ideas.* (4 vols.) Ed. P. P. Wiener. New York: Scribner's, 1968, 1973.

　　Short essays, with topics ranging from abstraction to *Zeitgeist,* were solicited from various scholars judged to have an awareness of the cultural and historical affiliations of their disciplines. There is a short analytic table of contents. The history of ideas about human nature, and about history and historiography, are two of the six major categories. There is no index.

A15 *Dictionary of philosophy and psychology, including many* *of the principal conceptions of ethics, logic, aesthetics, philosophy of religion, mental pathology, anthropology, biology, neurology, physiology, economics, political and social philosophy, philology, physical science and education, and giving a terminology in English, French, German and Italian.* (Vols. 1 & 2) Ed. J. M. Baldwin. New York: Macmillan, 1901. (Reprinted Gloucester, Mass.: Peter Smith, 1960)

These monumental volumes were prepared with the assistance of an international panel from various fields, making up a distinguished list of collaborators numbering about 75. It is an authoritative source for the period preceding the turn of the century and still essential for many historical problems. In part it is a dictionary, in that words are defined; in larger measure it is an encyclopedia in that the articles go into considerable detail. The concepts, the meanings, and the like are presented within the context of the then current intellectual movements. It contains, roughly in order of entry length, concise definitions, very short biographies, definitions supplemented by some explanations and exemplifications, and longer essays of up to about 5,000 words. The inclusion of references to the pertinent literature tends to be confined to articles in the last two categories. Volume 3 of the *Dictionary,* the bibliography prepared by Rand (A48) in two parts, is considered in the section devoted to bibliographies.

A16   *Encyclopaedia britannica.* (14th ed.) (24 vols.) Ed. Walter Yust. Chicago: Encyclopaedia Britannica, 1973.

For factual accuracy on general matters beyond the specialized competence of the user, the *Encyclopaedia Britannica* is still the best authority. There has been too little experience with the entirely new format of the 1974 edition to give an informed opinion. This latest edition may prove to be needlessly complicated, since there are three sets of volumes: the *Macropaedia* (19 vols.) with extended treatment of alphabetically-arranged topics; the *Micropaedia* (10 vols.), short capsules (750 words or less), topically arranged; and the *Propaedia,* the "outline of knowledge and guide" to the main volumes of the *Britannica.* The *Propaedia,* planned under the direction of M. Adler, is highly reminiscent of his *Syntopicon* (A20). The purpose of the new edition and its format are purported to be a retention of the reference function and utility while providing more "educational" experience.

A17   *The encyclopedia of philosophy.* (8 vols.) Ed. P. Edwards, et al. New York: Macmillan, 1967.

For philosophy, this series is the successor to Baldwin's *Dictionary* (A48). It includes Eastern and Western philosophy from ancient to modern times, as well as a consideration of theories that have an impact upon philosophy, in the fields of mathematics, physics, biology, sociology, psychology, and religion. The articles included discuss nearly 1,500 pertinent concepts, words, schools, and themes in the above-mentioned fields, and include biographical material on 150 of the 538 *Contributors.* With respect to the schools of philosophical thought, it presents rather lengthy statements of their development, their major tenets, and criticisms. Short bibliographies follow most articles. A subject/name index is to be found in the last volume.

A18   *Encyclopaedia of the social sciences.* (15 vols.) Ed. E. R. A. Seligman. New York: Macmillan, 1930-1935.

A definitive survey of the social sciences, circa 1930, prepared under the auspices of many learned societies. Volume 1 presents an introduction in about 300 pages of the historical emergence of the social sciences and provides an analysis of national trends in these fields. Throughout the volumes, concepts and problems in political science, economics, anthropology, law, sociology, and psychology, and the social aspects of related subjects, are covered. It deals with history "only to the extent that historical methods or episodes are of especial importance to the student of societies" (1, p. xix). Brief biographical articles on 4,000 individuals make up a considerable portion of the contents. Bibliographies for all articles are provided. Cross-references and a subject index are included.

A19   *An encyclopedia of world history: Ancient, medieval, and modern, chronologically arranged.* (4th rev. ed.) Ed. W. L. Langer. Boston: Houghton Mifflin, 1968.

This volume is chronologically arranged in connected narrative form. Nine hundred pages are devoted to the modern period, divided into "Early Modern," "Nineteenth Century," "First World War," "Inter-War Period," and the

"World since 1939." Subdivisions vary according to the nature of the material. It is primarily devoted to political, diplomatic, and military history. Specific dates are often given. A detailed index is provided.

A20 *The great ideas: A syntopicon of great books of the western world.* (2 vols.) Ed. M. J. Adler. Chicago: Encyclopaedia Britannica, 1952.

While the *Syntopicon* is concerned with ideas and thus conventionally distinguishable from the dictionary (which is more concerned with words), and from the encyclopedia (which is more concerned with facts), it does no great violence to list this unique work in the present category. The *Syntopicon,* volumes 2 and 3 of the 54 volumes of the *Great Books,* takes 102 painstakingly selected "ideas" through time, with the ambitious aim of finding the unity and continuity of Western thought through its major common themes. Citations of the pages, paragraphs, and lines where particular topics are being discussed are given for the works included. Additional sources, both from additional works of authors of the literature in the volumes of the *Great Books* and from authors not so represented, are given at the end of each "idea" section. By a conservative estimate, at least one-third of the "ideas" are pertinent to the history of the behavioral sciences; a limited illustrative sample of these includes "animal," "cause," "desire," "experience," "habit," "idea," "man," "medicine," "mind," "philosophy," "science," "soul," and "will." A detailed outline for each "idea" has been prepared. The topics for the idea of "man," for example, are definitions of man; man's knowledge of man (including a subdivision on the science of human nature); constitution; and analysis of human nature into faculties, and their order and harmony, individual differences, and group variations. A detailed inventory of terms serves as an index at the end of the second volume.

A21 *Historical tables: 58 B.C.-A.D. 1963.* (8th ed.) Ed. S. H. Steinberg. Foreword G. P. Gooch. London: Macmillan, 1966.

A chronology is given of what was going on in a given age, in terms of events and persons living at that time. For most time periods, there is a six-column arrangement, showing relations of the major powers, ecclesiastical history, constitutional and economic history, and cultural life. There is no index.

A22   *Historisches Wörterbuch der Philosophie.* Ed. J. R. Ritter. Basel: Schwabe, 1971-.

This is a cooperative venture, involving more than seven hundred contributors, including a considerable number of psychologists. It is anticipated that one volume will be added each year. Both philosophically rooted and contemporary terms are defined, and the varieties or branches of psychology are discussed. There are no biographical entries, but bibliographies are provided liberally.

A23   *International encyclopedia of the social sciences.* (17 vols.) Ed. D. L. Sills. New York: Macmillan & Free Press, 1968.

This series is the successor to the *Encyclopaedia of the Social Sciences* (A18), but it is designed to complement, not to supplant it. This magnificently edited, well-written series coordinates the efforts of 1,500 social scientists from 30 countries. It is organized alphabetically, with extensive cross-references. Often specific articles are grouped under a more general title. It defines terms, concepts, theories, and empirical areas of research for various fields, including anthropology, psychiatry, psychology, sociology, and statistics. Major emphasis is upon the analytical and comparative aspects of the topic; historical material is included only as illustrative. Often the same topic is approached by different subject-matter specialists. Biographies number 600, including those for about 150 of the *Contributors.* Bibliographies and a detailed 350-page index are provided.

A24   *Psychologisches Wörterbuch.* (8th ed.) Ed. F. Dorsch, et al. Hamburg: Meiner, 1970.

More than a dictionary and less than an encyclopedia, this widely used book has the style of the latter in a manner reminiscent of the *Dictionary* of Baldwin (A15). Three-fifths of the volume deals with alphabetically-arranged terms and concepts, with numerous cross-references. The appendices include a 40-page listing of psychological books.

A25   *Wörterbuch der philosophischen Begriffe und Ausdrücke, quellenmässig bearbeitet.* (4th ed.) (3 vols.) Ed. R. Eisler & K. Roretz. Berlin: Mittler, 1927-1930. (1899)

By the time it had reached the fourth edition cited here, this work had gone beyond its beginning as a dictionary and emerged as the most influential German philosophical encyclopedia of its time.

BIBLIOGRAPHIES OF BOOKS, ARTICLES, AND RETRIEVAL SYSTEMS

For books, the printed catalogues of the great national libraries, the *British Museum* (A59), the *Bibliotheque Nationale* (A53), and the *Library of Congress* (A139) come closest to achieving bibliographic universality. The historical fact of the later national unification of Germany means that we lack a comparable German source, thus creating a problem still not completely overcome. For both books and articles in the behavioral sciences, *Psychological Abstracts* (A118) and the earlier *Psychological Index* (A120) are invaluable.

Since about 160 bibliographic items are to be cited, these major sources just mentioned and about 20 other bibliographies especially pertinent to a search for the literature concerning the history of the behavioral sciences have been identified by an asterisk following the reference number. Of course, under specific circumstances any reference may prove to be the most useful.

By the time a bibliography appears in book form, it is out of date. From the perspective of consideration of time lag, there are at least three kinds of bibliographies. An illustration from British sources will be used. There is a major source in the *British Museum Catalogue* (A59), which covers its holdings to 1955. A supplementary source is the *British National Bibliography* (A61), which is based on books from 1951 to date deposited in the *British Museum* and reported by annual and monthly cumulations. An annual source is in *British Books in Print* (A58). The *English Catalogue of Books* (A81) fills a gap of a century before *British National Bibliography* took over. There are even sources that announce books to be published in the future, as is the case with Whitaker's *Books of the Month and Books to Come* (A55).

A review of some of the kinds of sources of bibliographic information to be encountered is worthwhile, since foreknowledge makes for efficiency when consulting these references. In addition to the national bibliographies of books and articles already referred to, there is a great number of bibliographies concerned with special topics, such as philosophical literature, American history, psychohistory, or unpublished doctoral dissertations. Books and articles on bibliographies as tools are also cited.

Bibliographies from computer retrieval systems are cited. These are produced by entering a larger, more heterogeneous reference storage unit with some entry key that isolates the titles pertinent to the problem for which the search is being made. Their major current weakness is the relatively short time span covered by the available data banks. Few, if any, take bibliographic material back ten years into the past. Retrieval systems for quantitative material will be referred to in later sections concerned with quantitative methods.

Bibliographies of biographies and autobiographies are presented in the next category, "Biographical Collections," although certain major biographical sources are cross-referenced. Similarly, bibliographies of journals as such (as distinguished from articles in the journals) are given in a still later section, "Journal Bibliographies."

In the references that follow, alphabetical entry by title or by institutional source rather than by author or editor is the most convenient and meaningful one to follow, despite an awkwardness created for a few sources. This arrangement is made even more desirable by the fact that some publishers do not list editors or compilers by name.

A26   *American bibliography: A chronological dictionary of all books, pamphlets and periodical publications printed in the United States of America from the genesis of printing in 1639.* (12 vols.) Ed. C. Evans, et al. New York: Peter Smith, 1941-1942.

    A year-by-year record to 1800 is provided with subject, author, and publisher's index. See *American Bibliography: A Preliminary Checklist for 1801-1819* (A27) for a continuation.

A27   *American bibliography: A preliminary checklist for 1801-1819.* (23 vols.) Comp. R. R. Shaw & R. H. Shoemaker. New York: Scarecrow Press, 1958.

    A continuation of *American bibliography* (A26), covering the period between 1801 and 1819, this listing includes specifications of locations of copies. Title, author indices, and corrections and addenda are provided. No annotations are given. See *A Checklist of American Imprints* (A65) for a continuation.

A28   *American catalog of books, 1876-1910.* (9 vols. in 13 parts) Ed. F. Leypoldt. New York: Publishers Weekly, 1876-1910. This is a standard catalog for the period in question.

A29   *American social history before 1860.* Comp. G. N. Grob. New York: Appleton-Century-Crofts, 1970.
       A bibliography is supplied in which the compiler deliberately excluded material on intellectual history by using categories of classification that stressed the social institutions, e.g., immigration, religion, reform, education, medicine and health, and journalism (but not science). It is a companion volume to *American Social History since 1860* (A30).

A30   *American social history since 1860.* Comp. R. H. Bremner (assist. R. M. Friedman & D. B. Schewe). New York: Appleton-Century-Crofts, 1971.
       Social history is an admittedly loosely-defined area. For present purposes, it is defined by the following account of the volume's content headings: bibliographic guides, general surveys by periods such as "Civil War and Reconstruction"; sectional histories, such as "New England," the "southern States," and so on; "The Rise of the City"; "The American People," including sections on "Social Classes," "Immigration," "Negroes," "Women"; "The American," "His Work," "His Attitudes Toward Other Americans"; "His Religious Life"; "Social and Political Thought"; "Social Problems and Reform Movements"; "Cultural Life"; "Education and Intellectual Trends"; "Communication"; and "Science" with 17 references in the subsection "Social and Behavioral Sciences." It is a companion volume to *American Social History Before 1860* (A29).

A31   *L'Année psychologique,* 1894-, *1-.*
       Each volume of this journal contains a bibliography. Between 1894 and 1904, citations only are given; thereafter, abstracted French references predominate, but a certain number of English and German ones are also included.

A32   Annotated bibliographic sources in the history of psychol-

ogy. R. A. Bagg. In Mary Henle, J. Jaynes, & J. J. Sullivan
(Eds.), *Historical conceptions of psychology.* New York:
Springer, 1973, pp. 295-304.

A compact statement of the important and commonly-
available biographic and bibliographic sources for the psychologist.

A33   *Annual review of psychology.* Stanford, Calif.: Annual
Reviews, 1950-.

These solicited evaluative reviews of current work in
research areas in psychology cover a specified number of
years on a regular, scheduled basis, with excellent bibliographies, each with a limited time span as a by-product.
Hence, historical setting is ignored except for the very
immediate past just preceding the period being considered.

A34   *Author index to Psychological index (1894-1935) and
Psychological abstracts (1927-1958).* (5 vols.+supplements).
Boston: Hall, 1960-1968. (Supplements. Washington, D.C.:
American Psychological Association, 1969-.)

This is exclusively an author index, in which published
works by an individual from 1894 onward are cited. In
cases of joint authorship, only the primary author is credited. The use of "anon.," "Various," etc., for entry identification, errors in alphabetical placement, inconsistencies
in citations, and different spellings for foreign names are
among sources of difficulty in using it to find references.
The original five volumes brought together 320,000 entries
into a single alphabetical arrangement. Supplements bring
the literature coverage up to the recent past. The *Psychological Abstracts* (A118) themselves have to be used for
the years not yet covered by supplements.

A35   *Bibliographic index: A cumulative bibliography of bibliographies.* New York: Wilson, 1938-.

Published semiannually since 1951, bibliographies
found from a search of nearly 2,000 periodicals, parts of
books, and books are reported. They are mainly in English
and cover at least a specified minimum number of titles
(which has varied). Subject headings for many fields of
knowledge under which the bibliographies are presented
narrow the search process considerably.

A36*   *Bibliographie der deutschen Zeitschriftenliteratur.* (128 vols.) New York: Kraus Reprint, 1961-1964. (1896-1964)

   This is an annual, reporting articles in periodical sources in all fields from 1861 to 1964, by subject and author entry. Many means of saving space are utilized, making it difficult to use until the citation system is mastered. Journal titles are truncated, with a table for the finding of full titles. Author index refers to a key word within the title, which necessitates going back to the subject index. There is a companion series for non-German periodicals, *Bibliographie der fremdsprachigen Zeitschriftenliteratur* (A38). As of 1965, this series became part of *Internationale Bibliographie der Zeitschriftenliteratur* (A102).

A37   *Bibliographie der deutschprachigen psychologischen Literatur.* Ed. J. Dambauer. Frankfurt: Klosterman, 1971-.

   An annual of German psychological literature for books and articles, beginning with the literature of 1971.

A38*   *Bibliographie der fremdsprachigen Zeitschriftenliteratur.* (51 vols.) New York: Kraus Reprint, 1961-1964. (1911-1964)

   This is a companion series to *Bibliographie der deutschen Zeitschriftenliteratur* (A36) for the citation of scientific periodical literature other than in German sources. See its annotation for comments about arrangement and use. As of 1965, it was incorporated into *Internationale Bibliographie der Zeitschriftenliteratur* (A102).

A39   *Bibliographie de la litterature française du dix-huitième siècle.* (3 vols.) Ed. A. Ciorianescu. Paris: Centre Nationale de la Recherche Scientifique, 1969.

   Selected French references, including articles, chapters, and books, for literature published during the 18th century. Primary references of eminent individuals (e.g., Voltaire) are followed by relevant secondary references, their works, presented alphabetically by author under subheadings (e.g., *L'homme*). There is an author index.

A40   *Bibliographie de la philosophie.* (10 vols.) Paris: International Institute of Philosophy, 1937-1953.

Abstracts of philosophical books published throughout the world, superseded after 1953 by *Bibliographie de la philosophie* (A41).

A41   *Bibliographie de la philosophie.* Paris: Vrin, 1954-.

This quarterly presents abstracts of new philosophical books and bibliographical information on reprint editions throughout the world. See *Philosopher's index* (A114) for articles almost exclusively from British and American periodicals. It supersedes *Bibliographie de la philosophie* (A40).

A42   *Bibliographie der psychologischen Literatur der sozialistischen Länder.* Berlin: Volk u. Wissen, 1961/62-.

This series gives a yearly coverage of books and articles from East Germany, the Soviet Union, Bulgaria, Czechoslovakia, Hungary, and Poland and presents details in either German or Russian. Volume contents run two or three years behind dates of publication.

A43*   *Bibliography of bibliographies on psychology, 1900-1927.* Comp. C. M. Louttit. Washington: National Research Council, 1928. Reprinted Franklin, 1970.

Over 2,000 bibliographies that meet the criteria of no less than 50 references, a high rating for completeness of coverage, and a historical orientation are identified. It is arranged by author, with subject index, including numerous cross-references. Since the *Psychological Abstracts* (A118) has been published since 1927 and carries an index entry on bibliographies, a reasonably complete coverage from 1900 is assured if both are used. See also *Cumulated Subject Index to Psychological Abstracts, 1927-1960* (A69).

A44   *Bibliography: Current state and future trends.* Ed. R. B. Downs & F. B. Jenkins. Urbana, Ill.: University of Illinois Press, 1967.

A general review of bibliographic control is presented in a collection of papers. It includes selected bibliographies as examples of recommended procedure. The articles on problems in psychology by Daniels capture very well the current concern with informal methods of information exchange, especially the efforts to keep up with the very latest developments and the need for cooperative efforts to improve efficiency in information retrieval.

A45 *Bibliography and the historian: The conference at Belmont of the Joint Committee on Bibliographical Services to History, May 1967.* Ed. D. H. Perman. Santa Barbara, Calif.: CLIO, 1968.

A series of articles on bibliographic aids for the historian, with emphasis on new and emerging technologies and services.

A46* *Bibliography of the history of medicine, 1964-1969.* (Annual supplements) Bethesda, Md.: National Library of Medicine, 1971-.

A cumulation volume for four previous yearly volumes starts the series, with annual supplements provided thereafter. It is divided into sections devoted to biographies (medical and related nonmedical); subjects (various diseases, specialties, and institutions by chronologic or geographical subheadings); and the authors of publications cited in the earlier two parts. Cross-references are given. The more relevant subject headings are historiography, neurology, philosophy, physiology, psychiatry, and psychology. Coverage is excellent.

A47 *Bibliography of the history of medicine of the United States and Canada, 1939-1960.* (2nd ed.) Ed. Genevieve Miller. Baltimore, Md.: Johns Hopkins, 1964.

A one-volume consolidation of the bibliography that has been published annually since 1940 in the *Bulletin of the History of Medicine.* Included are sections on biography, journals, diseases, libraries, museums, local history, medical education, medical science and specialties, primitive medicine, professional history, and public health. A section for psychiatry is conspicuously absent, although a few pertinent references are to be found.

A48* Bibliography of philosophy, psychology, and cognate subjects. Ed. B. Rand. In J. M. Baldwin (Ed.), *Dictionary of philosophy and psychology.* (Vol. 3 in 2 parts.) New York: Macmillan, 1905.

A definitive, pioneer effort, this listing was unsurpassed

for its time. The first part lists unannotated general bibliographies, dictionaries, and periodicals and then turns to
histories of philosophy, classified by period and country:
the bulk of the volume, however, is taken up with primary
and secondary books and articles of individual philosophers,
including about 70 individuals from among the *Eminent
Contributors.* The second part gives unannotated references for various systematic fields of philosophy: logic,
aesthetics, philosophy of religion, ethics, and psychology.
The bibliography on psychology takes up nearly half the
volume. The general sections are labeled bibliography,
dictionaries, periodicals, collections and proceedings,
history, systems and essays, experimental and physiological
psychology, child psychology, individual and social psychology, comparative psychology, abnormal and criminal
psychology. The 26 so-called "special bibliographies" that
follow are content-oriented. Representative are the brain
and its functions, emotion and feeling, memory and association, mind and body, nervous system, psychophysics,
self-consciousness and personality, sensation and the senses,
will, work, and fatigue. For Part 2, a lack of author index
and the vagaries of classification make it relatively hard to
search for the work of a particular individual.

A49   A bibliography of psychohistory. Faye Sinofsky, J. J. Fitz-
        patrick, L. W. Potts, & L. de Mause. *Hist. Childhood Quart.,*
        1975, *2,* 517-562.
            This is the most comprehensive bibliography with this
        approach that has yet been published, including, as it does,
        1300 citations without annotations. It is divided into sev-
        eral areas: Methodology and General; History of Child-
        hood; Ancient, Medieval and Renaissance; Modern; and
        Asia. Future bibliographies will presumably be able to im-
        prove upon these rather uninformative, loose, descriptive
        area categorizations.

A50   *Bibliography and research manual of the history of math-
        ematics.* K. O. May. Toronto: University of Toronto Press,
        1973.
            This bibliography is preceded by an introductory
        manual on methodology, which considers problems of in-
        formation retrieval, developing one's personal store of in-
        formation, and historical analysis. The bibliography pri-

marily lists citations, but there are a few annotations. It is divided into sections devoted to biography (biographical collections, reference sources, and, in the case of the majority of references, listing by persons); mathematics, topics in mathematics (algebra, calculus, statistics, etc.), topics external to, but related to mathematics (astronomy, calculating machines, education, instruments); historical (temporal period, countries, organizations) and information retrieval (bibliography, collections, historiography, information systems, libraries, manuscripts, museums, and reference materials). An annotated list of serials closes the volume.

A51   Bibliography of works in the philosophy of history, 1945-1957. J. C. Rule. *Hist. Theory.*, 1961, Beiheft 1.

A definitive bibliography for the aspects and years covered, but the announced exclusions, e.g., Marxist interpretations, should be taken into consideration. It is arranged alphabetically by authors within each calendar year, with books preceding journal articles. An index of names and subjects is supplied.

A52   Bibliography of works in the philosophy of history, 1958-1961. M. Nowicki. *Hist. Theory*, 1964, Beiheft 3.
See (A51) for details.

A53*   *Bibliothèque Nationale: Catalogue general des livres imprimés.* Vols. 1-80, Paris: Catin. Vols. 81-, Paris: Imprimerie Nationale, 1924- (+ supplements, Paris: Bibliothèque Nationale, 1965-).

Although there are over 200 volumes in the main set, this reference work is still not complete. Books (mainly in French but also including some in English, German, and other languages) are arranged alphabetically by author. Supplemental volumes begun in 1960-1964 are planned quinquennially, to keep the catalogue up to date.

Bibliographical memoirs: National Academy of Sciences.
(A158)

A54*   *Biographisch-literarisches Handwörterbuch.* (7 vols. in 21 parts +) Ed. J. C. Poggendorff, et al. Leipzig: Barth, 1863-.
The biographical information that is given is just

enough to identify the individual. The intent of this series is to supply a complete primary bibliographical listing of articles and books for each individual. One special volume is devoted to a listing of secondary literature about some of the individuals. Emphasis is on German-language publications.

A55 *Books of the month and books to come.* London: Whitaker, 1970-.
This is a monthly publication.

A56 *Bowker serials bibliography supplement 1974. To Ulrich's International periodicals directory, 15th edition and Irregular serials and annuals, 3rd edition.* New York: Bowker, 1974.
The purpose of this supplement, which is published intermittently, is to add to and expand information provided by *Ulrich's Directory* (A138) and *Irregular Serials & Annuals* (A103). The current volume provides information for over 7,200 current serials. The arrangement includes a Key-Title index, an ISSN index, new serials listing (1972-1974), and a title index (with cross-referencing).

A57 *British books.* London: Publishers' Circular, 1837-.
A weekly record of books published.

A58 *British books in print, the reference catalogue of current literature.* London: Whitaker, 1965-.
An annual that covers the literature since 1965.

A59* *British Museum: General catalogue of printed books.* (263 vols. + suppl.) London: Trustees of the British Museum, 1965/1966-.
This source lists the contents of the British Museum Library, alphabetically by author, from the fifteenth century to 1965. Annual and cumulative supplements have followed. Because of copyright privileges vested in it for all British publications, this is the most complete collection of its kind in the world. In almost all instances, it cites the city of publication but does not provide the name of the publisher.

A60 *British Museum. Subject index of the modern works added* *to the library, 1881-1950.* (17 vols.) London: British Museum, 1902-1961.

A valuable tool for searches for a particular subject matter.

A61 *British national bibliography, 1950-.* London: British Museum, 1951-.

This is a weekly based on copyrighted books deposited in the British Museum, with periodic cumulations; hence it is the official catalogue of British publishing. It has alphabetical author, title, and subject indices.

Bry, Ilse. Bibliographic foundations for an emergent history of the behavioral sciences. (D41)

A62 *Bücher-Lexikon.* (36 vols.) Ed. C. G. Kayser. Graz: Akademischer Druck, 1961-1962.

While it is essentially a book-dealers' catalogue, this series is very useful to the historian. Extensive bibliographies for German books, arranged by author for the period 1750-1910, are provided. It is especially valuable, because for the years covered, it would otherwise be difficult to verify or complete references. Some Swiss and Austrian publications are included.

A63 *Bulletin signalétique.* Paris: Centre Nationale de la Recherche Scientifique, 1940-.

The changes instituted in this abstracting service over the years since 1940 are impossible to summarize in short compass. See the relevant pages in *Sources of Information in the Social Sciences* (A12) for a succinct summary. In recent years there has been a monthly section on psychology and psychiatry and quarterly sections on education, sociology, history of science, and philosophy.

A64 Changes in the concept of "scientific literature." Editorial Committee, *Mental Health Book Review Index. J. Hist. behav. Sci.,* 1965, *1,* 235-243.

This is a discussion of the distinction and relation between "scientific information" and "scientific literature," with a plea that the latter be strengthened.

A65 *A checklist of American imprints.* (10 vols. +) Ed. R. Shoemaker. New York: Scarecrow Press, 1964-.

One volume for each year is being issued, covering material from 1820 onward.

Citation indexes. M. Weinstock. (C63)

A66   Citation indexing: A natural science literature retrieval system for the social sciences. E. Garfield. *Amer. behav. Scientist,* 1964, 7(10), 58-61.

This paper by the Director of the Institute for Scientific Information describes the Institute's approach to the retrieval problem. Despite a rapidly changing field, it is still a basic reference.

A67   *Comprehensive dissertation index.* (Microfiche) Ann Arbor, Mich.: Xerox University Microfilms, 1973- (1961-1972-).

See also *Dissertation Abstracts International* (A73) and *Dissertation Abstracts International: Retrospective Index* (A74).

A68   *A critical bibliography of French literature.* Vol. 4, Suppl. 4. *The eighteenth century.* Gen. ed. D. C. Cabeen. Syracuse, N.Y.: Syracuse University Press, 1951, 1968.

Annotated references are given to books, articles, and chapters dealing with issues and significant figures of eighteenth-century France. References are arranged under topic headings, but a subject/author index is provided.

A69*   *Cumulated subject index to Psychological Abstracts, 1927-1960.* (2 vols. + suppls.) Boston: Hall, 1966-1968.

The definitive *subject* bibliography of psychology, bringing together in the first publication the abstracts of the first 34 volumes of the *Psychological Abstracts* (A118), followed by periodic supplements. Subject headings include "Bibliography" (7,000 entries), "Biography," and a severely limited number by individual names. Supplements for 1969 onward are published by American Psychological Association.

A70   *Cumulative book index: A world list of books in the English language.* New York: Wilson, 1928-.

A world list of books in the English language is given. Some are "back volumes" resulting from retrospective searching going on at the same time as a current volume is being prepared. Alphabetical arrangement is provided for author, subject, and title. Biennial, annual, and monthly supplements are issued.

De George, R. T. *A guide to philosophical bibliography and research.* (A6)

A71* *Deutsches Bücherverzeichnis.* (38 vols.) (Vols. 1-22, Leipzig: Verlag des Börsenvereins der Deutschen Buchhändler.) Leipzig: Verlag für Buch und Bibliothekswesen, 1916-.

A bibliography of German books published from 1911 onward, in Germany, Switzerland, and Austria, and successor to Kayser's *Bücher-Lexikon* (A62).

A72 *The development of medical bibliography.* Estelle Brodman. Chicago: Medical Library Association, 1954.

A systematic examination of medical bibliographies from the sixteenth century onward, arrived at through a thorough search of the literature. Especially useful when search is for material published earlier than this century.

Dictionary of national biography. (A163)

Dictionary of scientific biography. (A164)

A73 *Dissertation abstracts international.* Ann Arbor, Mich.: University Microfilms, 1938-.

A monthly publication. Almost 300 universities cooperate in submitting abstracts. It was originally a single list, but since 1966 it has been divided into (a) humanities and social sciences; and (b) sciences and engineering. Since 1969 there is a key-word title index. Author index cumulates annually. See also *Comprehensive Dissertation Index* (A67) and *Dissertation Abstracts International: Retrospective Index* (A74).

A74 *Dissertation abstracts international: Retrospective index, volumes 1-29.* (9 vols.) Ann Arbor, Mich.: University Microfilms, 1970.

Cumulative subject index for abstracts through 1969, grouped by academic subject. Vol. 4, is devoted to psychology, sociology, political science; Vol. 5 to the other social sciences; Vols. 6 and 7 to education; Vol. 8 includes communication, information sciences, linguistics, and folk-lore. Each academic subject is subdivided by key-word in-dexing. Vol. 9 is a cumulative author index. See also *Comprehensive Dissertation Index* (A67) and *Dissertation Abstracts International* (A73).

A75   Dissertations relevant to the history of the behavioral sciences. Anon. *J. Hist. behav. Sci.*, 1973, *9*, 393-396.

A Datrix search by Xerox University Microfilm yielded 30 relevant dissertations between 1938 and 1970. Details for each are given.

A76   *Dix années de psychologie française*, 1947-1956. Ed. D. Voutsinas. Paris: Editions du "Bulletin de Psychologie," 1957.

This volume cites articles in French periodicals for the years 1947 to 1956. See *Documentation sur la psychologie française* (A77) for a continuation.

A77   *Documentation sur la psychologie française*. Ed. D. Voutsinas. Paris: Group d'Etudes de Psychologie de l'Université de Paris, 1958.

This series of fascicles continues *Dix années de psychologie française, 1947-1956* (A76). They cover the French books and literature to 1960. In addition, articles published between 1843 to 1946 and books between 1746 and 1946 are included in III and VI respectively.

Ellenberger, H. F. *The discovery of the unconscious.* (B128)

Elliott, C. K. *A guide to the documentation of psychology.* (A7)

A78*   *Eminent contributors to psychology.* Vol. 1.*A bibliography of primary references.* Ed. R. I. Watson, Sr. New York: Springer, 1974.

For each of more than 500 deceased individuals of the modern period (i.e., after 1600) chosen by a panel of specialists, there are selected bibliographies, totaling over 12,000 primary references, including autobiographies and self-prepared bibliographies. See pages 1-3 for further details.

A79* *Eminent contributors to psychology.* Vol. 2. *A bibliography of secondary references.* Ed. R. I. Watson, Sr. New York: Springer, 1976.

This is a selected bibliography of 55,000 secondary references including biographies (for 530 of the 538 individuals included) and other bibliographies. A bibliography is provided for each of over 500 deceased individuals of the modern period, arranged alphabetically by name of authors. See pages 1-3 for further details.

A80 *Encyclopedia of information systems and services.* (2nd ed.) Ed. A. T. Kruzas. Ann Arbor, Mich.: Edwards Brothers, 1974.

This is a basic general source for the topic. It lists computerized services available through university and college centers.

The encyclopedia of philosophy. (A17)

Encyclopedia of the social sciences. (A18)

A81 *The English catalogue of books.* London: Low, 1864-1901; London: Publishers' Circular, 1906-.

Although first issued in 1864, this catalogue covers the period from 1801 and was published for a century before *British National Bibliography* (A61) and *British Books in Print* (A58) and hence fills a gap.

A82 European background (1600-1900) for American psychology. S. H. Britt. *J. gen. Psychol.,* 1942, *27,* 311-329.

Its major table, 14 pages long, presents a selection of works that influenced the history of psychology, arranged by date of birth of author and giving publication dates.

A83* *Excerpta medica: Neurology and psychiatry.* Amsterdam: Excerpta Medica, 1948-.

This provides an international abstracting index not only for these areas but for related ones, e.g., endocrinology. For the historian, this source contains a section on "history and general aspects."

A84   *La France litteraire ou Dictionnaire bibliographique.* (12
vols.) Ed. J. M. Querard. Paris: Maisonneuve & Larose,
1827-1864. (Reprinted 1964)
    Alphabetical listing, by name of author, of books
written in or translated into French during the eighteenth
and nineteenth centuries.

A85   *Gesamtverzeichnis der deutschsprachigen psychologischen
Literatur der Jahre 1942 bis 1960.* Ed. A. Wellek. Göttingen:
Verlag für Psychologie, 1965.
    Continues the listing of the bibliography of psycho-
logical books and articles in German, from the point in
time that the *Zeitschrift für Psychologie* (A147) stopped
publishing bibliographies. Materials listed by year, with
subdivisions of subject matter. Author index for the
volume facilitates search for the work of a specific individual.

A86   *Grundiss der Geschichte der Philosophie.* (11th-12th ed.)
(5 vols.) F. Ueberweg. Berlin: Mittler, 1923-1928.
    Although the lengthy text should not be neglected,
these volumes are more used today for bibliographic reference search. The bibliographic apparatus is very extensive
and needs to be consulted for studies in depth, especially
for nineteenth-century German philosophy.

A87   *Guide to microforms in print.* Washington, D.C.: Microcard Editions, 1961-.
    Annual cumulative guide to books, journals, and other
materials available in microfilm, microcard, and microfiche from publishers in the U.S.; arranged alphabetically,
with books by author's name and journals and sets by title.
Price and publisher are given. There is a companion *Subject
Guide to Microforms in Print.*

A88   *Guide by PAIS.* Psychological Abstract Information Services, American Psychological Association. Washington,
D.C.: American Psychological Association, 1975.
    A guide to the various means of finding relevant ab-
stracts from the *Psychological Abstracts* (A118). One of
the services for the individual user is a description of how a
search procedure for automated retrieval may be instituted.

The data base at the time of writing were abstracts published in that journal from 1967 onward.

A89* *Guide to reference books.* (9th ed.) Ed. Eugene P. Sheehy. Chicago: American Library Association, 1976.

The standard American guide to annotated general reference works, including the social sciences, to about 1976. Semiannual supplements and annotated lists in January and July issues of *College and Research Libraries* keep it up to date.

A90 *Guide to reference material.* (2nd ed.) (3 vols.) Ed. A. J. Walford. London: Library Association, 1966-1970.

About 12,000 annotated sources, with an emphasis on material of recent years and expressing a British viewpoint. Volume 1 is devoted to science and technology; volume 2 to philosophy, psychology, social science, and history; volume 3 to general works, fine arts, and literature. Literature surveys and lists of subject materials published in specified journals are included.

A91 *Handbuch der philosophischen Literatur der Deutschen von der Mitte des achtzehnten Jahrhunderts bis zum Jahr 1850, von Ersch und Geissler.* (3rd ed.) Foreword & index L. Geldsetzer. Dusseldorf: Stern-Verlag Janssen, 1965. (1850)

Ersch's *Handbuch* lists philosophical books and articles in Germany from 1750 to 1850, a century that represents its heyday. From among the *Contributors,* Fichte, Fries, Hegel, Herbart, and Kant receive extensive attention.

A92 *Handwörterbuch der Socialwissenschaften.* (12 vols. + index) Ed. E. V. Beckerath, et al. Stuttgart: Fischer, 1956-1968.

This series concerns all fields of social science, is international in scope, contains long, signed articles, and gives excellent bibliographies. About 20 percent of the entries are biographical. Indices are arranged by contributors, names, and subjects.

A93 *The Harvard list of books in psychology.* (4th ed.) Comp.

& annot. psychologists in Harvard University. Cambridge: Harvard University Press, 1971.

A prestigious, careful selection of about 700 annotated books by a group of knowledgeable psychologists, with psychology classified into thirty or so branches. It is kept relatively current by periodic new editions.

A94   *A history of the bibliography of philosophy.* M. Jasenas. New York: Olms, 1973.

Jasenas traces the history of bibliographies in philosophy from the Renaissance to the present day. The background of the compilers, the influence of still earlier bibliographies, and the changes in the subject matter of philosophy are stressed. It is an important source for several kinds of bibliographies not cited here, particularly for those compiled before the present century, those that appeared for a relatively short period of years, and those organized around some special philosophical-bibliographic principles such as those prepared by Bochenski and Varet. It includes an appendix of short titles of major philosophical books discussed in standard histories of philosophy.

A95   *Humanities Index.* New York: Wilson, 1974-.

Continues on a quarterly basis the *Social Science and Humanities Index* (A135), which had covered the literature from 1907 until this source took over. It monitors publications selected as widely used in these fields. It is a companion series to the *Social Science Index* (A134).

A96*   *Index-Catalogue of the Library of the Surgeon General's Office.* (61 vols.) Washington, D.C.: Government Printing Office, 1880-.

This is an author and subject index to book and periodical material now contained in the U.S. National Library of Medicine. Various series of the *Index-Catalogue* have been published, starting in 1880 under the auspices of the U.S. Army and its Surgeon General. The National Library of Medicine now sponsors the series. All fields of medicine and some related areas are covered.

A97   The *Index-Catalogue* as a tool of research in medicine and history. C. F. Mayer. In E. A. Underwood (Ed.), *Science, medicine and history.* Vol. 2, pp. 482-493. (B179)

It discusses how the *Index-Catalogue* (A96) may be used.

A98 *Index medicus.* Washington, D.C.: National Library of Medicine, 1879-.

This is the most comprehensive index to medical literature extant. Thousands of journals are searched systematically, and the titles are published monthly. Despite the date of 1879 given, the series published by the National Library of Medicine did not commence until 1960. The *Quarterly Cumulative Index Medicus* took over from *Index Medicus* until 1956, and the *Current List of Medical Literature* overlapped from 1950 and ceased publication in 1959. An annual cumulation, *The Cumulated Index Medicus,* has also been published since 1960. The relation to the information retrieval system, *Medlars,* used in connection with it should be noted.

A99* *The index of psychoanalytic writings.* (13 vols. so far) Ed. A. Grinstein. New York: International Universities Press, 1956-.

Books and articles, even those only remotely related to psychoanalysis, are listed. Citations, covering the literature to 1969, number over 100,000. All members of the International Psychoanalytic Society were originally solicited for complete biographies and titles of articles, books, etc., through 1952 and listed in an earlier book edited by J. Rickman, *Index Psychoanalyticus.* They have been incorporated by Grinstein in his volumes. Volumes 1-5 cover the literature up to 1952; Vols. 6-9, 1952-1959; Vols. 10-13, 1960-1969. All known reviews and abstract sources are cited. There are also chronological listings of references for especially eminent individuals, e.g., Freud and Abraham in Vol. 1.

A100 *International bibliography of the social sciences.* Chicago: Aldine, 1951-.

Various fields covered in this series of annual bibliographic sources under UNESCO sponsorship began in different years: anthropology in 1955, economics in 1952, political science in 1952, and sociology in 1951. Books and articles are indexed within subject and by author. It now draws upon nearly 2,500 journals and, instead of four independent bibliographies, there is a single comprehensive selection and index program for the series.

A101   *International catalogue of scientific literature, 1901-1914.* (254 vols.) Published for the International Council by Royal Society of London, 1902-1921. London: Dawsons, 1935.
   Articles and books are cited. Only a severly limited number of sets is available: consult *National Union Catalog* (A112) for location. To some extent, it extends *Catalogue of Scientific Papers* (A130).

International encyclopedia of the social sciences. (A23)

A102* *Internationale Bibliographie der Zeitschriftenliteratur.* Ed. O. Zeller. Osnabrück: Dietrich, 1965-.
   Periodical citations from nearly 8,000 periodicals in practically all fields of knowledge. Author and subject indices are provided, with the latter appearing in German, but with French and English equivalents. It was preceded by *Bibliographie der fremdsprachigen Zeitschriftenliteratur* (A38) and *Bibliographie der deutschen Zeitschriftenliteratur* (A36). For comments about arrangement and use see the latter annotation.

A103   *Irregular serials & annuals: An international directory, 1974-1975.* (3rd ed.) New York: Bowker, 1974.
   A companion volume to Ulrich's *Directory* (A138), it is also published biennially but in the alternate years. This volume includes titles to serials issued annually or less frequently. It contains four main sections: Section 1 provides information under subject headings on over 25,000 current serials published throughout the world; Section 2 records (for the first time in this edition) those serials that have ceased or suspended publication; Section 3 gives a selected index to publications of international organizations, and Section 4 provides a serials index by title, including extensive cross-referencing to variations of serial titles.

A104* *Isis: International Review Devoted to the History of Science and Civilization,* 1913-, 1-.
   The leading journal for the history of science, with magnificent critical bibliographies as a regular feature; these

now number about 100, the first 90 of which were cumulated (A105).

A105* *Isis cumulative bibliography: A bibliography of the history
of science formed from Isis critical bibliographies 1-90,
1913-1965.* (2 vols.) Ed. Magda Whitrow. London: Mansell,
1971.

A bibliography, arranged alphabetically, containing
references about or by various scientists (including over 200
Contributors) reported previously in 90 bibliographies
published in *Isis* between 1913 and 1965. An accompanying
subject bibliography was issued in 1976 by the same publisher.

A106 *Journal of the History of the Behavioral Sciences,* 1965-, 1-.
Biennial bibliographies were published from 1966 to
1975, divided into book and article sections.

A107 *Koehler & Volckmar-Fachbibliographien: Philosophie und
Grenzgebiete 1945-1964.* Stuttgart: Koehler & Volckmar,
1965.
An extensive book catalogue and a list of periodicals.

A108 Lauden, L. Theories of scientific method from Plato to
Mach. (D61)

A109 *Die Literatur der Psychiatrie, Neurologie und Psychologie
von 1459-1799.* (3 vols. in 4) Ed. H. Laehr. Berlin: Rimer,
1900.
Reports titles of books only but is valuable for the
temporal period in question.

A110 *A medical bibliography (Garrison and Morton): An annotated checklist of texts illustrating the history of medicine.*
(3rd ed.) Ed. L. T. Morton. Philadelphia: Lippincott, 1970.
Over 7,000 references, classified into basic medical
science and medical speciality areas. Since there are so
many detailed fields, each has relatively few entries, e.g.,
medical psychology has 31 entries from Aristotle to Köhler
and the history of psychiatry has 26 from Bucknell to
Eldridge. Most useful as a beginning in a field with which
one is unacquainted.

A111 *Mental measurements yearbook.* (7 vols. in 8 so far) Ed.
O. K. Buros. New Brunswick: Rutgers University Press,
1938-. (7th ed., 2 vols. Highland Park, N.J. Gryphon Press,
1972).
     The standard review of tests and test literature is
given in these volumes. An index of tests is given.

Mora, G. The historiography of psychiatry and its development. (D81)

Mora, G. The history of psychiatry: A cultural and bibliographic survey. (D82)   .

A112* *National Union catalog: Pre-1956 imprints.* London: Mansell, 1968-.
     This series provides a cumulative author list representing
Library of Congress printed cards *and* titles reported by
other American libraries. Still in progress, it is the best
source for period covered. Corrects and supplements chronologically earlier *Library of Congress* (A139) edition.

A112a *The new Cambridge bibliography of English literature.* Vol.
2. *1660-1800.* Vol. 3. *1800-1900.* Ed. G. Watson. Cambridge: Cambridge University Press: 1969-1971.
     Useful for behavioral scientists who are working on a
problem that has some relation to literature in the conventional sense.

Nouvelle biographie générale. (A175)

A113 *On documentation of scientific literature.* T. P. Loosjes.
Trans. A. J. Dickson. Hamden, Conn.: Archon, 1967.
     Documentary practices of librarians in terms of the
ways material is organised for use, documents are kept
track of, and retrieval systems are installed. Knowledge of
these practices will aid the user of the work of librarians in
finding the document he is searching for from the description provided.

Philosophen-Lexikon (A176)

A114 *The philosopher's index: An international index to phi-*

losophical periodicals. Bowling Green, Ohio: Philosophical Documentation Center, Bowling Green University, 1967-.

A quarterly review of the contents of periodicals, with annual cumulative editions. Author and key-word subject index to articles in 90 American and British journals and severely selected from others. Abstracts prepared by the authors themselves are provided from Volume 3 onward.

A115 *Philosophical books: A quarterly review.* Leicester: Leicester University Press, 1960-.

Review of books only included.

Die Philosophie der Gegenwart in Selbstdarstellungen. (A177)

A116 *Poole's index to periodical literature, 1802-1907.* (7 vols.) Boston: Houghton, 1882-1908.

Lists about 600,000 articles in several hundred American and English periodicals. Despite breadth of coverage it includes very, very few of the journals that are primarily historical in nature. Consequently, while less useful than at first might be inferred, it does contain the literature on how the sciences are seen in the popular magazines of the day. A companion volume subject index only is provided, but much needed is the new *Cumulated Author Index, 1802-1906.* Ed. C. E. Wall. (Ann Arbor, Mich.: Pierian Press, 1971), which lists over 300,000 references to authors formerly not so listed in original volumes of Poole's Index. Joint authorship is listed under both names; multiple authors are also included. See also *Reader's Guide to Periodical Literature* (A127) for similar coverage in more recent years to the more popular rather than scientific periodicals.

Poulton, Helen J. *The historian's handbook.* (A10)

A117 Problems and projects in the bibliography of psychiatry and psychology. Helen Bayne & Ilse Bry. *Libri,* 1953, *3,* 363-387.

A brief history of bibliography. Attention is given to the literature of psychology and psychiatry and of bibliographic projects on serials and monographs in which they are engaged. An extensive bibliography is provided.

A118* *Psychological abstracts.* Washington, D.C.: American Psychological Association, 1927-.

The series attempts to abstract monthly all published psychological material. Definitive source for psychological literature, but also widely used in other social sciences, psychiatry, and psychoanalysis. There are now cumulative indices for each six months. The time lag between the publication of books or articles and their appearance in the *Abstracts* is from 3 to 9 months. The format and organization have changed several times since 1927, which means that the user must be alert to these differences when planning a search strategy. For the current format in use, see the *Thesaurus of Psychological Index Terms* (A189) whose 17 hierarchical content areas are used. For abstracts prior to 1927, see *Abstract References* (A121) and for citations see *Psychological Index* (A120). For cumulated author and subject indices respectively see (A34) and (A69).

A119 *Psychological bulletin,* 1904-, 1-.

While not confined to them, the journal publishes a large number of reviews of areas of research, from which rather detailed bibliographies emerge.

A120* *The psychological index.* Vols. 1-11, New York: Macmillan; Vols. 12-17, Baltimore, Md.: Psychological Review; Vols. 18-42, Princeton, N.J.: Psychological Review, 1895-1935.

The series provides a listing by subject categories of titles of all known articles and books in the psychological literature, in most languages, from 1894 to 1935. The *Index,* Volume 42, list 150,000 items. The series overlaps the bibliographic service rendered by Rand's *Bibliography* (A48) for a few years; then it overlaps with the *Psychological Abstracts* (A118), which, after cessation of the *Index,* carried on the task of not only regularly listing, but also abstracting psychological literature. Author indices at the end of each volume were cumulated in (A34). See *Psychological Index: Abstract References* (A121) for the abstracts that retrospectively have been found.

A121 *Psychological index: Abstract references.* (2 vols.) Ed. H. L. Ansbacher. Columbus, Ohio: American Psychological Association, 1940-1941.

This volume is a retrospective attempt to find one or more abstracts for each of the titles of the psychological literature from 1894 to 1928 contained in the *Psychological Index* (A120), which contains no abstracts. Abstracts for 43 percent of the over 100,000 titles were found and related to the *Index* item in question by its number, requiring one to use these volumes simultaneously with the *Index* itself.

A122* *The psychological register.* Vol. 3. Ed. C. Murchison. Worcester, Mass.: Clark University Press, 1932.

An invaluable but somewhat untrustworthy source. From each of 2,400 then-living psychologists a selected but relatively extensive bibliography of books and articles to about 1930 was secured, along with a very short vita akin to that carried in directories. Although an impressive array of international authorities helped select those invited to participate, the rationale for selection of references for a given person or given country is not made clear. Evidently at some point works of a "philosophical" nature were excluded. The psychologists themselves prepared their lists, some with care, others in haste. Many titles are incompletely cited, and although the editor and his staff made efforts to complete these, they were not always successful. Experience in working on the *Eminent Contributors* (A78) results in the conviction that errors in the *Register* were numerous and that inexplicable omissions of "important" titles occurred. Within each of 40 countries, the names of the psychologists are arranged alphabetically and references cited chronologically. About one half of the individuals whose works are cited are from outside the United States. Only Volume 3 is cited here, because Volume 2 was a preliminary and shorter run, with the same area of coverage, while Volume 1, never published, was to have surveyed deceased psychologists from the time of the early Greeks. The passage of 40 years since its publication results in nearly 250 individuals cited being included in *Eminent Contributors* (A78), despite the fact that in spirit the latter is more similar to the contemplated Volume 1 and with the added advantage of being able to include works published since 1930. By no means are all of the pre-1930 references included in the *Eminent Contributors,* so for that literature the *Register* is still very useful. For the 2,150 individuals not among the 538, it is still an essential reference source.

A123 *Psychology book guide: 1974.* Ed. G. L. Swanson. Boston: Hall, 1974-.

A source citing books catalogued by the Library of Congress for a particular year. The majority of those in the first volume bear the copyright date of 1973, but casual inspection showed one as early as 1912-1921. Main entries are by author, but a subject and title index are included. It is planned as an annual. There are similar guides for law, medicine, technology, and business and economics.

A124 *Publishers' trade list annual.* New York: Bowker, 1873-.

Alphabetically arranged by publisher, with separate indexes: *Books in Print,* an *Author-Title-Series Index,* and *Subject Guide to Books in Print, An Index.*

A125 *Publisher's weekly.* New York: Bowker, 1872-.

Weekly record of books published in the United States. A semiannual issue announces books scheduled for the subsequent six months.

A126 *Quarterly check-list of psychology: An international index of current books, monographs, brochures & separates.* Darien, Conn.: American Bibliographic Service, 1960-.

A survey of recent publications in psychology arranged by author is provided. It includes citations not only to books but also to articles and chapters within books. One volume of 4 issues per year is published, with an author/editor/translator index in last issue of each volume.

A127 *Reader's guide to periodical literature, 1900-.* New York: Wilson, 1905-.

An author-subject and a title index are given for more than 100 leading general magazines published since 1900, thus slightly overlapping *Pooles'* (A116) but going beyond to the present; it is even less valuable than *Poole's,* since the periodicals indexed tend to be even more "popular" rather than "scholarly." This is published semimonthly and cumulated annually.

A128 Recent international documentation in philosophy: A survey of select reference works. D. H. Borchardt. *Int. Libr. Rev.*, 1972, *4*, 199-212.

 The article gives afterthoughts and additions to *How to find out in philosophy and psychology* (A1).

A129 *Repertoire bibliographique de la philosophie.* Louvain: Societé philosophique de Louvain, 1949-.

 This series supersedes the *Repertoire bibliographique* issued as a supplement to the *Revue philosophique de Louvain.*

A130* Royal Society of London. *Catalogue of scientific papers compiled by the Royal Society of London, 1800-1900.* (19 vols.) New York: Kraus Reprint, 1965. (1867-1925)

 Scientific articles for the nineteenth century, listed alphabetically by author, are given. Biographies and secondary works sometime precede the listing of a particular author's works. Continued by *International Catalogue of Scientific Literature* (A101) for the years 1901-1914.

Royal Society of London. *Obituary notices of Fellows.* (A180)

A131 *Science citation index.* Philadelphia: Institute for Scientific Information, 1963-.

 This index cites literature on the natural and biological sciences and uses over 2,000 journals as base for collection. Chemical, pharmaco-medical, life sciences, space, electronic, and physical sciences are major rubrics of classification of content. See *Social Sciences Citation Index* (A133) for details about its nature and use.

A132 Selective reading list, on historiography and philosophy of history. R. Thompson, in Social Science Research Council, *Theory and practice in historical study: A report of the committee on historiography, Bulletin No. 54.* New York: Social Science Research Council, 1946, pp. 141-172.

 This is an admirably selected bibliography that has become rather influential. It is divided into five major sections: profession of historian (historical method, history of history, history and the social sciences); philosophical approaches (early syntheses, persistent problems, current trends); contending schools (economic and spiritual interpretations); national developments (Germany, other parts of Europe, United States); and new interpretations (general, social interpretation, cyclical interpretation, historical sociology).

A133   *Social sciences citation index.* Philadelphia: Institute for Scientific Information, 1973-.

Annual cumulative volumes of three issues per year. Beginning in 1973, every article in about 1,000 journals and relevant articles in about 2,000 more journals are cited. As a technique, citation indexing assumes that an author's citations indicate subject relationships with which he is concerned. Articles that cite the same publication usually have subject relationships with each other although they do not necessarily reciprocally cite one another (especially nearly simultaneous publications). The citation index identifies a particular article that cited the same earlier publication. It will increase in value as the literature years covered increase in number. The fields of the journals that are cited include anthropology, educational research, history, philosophy, psychiatry, psychology, sociology, and statistics. See article, "Citation indexes," by Weinstock (C63) for a survey of the earlier literature on this approach.

A134   *Social science index.* New York: Wilson, 1974-.

The series continues on a quarterly basis parts of the *Social Sciences and Humanities Index* (A135), which had covered the literature from 1907. It monitors publication selected as widely used in these fields. A companion series to that of the *Humanities Index* (A95).

A135   *Social sciences and humanities index.* (Title varies over the years) New York: Wilson, 1916-.

The index cites from the 200 best-known English periodicals in the social sciences, language and literature, religion, and philosophy (but not psychology).

A136   *Les sources du travail bibliographique.* (3 vols. in 4). Ed. Louise-Noëlle Malcles. Geneva: Droz, 1950-1958.

This source emphasized French and other European works. The first volume includes bibliographies of bibliographies, library catalogues, and society publications; the second, dictionaries, encyclopedias, periodicals, and bibliographies in the humanistic and social sciences; the third, bibliographies in the exact sciences and technology. Each volume is indexed separately by author, title, and subject.

A137 *Sources for the history of science, 1660-1914.* Ed. D. Knight. Ithaca, N.Y.: Cornell University Press, 1975.

An introductory chapter on the historiography of the physical sciences is followed by chapters devoted to histories of science, manuscripts, journals, books related to contemporary science, and models and apparatus. Perhaps more than is usually the case, volumes discussed are idiosyncratic choices.

Sury, K. V. *Wörterbuch.* (A202)

A138 *Ulrich's international periodicals directory, 1973-1974.* (15th ed.) New York: Bowker, 1973.

A directory that contains entries for approximately 55,000 current periodicals published throughout the world; an index by title of new periodicals (1971-1973); a listing of over 1,800 periodicals that have ceased publication; and an index of all titles and subject entries, with extensive cross-referencing. It is published biennially. See also *Bowker Serials* (A56) and *Irregular Serials & Annuals* (A103).

A139* U.S. Library of Congress. *A catalog of books represented by Library of Congress printed cards issued to July 31, 1942.* (167 vols.) Supplements: 1942-1948 (42 vols.) & 1948-1952 (23 vols.) Ann Arbor, Mich.: Edwards, 1942-1946.

This is a major source. Continued by *The National Union Catalog* (A140) in 1953. See also *National Union Catalog, Pre-1956 Imprints* (A112).

A140* U.S. Library of Congress. *The National Union Catalog: A cumulative author list representing Library of Congress printed cards and titles reported by other American libraries.* Washington: Library of Congress, 1953-.

The current major source, presented in nine monthly issues and three quarterly cumulative annual publications for four years and a quinquennial in the fifth year.

A141   Wellcome Historical Medical Library. *A catalogue of printed books in the Wellcome Historical Library.* Vol. 1 *Books printed before 1641.* Vol. 2 *Books printed from 1641 to 1850,* A-E. London: Wellcome Historical Medical Library, 1962, 1966.

   This is an excellent source because selection for purchase for the library and consequent inclusion was done in a very discriminating fashion.

A142* Wellcome Institute for the History of Medicine. *Current work in the history of medicine.* London: Wellcome Institute, 1954-.

   Invaluable quarterly listing of articles and books on the history of medicine and allied fields.

White, C. M., & Associates. *Sources of information in the social sciences.* (A12)

A143   Widener Library Shelflist (Harvard University). *Philosophy and psychology.* (2 vols.) Cambridge: Harvard University Press, 1973.

   A two-volume listing (vols. 42-43 in the Widener Library Shelflist series) of works present in Harvard's central research collection. These volumes contain nearly 59,000 books, periodicals, and pamphlets concerning metaphysics, cosmology, ontology, epistemology, logic, aesthetics, and psychology. The first volume is arranged chronologically, in terms of topics; the second contains an author and title listing.

A144* *A world bibliography of bibliographies and bibliographical catalogues, calendars, abstracts, digests, indexes and the like.* (4th ed.) (5 vols.) Ed. T. Besterman. Lausanne: Societas Bibliographica, 1965-1966.

   A stupendous accomplishment of an alphabetical subject listing of nearly 120,000 bibliographies of books and manuscripts, with cross references. Only American, British, and French national bibliographies are annotated in this volume, but it is especially valuable for finding citations of bibliographies of other countries.

Wörterbuch der philosophischen Begriffe. (A25)

Wörterbuch der Psychologie. (A197)

Yearbook of the American Philosophical Society. (A188)

A145 *Zeitschrift für gesamte Neurologie und Psychiatrie, 1910-, 1-.*
Bibliographies are included until 1920. From 1921 on they appear in *Zentralblatt für die gesamte Neurologie und Psychiatrie, 1910-, 1-.*

A146 *Zeitschrift für philosophische Forschung, 1946-, 1-.*
This journal began reporting biographies and bibliographies in 1966.

A147* *Zeitschrift für Psychologie und Physiologie der Sinnesorgane, 1890-1906, 1-40,* and *Zeitschrift für Psychologie, 1906-1944, 41-156, 1954-, 157-.*
The first indexing of psychological literature, beginning with that of 1889 under the first title above. In 1906 the title was changed to *Zeitschrift für Psychologie.* Between 1890-1916 coverage of literature was international; 1917-1924 interrupted; 1925-1941 only German literature was indexed; thereafter it stopped publishing bibliographies. From 1921 on the present reference contains bibliographies in *Referate* section, formerly published in *Zeitschrift für gesamte Neurologie und Psychiatrie* (A145). The literature for the period from 1942 to 1960 is found in *Gesamtverzeichnis der deutschsprachigen psychologischen Literatur* (A85).

BIOGRAPHICAL COLLECTIONS

Biographies in the sources to be cited range in length from a few lines to monographic essays. Some citations are to volumes of autobiographies. The scope of a particular biographical collection may be general, occupational, national, or regional. They may be retrospective, or contemporary, or both. Biographies of specific persons are not cited individually; they are to be found in these collections.

Alphabetical entry by title, rather than by author or editor, is followed, since again it is most convenient and meaningful, despite the awkwardness of a few sources.

Biography as a method is considered to be an aspect of historiography, and relevant references are found in a part of Section C: "Methods of Historical Research."

A148 *Allgemeine deutsche Biographie.* (56 vols.) Leipzig: Duncker & Humblot, 1875-1912.

A retrospective source that covers the period from the earliest accounts to about 1900. The last volume is an index. It is supplemented in later years by the *Biographisches Jahrbuch und deutscher Nekrolog* (A155) and the *Deutsches biographisches Jahrbuch* (A160).

A149 *American men and women of science: Formerly American men of science: The physical and biological sciences.* (12th ed.) (7 vols.) New York: Bowker, 1971-1973.

This is the most comprehensive American and Canadian contemporary directory that is available. It was very carefully prepared with the aid of an advisory committee and maintains high standards of selection of those included. Entries are checked for accuracy by the biographer himself. Over 171,000 entries in this and the other volumes in the series. Includes a discipline index. Physiological psychologists are cited in this series, other psychologists in the companion volumes for the social and behavioral sciences (A150).

A150 *American men and women of science: Formerly American men of science: The social and behavioral sciences.* (12th ed.) (2 vols.) New York: Bowker, 1973.

See comments on *American Men and Women of Science: The Physical and Biological Sciences* (A149). Provides biographical data on contemporary American and Canadian anthropologists, economists, political scientists, psychologists, sociologists, and statisticians. A discipline index is forthcoming.

A151 American Psychiatric Association. *Biographical directory of fellows and members.* New York: Bowker, 1975.

An alphabetical listing of 21,000 contemporary American psychiatrists and a few from foreign countries now issued bi-yearly. Professional training, experience, specialty, selection of publications, and address are given for each entry. A geographical listing is appended.

A152 American Psychological Association. *Biographical directory.* Washington, D.C.: American Psychological Association, 1916-.

This directory is issued irregularly (but at time of writing every other year) supplying information at time of writing on about 40,000 contemporary members. In alternate years a shorter *Membership Register* of names, addresses, membership status, and divisional affiliations is provided. The *Directory* supplies, in addition, biographical data including chronological listing of academic and professional appointments. Geographical listing by states is appended. Some earlier editions gave more detailed information.

A153 *A biographical history of medicine: Excerpts and essays on the men and their work.* J. H. Talbott. New York: Grune & Stratton, 1970.

A retrospective source that, among others, includes, from the *Contributors:* Babinski, Bell, Bernard, Bowditch, Broca, Brown-Séquard, Cannon, Charcot, Descartes, DuBois-Reymond, Galton, Golgi, Haeckel, M. Hall, Harvey, Head, von Haller, von Helmholtz, Jackson, Kraepelin, Kretschmer, Lavoisier, Linnaeus, Ludwig, Magendie, J. Müller, Pavlov, Pinel, Priestley, Ramon y Cajal, Rush, Sherrington, Swedenborg, and Young.

A154 *Biographie universelle, ancienne et modern.* (New ed.) (45 vols.) Ed. M. Michaud. Paris: Desplaces, 1843-1865.

An important retrospective dictionary of universal biography, carefully edited for its time.

A155 *Biographisches Jahrbuch und deutscher Nekrolog, 1896-1913.* (18 vols. + index) Ed. A. Bettelheim. Berlin: Reimer, 1897-1917.

An annual that fills the temporal period after *Allgemeine deutsche Biographie* (A148) and covers the years 1896-1913.

A156 *Biographisches Lexikon der hervorragenden Ärzte aller Zeiten und Völker.* (3rd ed.) (5 vols. + suppl.) Ed. A. Hirsch, et al. Munich: Urban & Schwarzenberg, 1962. (1883)

Biographies of physicians and naturalists down to about 1880 are its contents. The *Biographisches Lexikon* (A157) edited by Fischer continues the chronology until about 1930.

A157 *Biographisches Lexikon der hervorragenden Ärzte der
letzten fünfzig Jahre (1880-1930).* (2nd & 3rd ed.) (2 vols.)
Ed. I. Fischer. Berlin: Urban & Schwarzenberg, 1962.
(1931)
The volumes are devoted to biographies of physicians
for the period 1880-1930. It therefore includes many
naturalists. Short bibliographies are given.

A158 *Biographical memoirs: National Academy of Sciences.* New
York: Columbia University Press, 1877-.
The basis of publication policy is to give monographic
biographies for each deceased member. Exhaustive, definitive bibliographies are provided for each memoir.

A159 *Chamber's biographical dictionary.* Ed. J. O. Thorne. New
York: St. Martin's Press, 1962.
This is the British counterpart to *Webster's Biographical Dictionary* (A183). There are approximately 15,000
short biographies in this edition, which is world-wide in
coverage.

A160 *Deutsches biographisches Jahrbuch.* (12 vols.) Berlin:
Deutsche Verlagsanstalt, 1925-.
This series continues *Biographisches Jahrbuch* (A155);
it covers in the first two volumes the years 1914-1920, and
volume three begins the regular series for 1921 on.

A161 *Dictionnaire de biographie française.* Paris: Librairie
Letouzey et Ane, 1933-.
This French biographical source is far from completion.
Begun in 1933 with Volume 1, by 1973 it had reached
Volume 13, fasc. 76, with the last entry being that for
Féréol.

A162 *Dictionary of American biography.* (24 vols.) New York:
Scribner's, 1928-1973.
Volumes 1-20 make up the original set; there are supplemental volumes, 21-23; and volume 24 is the index to
1-20. Contains approximately 15,000 entries. Individuals
eligible for inclusion only when deceased, must have lived
in the United States at some time in their lives, and must
be judged to have made "contributions to the American
way of life." In 1964, the one volume, *Concise Dictionary*

of American Biography, appeared, which presents essential facts contained in the parent work plus entries from then available supplementary volumes.

A163 *The dictionary of national biography.* (22 vols. + suppl.) Ed. L. Stephen & S. Lee. London: Oxford University Press, 1959-1965.

Authoritative retrospective source for Englishmen and persons who have lived in the colonies. Selections range from early times to 1900, and supplementary volumes update the 30,000 articles of the basic set. Bibliographies accompany each biography.

A164 *Dictionary of scientific biography.* Ed. C. C. Gillespie. New York: Scribner's, 1970-.

This multivolumed work will be the definitive biographical source for the natural sciences for many years to come. It is being published under the auspices of the American Council of Learned Societies, which has as member organizations the relevant scientific and philosophical societies. Except when unusually influential outside the field itself, psychologists are not included. On this basis Bain, Binet, Cattell, Gesell, Hall, and Lashley are included in the first half of the series. By contrast, physiologists are well represented. Bekhterev, Bernard, Bowditch, Brown-Séquard, Brücke, Carlson, Carpenter, DuBois-Reymond, Flourens, von Frey, Fulton, Gall, Goltz, von Haller, Harvey, Helmholtz, Herrick, C.G. Lange, Lapicque, Loeb, and Ludwig are included. Similarly, anatomists, biologists, neurologists, and the older generations of philosophers are well represented.

A165 *A dictionary of universal biography.* (2nd ed.) Ed. A. M. Hyamson. New York: Dutton, 1951. (1916)

This volume limits biographical data to birth and death date, nationality, and profession, thus increasing the number of individuals included. Its value otherwise is in the references, where lengthier biographies can be found.

A166 *Directory of American scholars.* (6th ed.) (4 vols.) New York: Bowker, 1974.

Comparable to the *American Men and Women of Science* (A149, A150) series for contemporary historians, philosophers, English and foreign language specialists, as well as specialists in speech, drama, law, and religion.

Eminent contributors to psychology, Vol. 1. (A78)

Eminent contributors to psychology, Vol. 2. (A79)

The encyclopedia of philosophy. (A17)

Encyclopedia of the social sciences. (A18)

A167   *The founders of neurology: One hundred and thirty-three biographical sketches prepared for the Fourth International Neurological Congress in Paris by eighty-four authors.* Ed. W. Haymaker. Springfield, Ill.: Thomas, 1953.
        Succinct but relatively authoritative statements are given.

A168   *Die grossen Deutschen.* (5 vols.) Ed. H. Heimpel, T. Heuss, & B. Reifenberg. Berlin: Propyläen-Verlag, 1960-1961. (1935-1937)
        Chronologically arranged, and gives retrospective biographies for Germans in all fields from 672 to 1935.

A169   *Grosse Nervenärzte.* (Vols. 1 & 2, 2nd ed.) (3 vols.) Ed. K. Kolle. Stuttgart: Thieme, 1970, 1970, 1963 (1956, 1959)
        Drawing only from the *Contributors,* Volume 1 contains authoritative biographies on Bleuler, Ramon y Cajal, Charcot, Freud, Jackson, Jung, Kraepelin, Pavlov, Pinel, and Sherrington; Volume 2 on Babinski, Esquirol, Golgi, Head, Helmholtz, A. Meyer, and Meynert; and Volume 3 on Bethe, Binet, Gruhle, Janet, Lombroso, Maudsley, and Monakow.

Handwörterbuch der Sozialwissenschaften. (A92)

A170   *A history of psychology in autobiography.* Vols. 1-3. Ed. C. Murchison. Worcester, Mass.: Clark University Press, 1930-1936; Vol. 4. Ed. E. G. Boring, et al. Worcester, Mass.: Clark University Press, 1952; Vol. 5. Ed. E. G. Boring and G. Lindzey. New York: Appleton-Century-Crofts, 1967; Vol. 6. Ed. G. Lindzey. Englewood Cliffs, N.J.: Prentice-Hall, 1974.

Contributors whose autobiographies appear in successive volumes are as follows:

Volume 1: Baldwin, Calkins, Claparède, Dodge, Janet, Jastrow, Kiesow, McDougall, Seashore, Spearman, Stern, Stumpf, Warren, and Zwaardemaker. Volume 2 includes Bourdon, Drever, Dunlap, Franz, Heymans, Höffding, Morgan, Pillsbury, Terman, Washburn, Woodworth, and Yerkes. Volume 3 includes J. R. Angell, Bentley, Carr, De Sanctis, Judd, Klemm, Marbe, Myers, Scripture, Thorndike, Watson, and Wirth. Volume 4 includes Bingham, Gemelli, Gesell, Hull, Hunter, Katz, Michotte, Piéron, Thomson, Thurstone, and Tolman. Volume 5 has Allport and Goldstein. Volume 6 appeared after the cut-off date for the *Contributor* project, and consequently none are included; most of those listed, however, are of comparable stature.

A171 *International directory of psychologists exclusive of the U.S.A.* (2nd ed.) Ed. H. C. J. Duijker & E. H. Jacobson. Assen, Netherlands: Royal VanGorcum, 1966.

This is an international cooperative effort sponsored by the International Union of Psychological Science. It lists alphabetically by country about 8,000 contemporary psychologists with very brief statements of career data. There is a name index.

International encyclopedia of the social sciences. (A23)

A172 *Neue deutsche Biographie.* Berlin: Duncker & Humblot, 1953-.

This multivolumed work includes significant Germans who have died since the publishing of the *Allgemeine deutsche Biographie* (A148) and those overlooked in the original publication.

A173 *The New York Times biographical edition: A compilation of current biographical information of general interest.* New York: The New York Times, 1970-.

This is a weekly, with 12-week and annual cumulations, which uses the resources of the newspaper to organize the biographical information it has accumulated on contemporaries.

A174 *The New York Times obituary index, 1858-1968.* New
York: The New York Times, 1970.
Obituaries for deceased individuals are indexed. The
volume indicates precise location in the New York Times
where a given obituary is to be found. Very useful for
those individuals for whom biographies seem otherwise
unavailable.

A175 *Nouvelle biographie generale.* (3rd ed.) (46 vols. in 23) Ed.
E. Hoefer. Copenhagen: Rosenkilde & Bagger, 1963-1969.
Biographical data on eminent men, not exclusively
French, are given from the time of the ancients to ca
1850-1860. Secondary source material on most individuals
is provided.

A176 *Philosophen-Lexikon: Handwörterbuch der Philosophie
nach Personen.* (2 vols.) W. Ziegenfuss. Berlin: De Gruyter,
1949-1950.
Short biographies and bibliographies of works of and
about major philosophical figures are presented.

A177 *Die Philosophie der Gegenwart in Selbstdarstellungen.* (5
vols.) Ed. R. Schmidt. Leipzig: Meiner, 1923-1924.
From among the *Contributors,* Meinong, Stumpf,
Vaihinger, and Ziehen are represented. Bibliographies are
of primary references.

Psychological register. (A122)

A178 *Psychologie in Selbstdarstellungen.* Ed. L. J. Pongratz,
W. Traxel, & E. G. Wehner. Bern: Huber, 1972.
Rather lengthy autobiographies of a few contempo-
rary European psychologists.

A179 *The Psychologists.* (Vols. 1,2) Ed. T. S. Krawiec. New
York: Oxford University Press, 1972, 1974.
In the two volumes, about 25 contemporary psychologists from widely varying settings give their autobiographies. They had been encouraged to be frank, to report
"failures" as well as "successes," and to try to present
something about their life styles.

A180 Royal Society of London. *Obituary notices of Fellows.*
Vols. 1-8. Cambridge: The Society, 1932-1952.

Biographies of all deceased members that could be commissioned during the inclusive years. Definitive bibliographies are given.

A181   *Some apostles of physiology: Being an account of their lives and labours.* W. Stirling. London: Waterlow & Sons, 1902. Reprinted London: Dawsons, 1966.

The articles include biographies of Bell, Bernard, Bichet, Dalton, Descartes, Donders, DuBois-Reymond, Galvani, v. Haller, Harvey, v. Helmholtz, Huxley, Lavoisier, Leeuwenhoek, Ludwig, Magendie, J. Müller, Priestley, Purkinje, E. H. Weber, and Young. Portraits are given.

Sury, K. v. *Wörterbuch.* (A202)

A182   *Tafeln zur Geschichte der Philosophie.* (2nd ed.) C. Stumpf. Berlin: Speyer & Peters, 1900. (1896)

A biographic aid in the form of a schematic time chart of the history of philosophy from 600 B.C. to 1900 A.D., in terms of the names of the principal philosophers, arranged by philosophical schools through the Patristic period, then by schools and by countries for the Renaissance and modern periods. A valuable panoramic view in short compass.

A183   *Webster's biographical dictionary.* (2nd ed.) Springfield, Mass.: Merriam, 1960. (1943)

About 40,000 short biographies, with emphases on American and British figures, are included; it has its British counterpart in *Chamber's Biographical Dictionary.* (A159)

A184   *Who was who, 1897-1960.* (5 vols.) London: Macmillan, 1929-1961.

A companion volume to *Who's Who* (A186), containing the biographies of those who died during the years mentioned in the title.

A185   *Who was who in America* with world notables. (4 vols. & suppl. hist. vol.) Chicago: Marquis, 1943-1968.

A companion to *Who's Who in America* (A187), containing the biographies of those who died during the period mentioned in the title and supplemented by the historical volume, which contains 13,300 biographies of prominent

Americans who died before *Who's Who in America* began
to be published. Over 150 biographies of *Contributors* are
to be found in this and the current volume (A187).

A186   *Who's Who: An annual biographical dictionary with which
is incorporated "men and women of the time."* London:
Black, 1849-.
This is an annual that is the pioneer publication of its
kind. Each biographical entry supplies succinct material
checked for accuracy by its subject.

A187   *Who's who in America: A biographical dictionary of notable
living men and women.* Chicago: Marquis, 1899-.
This is the basic dictionary for contemporary Americans eminent in any area. It is issued biennially. The latest
edition contains a short biographical account including
educational background, awards, major achievements, and
current address for 70,000 individuals.

A188   *Yearbook of the American Philosophical Society.* Phila-
delphia: American Philosophical Society, 1938-.
Biographies of recently deceased members include
Hovland, Kluckhohn, and Stouffer, 1961; Bridgman and
Woodworth, 1962; Köhler, 1968. Bibliographies are pro-
vided.

DICTIONARIES

The date of publication of the source being consulted must always
be present in the mind of historians when they consider how words
are being used. Use of a series of dictionaries prepared at different
dates provides a needed temporal dimension. Psychologists and
philosophers are fortunate in having Baldwin's *Dictionary* (A15),
which defines terms at the turn of the century and also lists 35
earlier dictionaries. Baldwin was followed in 1934 by Warren
(A203) and in 1958 by English and English (A192). French and
German dictionaries are found to have similar histories, illustrated
here by inclusion of psychological dictionaries published between
1922 and 1975. A somewhat greater number of volumes in these
languages than is characteristic of other sections of this *Guide* is
annotated here, since they are indispensible for the historian when
he turns to material in these languages, even if he is relatively fluent
in them.

Contemporary philosophical, psychoanalytic, social science, and educational dictionaries are also annotated. For earlier dictionaries in these other fields, items from the earlier bibliographic section should be consulted. Irrespective of field, earlier editions of the dictionaries cited may be more important for some purposes than the latest, which are given here.

Entry for citations in this section is by the name of the editor or of the sponsoring editorial agency.

A189 American Psychological Association. *Thesaurus of psychological index terms.* Washington, D.C.: American Psychological Association, 1974.

Over 4,000 terms used in psychology and the behavioral sciences are analyzed. There are three sections: (1) "relationship among terms" identified as synonyms, as broader, as narrower, or as related; (2) "alphabetical" for each preferred term, particularly useful for the identification of terms for indexing; (3) "hierarchical" for 17 broad content areas corresponding to major ones of the current *Psychological Abstracts* (A118), with terms in descending order of breadth of concept.

Dictionary of philosophy and psychology. (A15)

A190 Drever, J.(Rev. H. Wallerstein), *A dictionary of psychology.* (3rd ed.) Baltimore, Md.: Penguin Books, 1969. (1952)

A convenient, succinct, pocket-size dictionary, British in origin, prepared with acumen and through scholarship.

A191 Duijker, H. (Ed.), *Trilingual lexicon of psychology.* Vol. 1. *English/French/German.* Bern: Huber, 1975.

Prepared under the auspices of the International Union of Psychological Societies. Two other companion volumes have French and German terms as points of entry.

A192 English, H. B., & English, Ava C. *A comprehensive dictionary of psychological and psychoanalytical terms: A guide to usage.* New York: McKay, 1958.

More recent and more comprehensive than Warren (A203), it is now the best contemporary source available. There are more than 11,000 entries, including extensive cross-references. Specialized usages for an individual or a school are so labeled.

A193 Fodor, N., & Gaynor, F. (Eds.), *Freud: Dictionary of psychoanalysis.* New York: Philosophical Library, 1950.

Freud's own definitions of terms quoted in English translation and the source references from which they are derived.

A194 Gauquelin, M., & Gauquelin, Françoise (Eds.), *La psychologie moderne de A á Z.* Paris: Centre d'Etude et de Promotion de la Lecture, 1971.

This is the newest of the French dictionaries and differs in organization from the usual ones. There are eight long papers devoted to broader topics e.g., history of psychology, personality, physiological bases of behavior, and psychoanalysis, and shorter entries devoted to psychological terms. Terms in the text for which there is a separate entry are underlined. Location of facts, information, and references is provided in the margin. A summary of opportunities to study psychology in France and an English-French index close the volume.

A195 Good, C. V. (Ed.), *Dictionary of education.* (2nd ed.) New York: McGraw-Hill, 1959. (1945)

This volume defines approximately 16,000 terms including those from foreign languages and related fields.

A196 Gould, J., & Kolb, W. L. *A dictionary of the social sciences.* New York: Free Press, 1964.

Defines 1000 concepts and terms from economics, political science, social anthropology, social psychology, and sociology.

A197 Hehlmann, W. *Wörterbuch der Psychologie.* (11th ed.) Stuttgart: Kröner, 1974.

The book is rich in historical information, including brief biographies. Appendices include a chronology of the development of psychology and a section on historical treatises.

A198 Hinsie, L. E., & Campbell, R. J. *Psychiatric dictionary.* (4th ed.) New York: Oxford University Press, 1970.

This volume consists of 7,500 entries, including names of eminent individuals in psychiatry and related fields and both current and obsolete terms. References are given for major definitions.

Historisches Wörterbuch der Philosophie, Ed. J. R. Ritter. (A22)

A199 Muller-Freienfels, R. (Ed.), *Handwörterbuch der Philosophie.* (2nd ed.) Berlin: Mittler, 1922. (1913)

In some ways this book is a condensation of Eisler's dictionary, *Wörterbuch der Philosophischen Begriffe* (A25), since it was Eisler who edited the first edition of this shortened dictionary after the *Wörterbuch* became increasingly detailed.

A200 Petrov, B. M. (Comp.), & Platonov, K. K. (Ed.) *(Short dictionary of psychology).* Moscow: Vysshaya Shkola, 1974.

A short dictionary of Marxist psychology, presenting brief, carefully identified excerpts, often from classic Marxist writers, of the meaning of basic psychological terms.

A201 Piéron, H. *Vocabulaire de la psychologie.* (2nd ed.) Paris: Presses Universitaries de France, 1957. (1951)

The French counterpart in arrangement to the American and German dictionaries.

Psychologisches Wörterbuch, Ed. F. Dorsch, et al. (A24)

A202 Sury, K. v. (Ed.), *Wörterbuch der Psychologie und ihrer Grenzgebiete.* (4th ed.) Olten: Walter, 1974. (1955)

This edition is a radical revision and extension of the third edition. Grouping of entries under master headings has been introduced for many more sections than before. Heavy emphasis is placed on the terminology, including that for psychology and psychopathology. Entomology is clarified. The names of individuals credited with having introduced a particular term are identified. Biographical and bibliographical data are provided for 300 living and deceased psychologists, including over 100 from the *Contributors.*

A203 Warren, H. C. *Dictionary of psychology.* Boston: Houghton Mifflin, 1934.

This was a group effort. Although superseded for many purposes by English and English (A192), it is worth consulting for terminology current in the thirties. It is an advance over Baldwin's concise articles in his *Dictionary*

(A15) at the turn of the century. It is cross-referenced, and French and German equivalents are given.

ARCHIVES AND MANUSCRIPT COLLECTIONS, INCLUDING ORAL HISTORIES

Depositories of unpublished documents, in the form of both official papers of organizations and of the private papers of individuals, characterize the substantive meaning of archives. Since oral histories are apt to remain in manuscript and to be filed in archives, references concerning them are included among the archival material.

A204   Bell, W. J., & Smith, M. D. Guide to the archives and manuscript collections of the American Philosophical Society. *Mem. Amer. phil. Soc.,* 1966, No. 66.
       Major collections of Boas, Cannon, Darwin, Franklin, and Rush are among their deposits.

A205   Benison, S. Reflections on oral history. *Amer. Archivist,* 1965, *28,* 71-83.
       Possibilities and limitations of oral history are discussed by an experienced specialist.

A206   Brichford, M. J. *Scientific and technological documentation: Archival evaluation and processing of university records relating to science and technology.* Urbana-Champaign, Ill.: University of Illinois, 1969.
       Consideration is given to the task of evaluating scientific and technological records for archival purposes, so as to select those appropriate to keep for research or administrative use. Their processing, once evaluated, the records kept, and kinds of publication about them follow in later chapters. The problems of what personal papers to place in archives and that of oral history are considered in later sections. A valuable bibliography closes the pamphlet.

A207   Brooks, P. C. *Research in archives: The use of unpublished primary sources.* Chicago: University of Chicago Press, 1969.
       This is an authoritative guide on use of archival materials and American sources.

A208 Colman, G. (Ed.), *The fourth national colloquium on oral history*. New York: Oral History Association, 1970.

This volume contains a considerable amount of information about the technical problem of oral history, but, by far, the most important chapter is the concluding one by Nathan Reingold. He raises many important questions, among others, what are the characteristics, requirements, and end-products of the oral history, what is its objective validity, and what objective tests of the methods and presuppositions can be made?

A209 Cutler, W. W. Accuracy in oral history interviewing. *Hist. Meth. Newsletter,* 1970, *3* (3), 1-7.

The author sketches some of the means whereby the historian can control the various sources of error in the taking of oral histories. Excellent bibliographic notes are included.

A210 Hamer, P. M. *A guide to archives and manuscripts in the United States, compiled for the National Historical Publications Commission.* New Haven, Conn.: Yale University Press, 1961.

An easily used guide to 1300 depositories and 20,000 collections of personal papers and archival groups. Depositories are listed alphabetically by state and city. Index of proper names and subjects closes the volume.

A211 *National union catalog of manuscript collections.* Washington, D.C.: Government Printing Office, 1962-.

This is a multivolumed continuing register of manuscript collections based on reports from manuscript repositories in the United States to the Library of Congress. Title, inclusive date, scope, and content are listed by source. Cumulative subject names and lists of contributing repositories are included.

A212 Popplestone, J. A., & Kult, M. L. The Archives of the History of American Psychology, January 1965-August 1966. *J. Hist. behav. Sci.,* 1967, *3*, 60-63.

This is an account of its founding and functions.

A213 Reingold, N., & Watson, R. I. The organization and preservation of personal papers. *Amer. Psychologist,* 1966, *21*, 971-973.

Advice to the individual is offered on the preservation of his personal papers, in the setting of customary archival practice.

A213a Saffady, W. Manuscripts and psychohistory. *Amer. Archivist,* 1974, *37,* 551-564.

The implications of psychohistorical research for appraisal of manuscripts and development of acquisition policies is a central theme of this article, but it is valuable in other ways as well, e.g., for his discussion of the general relationship between history and psychoanalysis.

A214   Schellenberg, T. R. *Modern archives: Principles and techniques.* Chicago: University of Chicago Press, 1956.

This has come to be a classic statement of archival practice in terms of institutions, library relations, records, management, appraisal, preparation, and description.

A215   Schellenberg, T. R. *The management of archives.* New York: Columbia University Press, 1965.

The author discusses the methodology of arrangement, the preparation of cards for finding material, and the like.

A216   Schippers, D. L., & Tusler, Adelaide. *A bibliography on oral history.* Los Angeles, Calif.: Oral History Association, 1968.

This is a description of 116 relevant, selected publications.

A217   Starr, L. (Ed.), *The oral history collection of Columbia University.* (3rd ed.) (1 vol. + suppl.) New York: Columbia University Press, 1964, 1968.

A218   Various. Archival research. *J. Hist. behav. Sci.,* 1975, *11,* 15-40.

This is a collection of papers given at a symposium concerned with various aspects of archival research: problems of retrieval of primary sources, research design questions, the unique values to be found, values and limitations of oral histories, and the frustrations and joys involved.

A219   Warner, R. M., et al. (Comps.), *College and university archives in the United States and Canada.* Ann Arbor, Mich.: Society of American Archivists, 1966.

A directory of university archives arranged alphabetically by state. It gives names and address of institution, name of archivist, description of quantity and nature of archives, and information on its availability for research.

A220 Wellcome Institute of the History of Medicine. *Catalogue of Western manuscripts on medicine and science in the Wellcome Historical Medical Library. Mss. written before 1650 A.D.* (2 vols.) Comp. S.A.J. Moorat. London: Wellcome Institute of the History of Medicine, 1962, 1973.

Indices are given that help to locate particular manuscripts in the Wellcome library. They are listed by order of date, subject, language, and the presence of illustrations, portraits, names of former owners, book plates, and the like.

A221 Woolf, E., et al. The conference on science manuscripts. *Isis,* 1962, *53,* 3-157.

This is a collection of papers given at a conference in 1960 concerned with fostering preservation and utilization of scientific manuscripts and involving historians, scientists, archivists and librarians.

JOURNAL BIBLIOGRAPHIES

The bibliographies included in this section list various kinds of journals by title and/or year of beginning publication, describe their content, and, in some instances, give the specific libraries where they may be found.

A222 A volume-year check list of psychological and allied journals. E. S. Conklin. *Univ. Oregon Publ., Psychol. Ser.,* 1931, *1* (2), 105-128.

This supplies a means of completing a journal reference for year and/or volume number or checking apparent discrepancy between volume number and date in a reference at hand.

A223 *British union-catalogue of periodicals: A record of the periodicals of the world, from the seventeenth century to the present day, in British libraries.* (4 vols. + suppls.) London: Butterworth, 1955-1958, 1962-.

With four volumes plus supplements, this series covers more than 40,000 periodicals from 1600 to the present and gives locations in 400 British libraries.

A224 *British union-catalogue of periodicals, incorporating World list of scientific periodicals: New periodical titles.* London: Butterworth, 1964-.

This is a quarterly with annual cumulations dated by year of preceding issues. It gives British library locations of the various periodicals.

A225 *New serial titles.* Washington, D.C.: Library of Congress, 1953-.

This is a monthly supplement to the *Union List of Serials* (A229).

A226 *Psychologie: Liste mondiale des periodiques specialisés. Psychology: World list of specialized periodicals.* Paris: Mouton, 1967.

An alphabetical list by country of journals with a psychological content, with a separate section for international publications. For each title, it gives location, editor, sponsor, details of title changes by year, size, and scope of interest.

A227 *Subject index to New serial titles, 1950-1965.* Ann Arbor, Mich.: Pierian Press, 1968.

See *New serial titles* (A225) for which it is the subject index.

A228 *Union list of serials.* Ed. Ruth S. Freitag. Madison, Wisc.: American Association for State and Local History, 1956.

This list includes as serials, periodicals, newspapers, annual proceedings, publications of learned societies, etc. It records selected 1500 union lists arranged in sections, geographically by region or county, and alphabetically within each section, for works pertinent to state and local history. Geographical, name (author, editor, compiler, or corporate body), and subject indices are provided.

A229 *Union list of serials in libraries of the United States and Canada.* (3rd ed.) (5 vols.) New York: Wilson, 1965.

This list gives about 1,000 library locations for over 150,000 serials (+ 75,000 serial cross-references) and is essential for making inter-library loans or planning a visit.

A230 *World list of scientific periodicals published in the years 1900-1960.* (4th ed.) (3 vols. + 3 suppls.) Ed. P. Brown & G. B. Stratton. Washington, D.C.: Butterworth, 1963-1965.

English and foreign-language periodicals relevant to the natural sciences and technology are listed. Location and date of publication are given, and cross-referencing for serials with name changes is provided. It includes periodicals published during the 20th century, whether initiated then or earlier.

B.   HISTORICAL ACCOUNTS

In consulting these annotations, one should keep in mind that while some are intended as more general surveys, others cover a relatively narrower span and are monographic studies in depth. The annotations try to suggest this distinction when it is appropriate to do so.

The historical accounts of psychology included in the first four sections that follow make up 79 or 34 percent of the references. The history of the other behavioral sciences and related fields has been selected in a fashion that supplies the remaining 151 or 66 percent. These are somewhat arbitrarily grouped as histories of science (including histories of the philosophy of science); philosophy; psychiatry and psychoanalysis; physiology, neurology, and anatomy; biology, medicine; anthropology; sociology; and education. Lastly, under the heading of "Readings" there is a section devoted to volumes containing excerpted sections of books or articles relevant to the history of the behavioral sciences.

In keeping with the intent of seeking general titles, references dealing with the contributions of a single individual are not cited, no matter how important the person in question may be. To include only a relatively few persons is a judgment I hesitate to make; to include more would begin to duplicate what has already been done in the *Eminent Contributors to Psychology* (A78, A79). These and other bibliographic sources need also to be consulted in literature searches involving specific individuals.

Books and articles considering the historiography of these fields are presented in Section D: "Historiographic Fields."

GENERAL PSYCHOLOGY

This section is devoted to books portraying the general history of psychology. Later sections are concerned with the history of branches and research problems of psychology, schools and systems in psychology, and psychology within national boundaries. The historical accounts annotated in this section may consider, with

varying degree of emphasis, fields, schools, national trends, and
the like, but nevertheless are broader in intent.

If the annotation does not refer to specific individuals, it may
be assumed that, within the limits of the theme of the title, a considerable number of major historical figures is considered. When
the work is more limited in scope, names are mentioned.

B1   Boring, E. G. *A history of experimental psychology.* (2nd
        ed.) New York: Appleton-Century-Crofts, 1950. (1929)
        A classic in the field due to a felicitous style and solid
        scholarship, this book remains an excellent resource volume,
        especially for the wealth of biographical and bibliographical
        data (primary and secondary) that is economically segre-
        gated in notes at the end of chapters. The format is a com-
        bination of the chronological and the topical. Overall, the
        emphasis is upon German and American contributions.
        There are two biases, however, of which readers should be
        made aware: (1) avowed emphasis on experimental criteria
        as deciding the history of psychology leads to subtle distor-
        tions of many thinker's actual emphases; and (2) repeated
        reference to the *Zeitgeist* as if it were a causal explanation
        or "push," rather than a summary statement that merely
        emphasizes similarity or commonality of preoccupations
        and assumptions.

B2   Brett, G. S. *Brett's history of psychology.* (Abridged) Ed.
        R. S. Peters. New York: Macmillan, 1953. (1912-1921)
        This abridgement of Brett's lengthy three-volume
        work *History of Psychology* by Peters excludes much of
        the unwieldly detail, yet maintains Brett's historical
        approach while integrating it into a theoretical framework
        previously lacking. It attempts to show the development of
        psychology from pre-Socratic thought to the modern times.
        The influence of medical, religious, and philosophical
        thought on psychological inquiry is emphasized as indicated
        by chapters dealing with the development of the ethico-
        religious tradition, the rationalist and observationalist tradi-
        tions, and the influences of physiology and biology. The
        final chapter, a contribution by Peters, briefly presents the
        main trends of twentieth-century psychology, showing the
        way in which these trends and theories represent reactions
        against the traditions of inquiry of the past. It is meant to

be complementary to, rather than a substitute for, other modern histories of psychology. An appendix lists the major sections from Bretts' three volumes that have been omitted.

B3   Flugel, J. C. *A hundred years of psychology*. New York: International Universities Press, 1970. (1933)

Originally published in 1933, this volume by Flugel examines psychology as it was in 1833 in the work of Herbart, Thomas Brown, James Mill, Beneke, Gall, Spurzheim, Bell, Magendie, Flourens, Rolando, Marshall Hall, Johannes Müller, E. H. Weber, and Mesmer, all from the list of *Contributors*. With this base, Flugel proceeds to consider the period from 1833 to 1860, with many of the same individuals but with the significant addition of the systematic psychologies of J. S. Mill, Bain, and Lotze. Events of 1860-1900 are crowded with *Contributors,* as might be expected, led by Darwin, Galton, Fechner, Helmholtz, Wundt, and James. From 1900 to 1933 the schools and the application of psychology made their appearance. Developments beyond 1933 were appended by J. West in a miscellaneous and disjointed selection of events and men.

B4   Hehlmann, W. *Geschichte der Psychologie*. (2nd ed.) Stuttgart: Kroner, 1967. (1963)

After two chapters devoted to the Greeks and the Middle Ages and a first section of the third chapter to the Renaissance, the author launches into a more detailed history, with consideration of the work of Descartes. In 450 small pages, the volume covers succinctly major aspects of the general history of psychology, organized around 50 themes such as positivism, psychometrics, folk psychology, animal psychology, psychopathology, characterology, and social psychology.

B5   Kantor, J. R. *The scientific evolution of psychology*. Vol. 2. Chicago: Principia Press, 1969.

The central theme is the war between scientific psychology and "transcendental systems" i.e., "idealistic, or spiritistic, ways of thinking." The author's major enthusiasm is reflected throughout the text—modern behaviorism *is* psychology. It is not surprising that a relatively large proportion of pages is devoted to the 20th century and to

America. The book is an excellent example of presentism
with its oppressive reiteration of the theme of "rooting
out" mentalism and the equation of psychology with be-
havioristic rationale and procedures.

B6   Klein, D. B. *A history of scientific psychology: Its origins
and philosophical backgrounds.* New York: Basic Books,
1970.
          The intent of the author is two-fold: to place the
major problems of psychology into historical perspective
and to explore the works and thought of the great founders.
Some of the philosophical issues discussed include the
mind-body problem and the challenge of positivism, problems of selfhood, free will vs. determinism, and the nature
of historical investigation. The anticipation of contemporary issues and concepts by the ancients is heavily emphasized. The psychological thought of the great figures since
the Renaissance—Hobbes, Descartes, Locke, Spinoza,
Leibniz, Wolff, Kant, Berkeley, Hume, Herbart, Lotze, Bain,
and Wundt—is examined, showing the elaborate interrelations of their philosophical thought to the emergence of
scientific psychology.

B7   Lowry, R. *The evolution of psychological theory: 1650 to
the present.* Chicago: Aldine, 1971.
          A short, concise portrayal is given of the evolution of
psychology in terms of major psychological theory during
the modern period. The contributions to psychology's
theoretical framework of Descartes' mechanical conception
of nature, of the Newtonian revolution in physics, of
physiological theory and discovery, of psychophysics, of
evolutionary theory, of psychoanalysis, of behaviorism,
and of Gestalt theory are discussed. The influence of the
past in determining our approaches to theory and problems
is shown very clearly.

B8   MacLeod, R. B. *The persistent problems of psychology.*
Pittsburgh, Pa.: Duquesne University Press, 1975.
          A posthumously published, incomplete account, end-
ing just beyond Herbart. The "problems" of the title are a
shifting panorama not to be specifically identified in a
word or two. It is clear that they are conceived as extending over time, arising from philosophy and the related

sciences, and being exhibited in different guises at different times.

B9   Metzger, W. *Psychologie; die Entwicklung ihrer Grundannahmen seit der Einführung des Experiments.* (4th ed.) Darmstadt: Steinkopff, 1968.

While prepared as a textbook in general psychology from a Gestalt point of view, this book is both systematically and historically organized. Metzger organizes the work around certain fundamental problems or concepts, such as wholes and parts, stimulus and response, and the phenomenological (man in the world) and physiological (the world in man) approaches. Its coverage goes beyond the figures of Wertheimer, Köhler, and Koffka to present Gestalt psychology in a broader perspective.

B10   Misiak, H. M., & Sexton, Virginia S. *History of psychology: An overview.* New York: Grune & Stratton, 1966.

This book, written almost in outline form, considers the roots of psychology, its growth in various countries, and its major systems. Special attention is given to topics of recent origin that are not covered systematically in other general historical textbooks i.e., the growth of psychology as a profession, the development of clinical psychology, psychology in Asia, phenomenological psychology, and existentialism and psychology.

B11   Müller-Freienfels, R. *The evolution of modern psychology.* Trans. W. B. Wolfe. New Haven, Conn.: Yale University Press, 1935.

Writing from the perspective of a European psychologist, the author emphasizes the rise of modern psychology as the study of consciousness. After a brief survey of ancient and medieval psychological thought, he provides a detailed history of psychology from the time of Wundt. It includes chapter topics of a somewhat different character than found in most other general histories on psychosociology, biopsychosociology, biopsychosociology, sociopsychology, and parapsychology.

B12   Murphy, G., & Kovach, J. K. *Historical introduction to modern psychology.* (Rev. ed.) New York: Harcourt, Brace & Jovanovich, 1972. (1949)

Murphy's social/cultural orientation to psychology is exemplified in this rather "Zeitgeistian" approach to the history of psychology. Most sections are delineated first according to chronological periodization, then current theoretical issues. Particularly unusual and noteworthy are the last two parts, which are devoted to contemporary psychological systems including field theory and to representative research areas with stress on child psychology, social psychology, and personality.

B13   Pongratz, L. J. *Problemgeschichte der Psychologie.* Bern: Francke Verlag, 1967.

Pongratz organizes the volume around three major themes stated in bipolar terms: soul as substance and as function; consciousness and the unconscious; and experience and behavior. While each theme could have been centered around three problems—'what' (subject matter); 'how' (methods); and 'why' (theory), Pongratz chose to emphasize the subject matter and does so from the time of the Greeks to that of the contemporary scene.

B14   Reuchlin, M. *Histoire de la psychologie.* (6th ed.) Paris: Presses Universitaires de France, 1967. (1957)

A short history comparable to those in English by Lowry (B7) and Wertheimer (B16) is presented in terms of specific fields. The section on individual differences is the most detailed. The pace is, of necessity, swift, since the book is only 125 pages in length.

B15   Watson, R. I. *The great psychologists.* (4th ed.) Philadelphia: Lippincott, 1977. (1963)

This volume is organized around both the individuals who contributed and a pattern of attitudes which, while shifting in a variety of ways, gave a continuity of themes. The first seven chapters cover the period from the ancient Greeks to the beginnings of the modern period and try to clarify the often confusing philosophical and physiological antecedents of the science of psychology (e.g., dualistic and deterministic attitudes, etc.) This is followed by discussion of the problems of the empiricism and associationism, those problems created by continental philosophical psychology, psychophysics, and neural physiology, which lead up to Wundt and his emphasis upon introspection and experiment. This is followed by chapters concerning Wundt's contemporaries and successors, the Darwinian evolutionary theory and its effect upon the study of individual differences, the French psychopathological tradition and Binet, the beginnings of psychology in the United States, functionalism, behaviorism, Gestalt psychology and psychoanalysis as schools of psychology. Chapters devoted to recent events in Europe and the United States follow. An epilogue is concerned with the contemporary status of psychology as a science.

B16   Wertheimer, M. *A brief history of psychology.* New York: Holt, Rinehart & Winston, 1970.

    A succinct presentation of the history of psychology is Wertheimer's goal. The important lines of development from science and philosophy that contributed to the birth of experimental psychology around 1860 are examined. After reporting on the work of Wundt and his immediate predecessors, the various schools of psychology—structural, functional, behavioral, Gestalt, and psychoanalytic—are reviewed. Brevity has led to a great economy of speech bordering on the telegraphic, but it is an excellent book for use in conjunction with other texts in teaching history/systems, as an introduction to the field, or as a quick review.

B17   Wolman, B. B. (Ed.), *Historical roots of contemporary psychology.* New York: Harper & Row, 1968.

    The chapters, each prepared by a specialist, center upon various *Contributors*—Bain, Brentano, Freud, Hartley, Herbart, Hume, James, Janet, Kant, Locke, McDougall, James Mill, Pavlov, Reid, Sechenov, Stern, Stout, Vygotsky, Ward, and Wundt.

PSYCHOLOGY:
BRANCHES AND RESEARCH PROBLEMS

Histories of branches of psychology and of research problems of psychology have in common that they concentrate on more limited areas than do accounts in the earlier section devoted to general histories. The distinction between branches and problems is only a matter of degree, since branches of psychology are apt to emphasize certain problems, while problems in psychology are characteristically associated with certain branches of the field. Nevertheless, some clarity is introduced by distinguishing between them.

The branches of psychology for which historical accounts are annotated include social psychology, child psychology, psychological testing, personality, clinical psychology, applied psychology, and physiological psychology.

Methodological problems include measurement, statistics, experimental control, introspection, and phenomenology along with the histories of the contentual problems of sensation and perception, thinking, feeling and emotion, intelligence, instinct, language, reflex action, the unconscious, and associationism.

B18   Allport, G. W. The historical background of modern social psychology. In G. Lindzey & E. Aronson (Eds.), *The handbook of social psychology*. Vol. 1. *Historical introduction: Systematic positions.* (2nd ed.) Reading, Mass.: Addison-Wesley, 1968, pp. 1-80. (1954)

This chapter is one of the very few contemporary evaluations of the history of social psychology. Major sections are devoted to Comte as a discoverer of social psychology, to the various unidimensional theories such as hedonism, egoism, sympathy, imitation, and the crowd that dominated the field at one time or another; the shift that occurred when, instead of these theories being sovereign, the unit of analysis in instinct, habit, attitude, or sentiment came to the fore; and, lastly, the beginnings of the predominance of the objective method in social psychology. Bentham, Durkheim, and McDougall also receive relatively full treatment.

Beach, F. A. The snark was a boojum. (C36)

B19   Blumenthal, A. L. *Language and psychology: Historical aspects of psycholinguistics.* New York: Wiley, 1970.

This book is designed to provide an overview of some important historical trends in the development of psycholinguistics. Beginning with nineteenth-century Europe as the background, it uses a Great Man approach in presenting the important trends that have occurred in the psychological study of language; with Wundt seen as the major contributor, it then proceeds to the modern period. For the contemporary scene, some similarities between the ideas that were pursued by the nineteenth-century experimentalists and those of the present-day psycholinguists (i.e., Chomsky, Lennenberg, and Miller) are emphasized.

B20 Boring, E. G. *Sensation and perception in the history of experimental psychology.* New York: Appleton-Century-Crofts, 1942.

This is the classic historical work in the history of sensation and perception from the seventeenth century until about 1930. It elaborates upon the relevant thinkers and schools by considering the actual experimentation and the related theory they expressed. Each of the senses is treated in separate sections.

B21 Boring, E. G. The influence of evolutionary theory upon American psychological thought. In S. Persons (Ed.), *Evolutionary thought in America.* New Haven, Conn.: Yale University Press, 1950, pp. 267-298. (Reprinted in *History, psychology, and science: Selected papers,* pp. 159-184.) (E2)

The author shows how the biological and mental concepts of certain Englishmen, primarily Darwin, Spencer, and Galton, combined with the physiological and associationistic concepts of the German psychologists to influence early American psychologists, notably James, Dewey, Hall, and Cattell. Representing the American pioneering spirit of survival, each of these individuals then transformed this European combination into the present American functionalistic thesis of the usefulness of mind to organism.

B22 Boring, E. G. A history of introspection. *Psychol. Bull.,* 1953, *50,* 169-189. Reprinted in *Psychologist at large: An autobiography and selected essays,* pp. 210-245. (E1)

The author traces various methods of studying consciousness from the time of Descartes. These methods include the classical introspection of Wundt and Titchener, the functional introspection of James and Dewey, the phenomenological observation of the Gestaltists, the free association of Freud, the psychophysics of Fechner, the verbal reports of Watson, and the observational operations of Stevens.

B23 Boring, E. G. The nature and history of experimental control. *Amer. J. Psychol.*, 1954, *67*, 573-589. Reprinted in *History, psychology, and science: Selected papers*, pp. 111-125. (E2)

This article, shows how 'control,' both as a concept and as a word, has been variously used in experimental psychology. He starts with Mill's "Method of Difference" and several less explicit antecedents in order to describe the use of the word in the sense of a check or comparison and concludes by considering the newest use of the word in the concept of the control group.

B24   Boring, E. G. The beginning and growth of measurement in psychology. *Isis*, 1961, *52*, 238-257. Reprinted in *History, psychology, and science; Selected papers,* pp.140-158. (E2)

The writer considers the measurement problems of Fechner in psychophysics; Donders in reaction time; Ebbinghaus in remembering; and Galton in individual differences. He shows how mental measurement offered solutions in each area through several kinds of progressive changes that typically emerge in the history of scientific quantification, no matter what the field in question.

B25   Burnham, J. C. Historical background for the study of personality. In E. F. Borgatta & W. W. Lambert (Eds.), *Handbook of personality theory and research.* Chicago: Rand McNally, 1968, pp. 3-81.

In a mere 80 pages, this is the most definitive contemporary history of the topic that is known to the writer. After presenting tentative definitions of personality; character, temperament, disposition, and habit, the author begins a historical account, progressing from the Greeks to Descartes—all in 14 pages. The major topic headings thereafter are: the Enlightenment; the early nineteenth century; the late nineteenth century (considered by him to be the low point of interest in the topic); and the "seed bed of modern personality theory and research," which he finds in instinct theories, environmentalism, the psychotherapy movement, hypnotism and suggestion, reeducation and persuasion as psychotherapy, behaviorism, the psychology of individual differences including mental testing, dynamic psychiatry, and the new physiology of personality.

B26   Carterette, E. C., & Friedman, M. P. (Eds.), *Handbook of perception.* Vol. I. *Historical and philosophical roots of perception.* New York: Academic Press, 1974.

An uneven publication bringing together original contributions related to perception, its philosophical roots, its historical background in research, and contemporary views. From among the *Contributors* Brunswik, Helmoltz, Hull, James, Köhler, Koffka, Locke, Royce, Tolman, and Wertheimer are given considerable attention.

B27 Dennis, W. Historical beginnings of child psychology. *Psychol. Bull.,* 1949, *46,* 224-235.

An historical survey of 42 publications dealing with observational studies of "normal" children, dating from 1787 to the publication of Wilhelm Preyer's *Die Seele des Kindes* (1882) and G. Stanley Hall's *Contents of Childrens' Minds* (1883).

B28 Dorsch, F. *Geschichte und Probleme der Angewandten Psychologie.* Bern: Huber, 1963.

The author emphasizes the history and problems of applied psychology in the German-speaking countries, although a few Frenchmen, Americans, and Englishmen are discussed.

B29 DuBois, P. H. *A history of psychological testing.* Boston: Allyn & Bacon, 1970.

Galton, Pearson, Cattell, and Kraepelin are regarded as prominent in early psychological testing. The individual scale introduced by Binet followed, along with the introduction of Stern's mental quotient. Spearman introduced the statistical concept of reliability, and Terman developed the Stanford-Binet Scale. Group tests, particularly the Army testing program, Thorndike's achievement tests, and the Strong Vocational Interest Blank, are then considered. A discussion follows of personality measures, both structured and projective. The last chapter concerns the modern period, roughly corresponding to the period of World War II and just beyond.

Fearing, F. *Reflex action: A study in the history of physiological psychology.* (B152)

B30 Gardiner, H. M., Metcalf, Ruth C., & Beebe-Center, J. G.

Feeling and emotion: A history of theories. New York: American Book, 1937.

   Approximately one-third of the book is concerned with emotion, through the period of the Renaissance. Thereafter, chapters are devoted to Descartes and Malebranche and Hobbes, Spinoza and Pascal, followed by one devoted to the British moralists and associationists including Locke, Hartley, Adam Smith, and Hume. Chapters devoted to France and Germany in the eighteenth century follow with Rousseau, Condillac, Helvetius, LaMettrie, Bonnet, Leibniz, Wolff, Tetens, and Kant prominently featured. The psychology of the emotions in the nineteenth and in the first decades of the twentieth century are the concern of the last two chapters.

B31   Hamlyn, D. W. *Sensation and perception: A history of the philosophy of perception.* London: Routledge & Kegan Paul, 1961.

   This survey extends from the pre-Socratic thought through the author's own view of the nature of sensation and perception. "Philosophical" views are emphasized.

B32   Hall, C. S., & Lindzey, G. *Theories of personality.* (2nd ed.) New York: Wiley, 1970. (1957)

   This is a comprehensive, authoritative survey of the major contemporary personality theories presented in a manner that makes it valuable as a historical source. Theories covered include psychoanalytic theory, Jungian analytic theory, individual psychology, and other social psychological theories (Fromm, Horney & Sullivan), Murray's personology, Lewin's field theory, Allport's psychology of the individual, organismic theories, (Goldstein, Angyal, Maslow & Lecky) constitutional psychology (Sheldon), factor theory (R. B. Cattell), stimulus-response theory (Dollard & Miller), operant reinforcement theory (Skinner), self theory (Rogers), and existential theory (Binswanger). Each theory is evaluated according to its position on personality structure, dynamics, development, followed by characteristic research. The current status and general evaluation of each theory is also included.

B33   Humphrey, G. *Thinking: An introduction to its experimental psychology.* New York: Wiley, 1951.

While dated in terms of present-day research in cognition, this account provides a thorough summary of many historically important trends that have evolved into cognitive research. An excellent evaluation of some important experimental research in the area of thinking is provided. It provides a thorough evaluation of the Wurzburg school, the theories of Selz and of Gestalt, and a chapter on thought in relation to motor reaction, language, and generalization.

B34   Karpf, Fay B. *American social psychology: Its origins, development and European background.* New York: McGraw-Hill, 1932.

Social psychology as a distinct field of scientific investigation is conceived as emerging from philosophy circa 1850. The author stresses the tenets of the famous Chicago school with its emphasis on function, adaptation, and social forces. While emphases of the text are explicitly American, one half of the book is devoted to sections on the influences upon it of German, French, and English social thought. Major themes covered include emergence from philosophy; concepts taken from other fields, e.g., folk psychology, anthropology and evolution; shifts in perspective, e.g., from commonsense or anecdotal to more scientific analyses. Attention is also paid to specific topics, e.g., instincts in relation to social psychological thought.

B35   Levine, M., & Levine, Adeline. *A social history of helping services.* New York: Appleton-Century-Crofts, 1970.

Various social institutions concerned with personal, social, and educational services are considered, including the psychological clinic, the settlement house, the visiting teacher movement, the Gary school system, the Chicago Juvenile Court and Juvenile Psychopathic Institute, the Denver Juvenile Court, and the child guidance clinic movement. Of the *Contributors* Bronner, Healy, and Witmer figure prominently.

B36   Miller, J. G. *Unconsciousness.* New York: Wiley, 1942.

This book is an attempt to unravel and clarify the diversity of meanings attributed at one time or another to the term 'unconscious' in order to arrive at a common feature or features. Consequently, it is a review of the liter-

ature concerning various concepts that deal with the unconscious.

B37   Misiak, H., & Staudt, Virginia S. *Catholics in psychology:
       A historical survey.* New York: McGraw-Hill, 1954.
          By extending the meaning to some extent, it is possible
       to include this volume under the rubric of "fields." Al-
       though not all of the following are stressed, because of
       church affiliation, it will suffice to say that from among
       the *Contributors* Bergson, Brentano, Cattell, Descartes,
       Fabre, Freud, Fröbes, Gemelli, James, Kiesow, Külpe,
       Lindworsky, Mercier, Michotte, G. E. Müller, J. Müller,
       Murchison, Ribot, Roback, Stumpf, Thorndike, Titchener,
       Wundt, and Zilboorg are major figures. Two other major
       Catholic figures are Edward A. Pace and Armand Thiery,
       who are not among the *Contributors.*

B38   Pastore, N. *Selective history of theories of visual percep-
       tion: 1650-1950.* New York: Oxford University Press,
       1971.
          The framework the author adopts unobtrusively is
       that of Gestalt theory. The book is 'selective' in the sense
       that certain individuals important in the history of percep-
       tion are singled out for exposition. Most of them are to be
       found among the *Contributors*—namely, Ames, Bain, Ber-
       keley, Condillac, Descartes, Hamilton, Herbart, Höffding,
       Humphrey, James, Koffka, Köhler, Lashley, Locke, Lotze,
       Malebranche, J. S. Mill, Molyneux, J. Müller, Pavlov, Reid,
       A. Smith, Spalding, Stewart, Sully, Taine, Wertheimer, and
       Wheatstone. Only T. K. Abbott, S. Bailey, A. H. Riesen,
       and M. Senden receive comparable attention.

B39   Pearson, E. S., & Kendall, M. G. (Eds.), *Studies in the his-
       tory of statistics and probability.* London: Griffin, 1970.
          This is a collection of historically-oriented papers
       selected from among those appearing in *Biometrika.* The
       contributions of Bernoulli, Fisher, Galton, Gauss, Gosset,
       Laplace, Pearson, and Yule are discussed.

B40   Peterson, J. *Early conceptions and tests of intelligence.*
       Yonkers-on-Hudson, N.Y.: World Book, 1925.
          The introductory third of the book considers early
       conceptions of intelligence and the attempts to use specific

sensory and motor skills for its measurement, particularly in the work of Galton and Cattell. Thereafter, the emphasis is upon the work and influence of Binet and his measurement of intelligence conceived as a complex of higher functions, a view that dominates the rest of the book. The contributions of Henri, Terman, Thorndike, and Simon receive some attention.

B41   Postman, L. (Ed.), *Psychology in the making: Histories of selected research problems.* New York: Knopf, 1962.

Original articles were prepared by researchers active in a particular field. The research topics chosen for historical presentation were drawn from biology, perception, learning, memory, intelligence, clinical and statistical prediction, the sucking behavior of mammals, repression, and hypnosis. The papers come off very well in that they are thorough, cogent, and well written. The number of *Eminent Contributors* whose work is discussed is quite extensive.

B42   Reeves, Joan W. *Thinking about thinking.* New York: Braziller, 1965.

The book is an interesting attempt to explain some of the relevant ideas on research in thinking in both its modern and its earlier trends. Starting with a reevaluation of Locke and Spinoza, Reeves discusses Freud's approach to thinking and the contributions of Galton and Binet. She includes a brief summary of some relevant modern trends in thinking, (i.e., Behaviorism, Gestalt, and the view of Piaget) and has chapters devoted to concepts in thinking such as insight, meditation, recognition, and a final summary that attempts an integration of diverse approaches as related to thinking research. The discussion and analysis of psychological trends is interpreted as refuting the simple associationist treatment of thought. This is a concise development of the process approach to conceptual thinking, as contrasted with the molecular, static approach prevalent in the nineteenth century.

B43   Reisman, J. M. *A history of clinical psychology.* (Enlarged ed.) New York: Irvington Publishers, 1976. (Originally published as *The Development of Clinical Psychology* in 1966.)

This is a history of the development of clinical psychology from the late nineteenth century to the late 1960s. After the first chapter, which is concerned with nineteenth-century antecedents, particularly psychiatric reform, each chapter thereafter covers a decade, beginning with that of 1890. Developments outside psychology are used to set the scene for a particular decade, then sections follow on normal personality functioning, diagnostic techniques, diagnostic formulations, treatment formulations, and professional developments.

B44   Robinson, E. S. *Association theory today: An essay in systematic psychology.* New York: Century, 1932. (Reprinted 1964)

    This is a summarization of the status of association theory, circa 1930. Since it does not stress the historical background, the author's contemporaries from the *Contributors,* H. L. Hollingworth, Thorndike, Warren, and Woodworth, receive emphasis. The only others as often mentioned are Thomas Brown and Ebbinghaus.

B45   Sahakian, W. S. *Systematic social psychology.* New York: Chandler, 1974.

    Despite its title and the attention paid to systematic issues, this is primarily a very much needed history of social psychology from the present perspective. Part 1 concerns the period from antiquity to 1908, part 2 from 1908 to about 1930, while parts 3 and 4 the thirties and thereafter. From the *Contributors,* sociologists Durkheim, Weber, Wallas, and Ross, anthropologist Benedict, socially oriented psychodynamicists Horney, Sullivan, and Adler and psychologists McDougall, Lewin, and several others receive detailed attention.

B46   Shakow, D. Clinical psychology: An evaluation. In L. G. Lowrey (Ed.) *Orthopsychiatry, 1923-1948: Retrospect and prospect.* New York: American Orthopsychiatric Association, 1948, pp. 231-247.

    This is an historical evaluation of clinical psychology from a psychodynamic perspective from about the time of the founding in 1896 of the psychological clinic at the University of Pennsylvania by Lightner Witmer to the immediate post-World-War-II years.

B47   Smith, R. The background of physiological psychology in natural philosophy. *Hist. Sci.*, 1973, *11*, 75-123.

Rather than considering the history of physiological psychology from a reductionistic stance, so common in the history of the physical sciences, the author related it to the mind-body problem of natural philosophy and to biological evolutionary theory. There are excellent bibliographic notes.

B48   Spiegelberg, H. *The phenomenological movement: A historical introduction.* (2nd ed.) (2 vols.) The Hague: Nijhoff, 1965. (1960)

This is an authoritative statement of the numerous ramifications of the phenomenological movement. The "preparatory phase" is seen to involve Brentano and Stumpf, from which it moves on to the focal figure of Edmund Husserl, and then to the older phenomenological movement centering at the Universities of Göttingen and Munich. Chapters devoted to Max Scheler, Martin Heidegger, and Nicolai Hartmann follow; the French phase then comes to the fore in the persons of Gabriel Marcel, Jean-Paul Sartre, and Maurice Merleau-Ponty. Current developments are next considered, first in France, and then in Europe and in the United States. The last section is devoted to a summary of principles and to an appraisal of the movement.

B49   Spiegelberg, H. *Phenomenology in psychology and psychiatry: A historical introduction.* Evanston, Ill.: Northwestern University Press, 1972.

A general orientation to the theme is provided through a brief examination on the thinking of Brentano, Stumpf, Husserl, and others. The author then considers phenomenological thought as affected by continental psychologists, particularly by the Germans, in the persons of Jaensch, Katz, Rubin, Messer, K. Bühler, Ach, Selz, Wertheimer, Köhler, and Koffka and by German and Swiss psychiatrists and psychopathologists, with Karl Jaspers as the early, and Binswanger as the later pivotal figures. A discussion of phenomenology in relation to psychoanalysis follows. The American scene is opened with a consideration of James and Allport. The perspective now shifts to the influence of individual contemporary leading figures in phenomenologi-

cal psychology and psychiatry, namely, Karl Jaspers, Ludwig Binswanger, Eugene Minkowski, Viktor Emil von Geb-
sattel, Erwin Strauss, Frederick J. J. Buytendijk, Kurt
Goldstein, Paul Schilder, Medard Boss, and Viktor Frankl.
The selected bibliography, arranged in terms of the leading
figures, is very well constructed.

B50   Van Hoorn, W. *As images unwind: Ancient and modern
       theories of visual perception.* Amsterdam: University Press
       of Amsterdam, 1972.
              A penetrating and original attempt to examine the
       history of visual perception in an effort to show that it is,
       in the main, a discontinuous affair, as differentiated from
       the situation prevailing in the history of the natural sciences.
       A different contextualistic background leads to a different
       theory of visual perception. The most decisive of these
       breaks with the past is seen as being due to Descartes and
       his theory of language. Newton and Goethe are other
       Contributors who figure prominently in the account.

B51   Walker, Helen M. *Studies in the history of statistical
       method: With special reference to certain educational
       problems.* Baltimore, Md.: Williams & Wilkins, 1929.
              As the title suggests, certain problems have been
       selected for exposition—the normal curve, moments, per-
       centiles, correlation, and the theory of two factors. An his-
       toriographic chapter on the teaching of statistics in Ameri-
       can universities is included. Bernoulli, Bessel, Boas, W.
       Brown, Fechner, Fisher, Galton, Gauss, Holzinger, Huygens,
       Jevons, Kelley, Laplace, Quetelet, Pearson, Spearman,
       Thorndike, and Yule from the *Contributors* figure promin-
       ently.

B52   Warren, H. C. *A history of the association psychology.* New
       York: Scribner's, 1921.
              Introductory material carries the early history through
       Aristotle, Descartes, Hobbes, Locke, Berkely, and Hume to
       a chapter on David Hartley, at which point the account be-
       comes more detailed. Successive chapters concern James
       Mill, evolutionary association through exposition of the
       views of Spencer and Lewes, a summarization, and, there-
       after, the topic of continental association through Con-
       dillac, Bonnet, and Helvetius. The last three chapters are

devoted respectively to experimental studies, to the current status of the nature and laws of association and, lastly, to the way the associative analysis of mental states relates to cognition, conation, and affectivity.

B53   Watson, R. I. A brief history of clinical psychology. *Psychol. Bull.*, 1953, *50*, 321-346. (Reprinted in I. N. Mensh (Ed.), *Clinical psychology: Science and profession.* New York: Macmillan, 1966, pp. 68-104.)

     Clinical psychology is examined historically, first in terms of its origin to about the end of the second decade of this century, through consideration of the psychometric and dynamic tradition, the founding of psychological clinics, work in child guidance and mental hospitals, and the beginnings of psychology as a profession. The same topics are then repeated for the decades of the twenties and the thirties. The work of psychologists in the Armed Services during the Second World War and its effect upon psychology in the immediate postwar period closes the paper.

B54   Watson, R. I. The experimental tradition and clinical psychology. In A. J. Bachrach (Ed.), *Experimental foundations of clinical psychology.* New York: Basic Books, 1962, pp. 3-25.

     The heritage of clinical psychology is shown to rest in the experimental tradition of the past, illustrated by the relevant works of Darwin, Pavlov, Kraepelin, and Franz. A closer examination follows of the influence of experimental problems in psychophysics, learning, and communication on clinical psychology. An account of how behavior modification is derived from experimental antecedents closes the chapter.

B55   Whyte, L. L. *The unconscious before Freud.* New York: Basic Books, 1960.

     The author's intent is to show both that Freud's theory of the unconscious was based upon prior work and that its later acceptance could be traced back to roots in a European cultural tradition that began as early as the seventeenth century. The thinking of a host of individuals is seen as contributing to this tradition: Carpenter, Descartes, Goethe, Hartmann, Hegel, Herbart, Herder, Kant, Leibniz,

Maine de Biran, Nietzsche, Pascal, Rousseau, Schelling, Schopenhauer, Spinoza, and von Wolff. Only Carl S. Carus receives attention similar to that given to the *Contributors.*

PSYCHOLOGY:
NATIONAL

Accounts of the history of psychology, even when not specifically intended, probably reflect some degree of national emphasis. Moreover, many of the general selections have chapters devoted to national accounts for a given period or problem. There are others intended to present accounts of psychological developments within a given country. It is to some of these histories that this section is devoted. American, German, British, French, and Soviet histories are included.

B56   Ben-David, J., & Collins, R. Social factors in the origins of a new science: The case of psychology. *Amer. Sociol. Rev.,* 1966, *31,* 451-465.

Using late-nineteenth-century Germany as the positive case and the United States, France, and Britain as negative ones, the authors explore how a new role, that of scientific psychology, came into being from new academic career opportunities, and the relatively low academic standing of philosophy and other factors resulted in psychology's emergence in Germany and not in the other countries. Quantitative data is used in presenting this case.

B57   Ben-David, J., & Collins, R. Reply to Ross. *Amer. Sociol. Rev.,* 1967, *32,* 469-472.

The authors' reply to Ross' critique (B68) of their work (B56), stating that she failed to take into account the difference between idea hybridization and role hybridization.

B58   Boring, Millie D., & Boring, E. G. Masters and pupils among the American psychologists. *Amer. J. Psychol.,* 1948, *61,* 527-534. (Reprinted in *History, psychology, and science: Selected papers,* pp. 132-139.) (E2)

The Borings trace the intellectual genealogy of over a hundred of the most eminent American psychologists, originating primarily from the first generation of Wundt, James, and Hall. The complete genealogy appears in chart form. Also identified are more than a dozen "self-starters," such as Köhler and Thurstone.

B59   Brozek, H., & Slobin, D. I. (Eds.), *Psychology in the USSR: An historical perspective*. White Plains, N.Y.: International Arts and Sciences Press, 1972.

The volume is made up of papers from various sources, including some translations from the Russian, from the later sixties. Articles summarize Soviet psychology in contemporary terms, its history including specific figures, and bibliographic aids; these are followed by a series of articles devoted to the various basic and applied fields, and a last section on Georgian psychology. The political motif is not prominent. From among the *Contributors,* Bekhterev, Kornilov, Pavlov, Rubinstein, Sechenov, and Vygotsky figure prominently. Also receiving considerable emphasis are P. K. Anokhin, P. P. Blonsky, Nadezhda N. Ladygina-Kots, B. M. Teplov, A. A. Ukhtomsky, and D. N. Uznadze. This is the most valuable source in English for leads on the history of Soviet psychology. There is no index.

B60   Dessoir, M. *Geschichte der neuren deutschen Psychologie. Von Leibniz bis Kant.* (3rd ed.) (2 vols.) Berlin: Duncker, 1902. (1894) Reprinted in 1 vol. Amsterdam: Bonset, 1964.

After a brief introduction, Dessoir begins a detailed presentation with Leibniz and von Wolff and continues through the eighteenth century. Hence the book does not extend into the period in which psychology was seen as an experimental science. Although the work of a considerable number of *Contributors* form aspects of the narrative, receiving equal or greater attention are individuals infrequently encountered, e.g., Alexander Gottlieb Baumgarten, Ludwig Heinrich von Jakob, Christian Thomasius, and Johann August Unzer.

B61   Fay, J. W. *American psychology before William James.* New Brunswick, N.J.: Rutgers University Press, 1939.

It can be inferred from the title that Fay is concerned with the preexperimental phase of American psychology, which extended until the 1880s. A whole host of otherwise relatively obscure mental philosophers is presented by him, one by one. However, James McCosh, Jonathan Edwards, and Noah Porter are also evaluated. The anticipations of later work attributed by him to the individuals with whom he is concerned are somewhat strained. This is, nevertheless, a valuable work since it is practically the only existing source for its period.

B62   Hearnshaw, L. S. *A short history of British psychology, 1840-1940.* London: Methuen, 1964.

The book opens with Bain, but his work is related to that of other earlier *Contributors,* such as J. S. Mill. Thereafter, sections are devoted to physiological and abnormal psychology to 1875, the relation of evolution and psychology, Galton and the beginning of psychometrics, development in neurology and physiology including the contributions of Jackson, Sherrington, and Head, the rise of comparative psychology, the founding of social psychology, changes in philosophical climate (scientific materialism, the religious reaction, and the influences of German idealism), systematic psychology at the turn of the century in the persons of Sully, Ward, and Stout, abnormal psychology again, the relatively late institutional beginnings, William McDougall, the London School represented by Spearman and Cyril Burt, British psychology between the Wars and, lastly, applied psychology.

B63   Leontiev, A. N. The historical approach to the study of the psyche of man. In B. G. Ananiev, et al. (Eds.), *Psychological sciences in the U.S.S.R.* Vol. 1. Washington, D.C.: U.S. Joint Publications Research Service, 1961, pp. 8-53. (1959)

A translation of an historical essay by a Soviet psychologist. From among the *Contributors,* Bekhterev, Kornilov, Marx, Pavlov, Rubinstein, Sechenov, and Vygotsky are evaluated.

B64   Rahmani, L. *Soviet psychology: Philosophical, theoretical, and experimental issues.* New York: International Universities Press, 1973.

This is the best source in English that we have for an account of the internal relations of the thinking of Soviet psychologists, one to another. As far as senior Soviet psychologists are concerned, it is by far the clearest and most detailed statement of their views, of Sergei Rubinstein and Leo Vygotsky in particular. Overall, it has the virtue of stressing the Soviet psychological, rather than physiological, orientation. Sechenov, Bekhterev, and Pavlov each have their place, but much more attention is given to the contributions of modern psychologists in the Soviet Union in sensory cognition, thought and language, memory, emotions and feelings, voluntary activity, and personality.

Reuchlin, M. *Histoire de la psychologie.* (B14)

B65   Ribot, T. A. *English psychology.* (3rd ed.) Trans. J. M. Baldwin. New York: Appleton, 1892. (1870)
Ribot prepared this volume to acquaint the French with developments taking place in then contemporary English psychology. He stressed the relatively recent associationism from Hartley to Lewes and utilitarianism in the persons of Bentham, J. Mill, J. S. Mill, and Spencer, as the major themes.

B66   Ribot, T. A. *German psychology of to-day: The empirical school.* (2nd ed.) Trans. J. M. Baldwin: pref. J. McCosh. New York: Scribner's 1886. (1879)
This volume was written to acquaint the French with contemporary developments, circa 1880, in German empirical and physiological psychology. It was subsequently translated into English. It opens with the work of Herbart and then turns successively to that of Lotze, Helmholtz, Fechner, J. Müller, Stumpf, E. H. Weber, and Wundt.

B67   Roback, A. A. *A history of American psychology.* (Rev. ed.) New York: Collier, 1964. (1952)
This book is divided into four sections: the eighteenth and the nineteenth centuries, until about 1885; the new psychology of James, Hall, Cattell, Baldwin, Scripture, Titchener, Münsterberg, and Witmer; the period from about 1900 of the schools the central figures of which were Dewey, Angell, Thorndike, Watson, McDougall, Prince, Woodworth, Lewin, Allport, Freud, Wertheimer, Köhler, Koffka, Hull, and Lashley; and growth of the branches of psychology, with Yerkes and Terman given prominence, though a considerably greater number of individuals is mentioned.

B68   Ross, Dorothy. On the origins of psychology. *Amer. Sociol. Rev.*, 1967, *32*, 466-469.

The author argues that Ben-David and Collins (B56) neglected the complexity of the historical situation in their emphasis on sociological factors, which led them into the error of failing to see that the professional "take-off" of the field of psychology in the 1870s occurred in the U.S. as well as in Germany.

PSYCHOLOGY:
SCHOOLS AND SYSTEMS

Although there are numerous shades of difference, one can characterize the references that follow as falling under the rubrics of Structuralism, Functionalism, Behaviorism, Gestalt psychology, Phenomenology, and Psychoanalysis. This last category involves citing again references from the section on "Psychiatry and Psychoanalysis," since it is an approach to psychiatry as well as a school of psychology. Phenomenology is sometimes considered to be primarily a method but does partake, in some of its manifestations, of a school. Hence, references from the section, "Psychology: Branches and Research Problems," are cited again.

Burnham, J. C. *Psychoanalysis and American Medicine.* (B124)

Hale, N. G., Jr. *Freud and the Americans.* (B132)

B69   Harrison, R. Functionalism and its historical significance. *Genet. Psychol. Monogr.*, 1963, *68*, 387-423.

Harrison explores the precursors of functionalism in the work of Brentano, Höffding, and James and then goes on to stress, as American functionalists, J. R. Angell, Carr, Dewey, and Judd, while using Titchener as a foil to their views.

B70   Hartmann, G. W. *Gestalt psychology: A survey of facts and principles.* New York: Ronald, 1935.

It is first argued by the author that antecedents of Gestalt psychology are found in Mach, von Ehrenfels, Dilthey, Katz, Karl Bühler, and Rubin. A theoretical section of several chapters then considers the physical bases, the physiological and philosophical foundations, and an exposition of varieties of Gestalt theory, including an exposition of the distinction between the Berlin and Leipzig Schools. Kohler, Wertheimer, Lewin, and Wheeler are considered the major Gestalt theoreticians, while the experimental work of non-Gestaltists Lashley, Driesch, and Coghill is seen as supporting the Gestalt position. Almost one-half of the work is devoted to the relevant empirical evidence in terms of studies of visual perception, audition, the skin senses, "the unity of senses," memory, learning, thinking, insight and action, emotion, and will. Practical applications considered thereafter are in terms of mental pathology (Gelb and Goldstein), industrial, and educational problems. Criticisms of the Gestalt position from outside of the school and then a short concluding statement close the volume.

B71   Heidbreder, Edna, *Seven psychologies.* New York: Apple-ton-Century-Crofts, 1933.

Although published in 1933 during the period when feelings still ran high about the schools, this is a remarkably balanced and temperate statement. The "seven psychologies" are structuralism, the psychology of William James, functionalism, behaviorism, the dynamic psychology of Columbia University in the person of Woodworth, Gestalt psychology, and psychoanalysis. Today opinion would have it that the contributions of James and Woodworth's Columbia group could be subsumed under the somewhat amorphous banner of functionalism, reducing it to five psychologies, but closeness to the scene made the author aware of distinctions she wished to bring out. From among the *Contributors* those receiving evaluation as representative of the schools, in addition to James, Woodworth, and Freud, are J. R. Angell, Carr, Cattell, Dewey, Koffka, Köhler, Lashley, Titchener, Watson, Wertheimer, and, as background for the period of the schools, Berkeley, Brentano, Fechner, Galton, Hume, Kant, Külpe, Locke, and Wundt.

B72   Helson, H. The psychology of Gestalt. *Amer. J. Psychol.*, 1925, *36*, 342-370, 494-526; 1926, *37*, 25-62, 189-223.

This is one of the first summarizations of the early work within the Gestalt movement and still an authoritative one.

B73   Krantz, D. L. (Ed.), *Schools of psychology: A symposium.* New York: Appleton-Century-Crofts, 1969.

This is an evaluation of the schools of psychology from the perspective of the later sixties written by individuals involved with one or another of the schools. Structuralism, functionalism, behaviorism, Gestalt psychology, and psychoanalysis are represented.

B74   Marx, M. H., & Hillix, W. A. *Systems and theories in psychology.* (2nd ed.) New York: McGraw-Hill, 1973. (1963)

This is an authoritative, widely used textbook that appeared recently in its second edition. After an introduction considering psychology as a science, and a statement of the strategy to be followed thereafter, associationism, structuralism, functionalism, behaviorism, Gestalt psychology, and psychoanalysis are each treated in a chapter. As background for their systematic treatment of the nature of the field, aside from their own theorizing, the conceptions of T. S. Kuhn, R. I. Watson, and R. W. Coan are used. This occupies the first half of the book. Contemporary theories, under the rubrics of S-R theories, field theories, and personality theories and a somewhat less parallel account of the engineering and mathematical influences in psychology make up the second half of the book. Appendices discuss comparable developments in various other parts of the world.

Metzger, W. *Psychologie.* (B9)

B75   Misiak, H., & Sexton, Virginia S. *Phenomenological, existential, and humanistic psychologies: A historical survey.* New York: Grune & Stratton, 1973.

It is the authors' thesis that phenomenological and existential philosophies have had a long and rich history that must be traced. Implications for, and application in, psychology have likewise been present, although phenomenology was sometimes relegated to the position of a method. As a movement with ill-defined boundaries, humanistic psychology drew its major inspiration from these sources. This historical survey culminates in a current account of humanistic psychology.

Munroe, Ruth L. *Schools of psychoanalytic thought.* (B138)

B76 Murchison, C. (Ed.), *Psychologies of 1925: Powell Lectures in psychological theory.* (3rd ed.) Worcester, Mass.: Clark University Press, 1928. (1926)

Accounts by leading protagonists of the schools at the time of their heyday—Watson and Hunter on behaviorism, Woodworth on "dynamic" (functional) psychology, Koffka and Köhler on Gestalt psychology, Prince and Mc-Dougall on purposive psychology, and Bentley on structural psychology.

B77 Murchison, C. (Ed.), *Psychologies of 1930.* Worcester, Mass.: Clark University Press, 1930.

This is a companion volume, five years later, to that for 1925 (B76). From among the *Contributors,* Adler, Bentley, Brett, Car, Dewey, Dunlap, Flugel, Hunter, Janet, Kelley, Koffka, Köhler, Kornilov, McDougall, Pavlov, Spearman, Troland, Washburn, Weiss, and Woodworth present their views. Four others participated.

B78 Wann, T. W. (Ed.), *Behaviorism and phenomenology: Contrasting bases for modern psychology.* Chicago: University of Chicago Press, 1964.

This is a collection of papers delivered at a conference by Sigmund Koch, R. B. MacLeod, B. F. Skinner, Carl R. Rogers, Norman Malcolm, and Michael Scriven, along with some of the discussion that followed each presentation.

Whyte, L. L. *The unconscious before Freud.* (B55)

B79 Woodworth, R. S., & Sheehan, Mary R. *Contemporary schools of psychology.* (3rd ed.) New York: Ronald Press, 1964. (1931)

Robert Woodworth's temperate account of the schools of psychology has become a classic. The collaboration of a coauthor in the third, posthumous edition, fortunately, did not remove its characteristic flavor. Functional and structural psychology are presented in the same chapter, so one is able to contrast them. The older and newer associationism, the latter represented by Thorndike and Pavlov, is then presented. Soviet psychology as a school integrates Pavlov into that amorphous movement. Three chapters on behaviorism follow and thereafter Gestalt psychology, "psychoanalytic" (Freud), "individual" (Adler), and "analytic" (Jung). Under the heading of "Motivation and the Unity of the Person," the positions of McDougall, Adolf Meyer, Goldstein, Calkins, Stern, Henry A. Murray, Spranger, Allport, and Carl Rogers are discussed.

Wyss, D. *Psychoanalytic schools from the beginning to the present.* (B146)

SCIENCE

As the term "science" is being used here, it refers to natural philosophy, the physical and/or natural sciences, the philosophy of science, and the "scientific method." The history of the social sciences and of biology are reserved for later sections.

B80   Buchdahl, G. *Metaphysics and the philosophy of science: The classical origins, Descartes to Kant.* Cambridge: MIT Press, 1969.
        Science, Buchdahl argues, was a crucial factor used by philosophers of this period for untangling their presuppositions and disagreements with one another. History, he says, is replete with analogies. Philosophical concepts, in point of fact, are reorganized and developed against a choice of analogies. A philosopher starts with a key concept (Locke's ideas, Hume's impression, Kant's appearance), for which a "metaphysical center of gravity" is also found (in God, in substance, in consciousness). The history of philosophy then shows shifts of centers of gravity from one model to another in a manner that can be called a "Kuhnian" interpretation. The expected *Contributors* are nearly all represented.

B81   Burnham, J. C. (Ed.), *Science in America: Historical selections.* New York: Holt, Rinehart & Winston, 1971.
        The history of scientific endeavor from the seven-

teenth century to the early seventies is presented through excerpts, including one from Franklin in the Colonial period, another from Agassiz in the nineteenth century, and Loeb, Thorndike, and Bridgman in the early twentieth century. An emphasis is placed on the relationships of the history of science to social and intellectual history.

B82   Burtt, E. A. *The metaphysical foundations of modern physical science.* (Rev. ed.) New York: Humanities Press, 1932. (1924)

Since the beginning of modern period, philosophers and scientists have had to be involved implicitly or explicitly with the issue of the nature and possibility of knowledge itself. This historical problem is traced from the beginnings of the new astronomy in Copernicus through Newton. Others receiving major attention are Kepler, Galileo, Descartes, and Hobbes from the *Contributors,* and in addition, More, Gilbert, and Boyle.

B83   Butterfield, H. *The origins of modern science, 1300-1800.* (2nd ed.) New York: Macmillan, 1957. (1949)

The author traces the interplay of the systems and theories that led to the origins of modern sciences, not only in terms of the new doctrines that are integral part of this view of sciences, but also of those theories that were to be overthrown. The views of Bacon, Descartes, Galileo, Harvey, Huygens, Kepler, Leibniz, and Newton from the *Contributors,* as well as those of Aristotle, Robert Boyle, Tycho Brahe, Copernicus, William Gilbert, and Vesalius receive major attention.

B84   Crombie, A. C. *Medieval and early modern science: Science in the later Middle Ages and early Modern times: XIII-XVII centuries.* Vol. 2. (2nd ed.) Garden City, N.Y.: Doubleday, 1959. (1952)

More than half the volume is devoted to the period pertinent directly to this *Guide,* but the earlier section is an excellent introduction as well. The major problems of early modern science taken up are atomism, the experimental method, gravity, induction, the mathematical method, the choice of units of measurement, the interrelation of logic, science, and philosophy, the nature of substance, and the relation of theology to science. The expected array of *Contributors* is to be found, with the greatest emphasis upon Descartes, Galileo, Kepler, and Newton. Biology, physiology, and zoology are not entirely neglected.

B85   Giere, R. W., & Westfall, R. S. (Eds.), *Foundations of scientific method: The nineteenth century.* Bloomington, Ind.: Indiana University Press, 1973.

The thinking of Bernard, Darwin, Kant, Maxwell, and Peirce as related to the scientific method is presented. Philosophers as well as historians of science contribute to the volume.

B86   Gillispie, C. C. *The edge of objectivity: An essay in the history of scientific ideas.* Princeton, N.J.: Princeton University Press, 1960.

Written in terms of the structural history of thought, this book is considered by the author to be ". . . a narrative which accepts the difference between the logical order and the historical order and seeks to discern a structure in the latter inhering in the relation of philosophy, technicality, personality, and circumstance" (p. 524). In this setting, the history of science is examined from Galileo to Einstein.

B87   Hall, A. R. *The scientific revolution: 1500-1800: The formation of the modern scientific attitude.* Boston: Beacon, 1954.

This is a conventional history of the physics, astronomy, biology, and chemistry of the first three centuries of modern science. Emphasis is not only on men, but equally on theories, methodologies, and attitudes.

B88   Hall, A. R. *From Galileo to Newton: 1630-1720.* New York.: Harper & Row, 1963.

Historical problems of astronomy, mathematics, physics, and biology are considered in that crucial ninety-year period in which modern science was born. Hall writes both in terms of problems and of men. Major issues treated are celestial mechanics, elements, experiments, instruments, microscopy, motion, optics, particulate theories of matter, and the scientific method. Receiving major attention are Bacon, Descartes, Galileo, Harvey, Huygens, Kepler, Leibniz, von Leeuwenhoek, Locke, Malebranche, Mersenne,

Newton, and Pascal from the *Contributors,* along with Robert Boyle, Samuel Clarke, Nicholas Copernicus, Edmond Halley, Johann B. von Helmont, Robert Hooke, Henry Oldenburg, Jan Swammerdam, and John Wallis.

B89   Hutten, E. H. *The origins of science: An inquiry into the foundations of Western thought.* London: Allen & Unwin, 1962.

This is an attempt to use psychoanalytic psychology, instead of the traditional epistemology, to understand the origin of science in the history of Western thought. Since it is relatively short, this volume is also sketchy and incomplete.

B90   Koyré, A. *From the closed world to the infinite universe.* Baltimore, Md.: Johns Hopkins Press, 1957.

A history of the scientific and philosophical thinking of the sixteenth and seventeenth centuries, which made the title an apt way to describe the change that had taken place. From among the *Contributors* the thinking of Descartes, Galileo, Kepler, Leibniz, Newton, and Spinoza is prominent. Although without explicit methodological discussion, this book is a masterly example of the appeal to ideas as dynamic.

Koyré, A. *Metaphysics and measurement.* (E58)

Laudan, L. Theories of scientific method from Plato to Mach: A bibliographic review. (D61)

B91   Losee, J. *A historical introduction to the philosophy of science.* London: Oxford University Press, 1972.

This is a sophisticated attempt to interrelate the history of science and the history of the philosophy of science. The author examines, among others, the contributions of Bacon, Berkeley, Bridgman, Charles Darwin, Galileo, Hume, Kant, Kepler, Locke, Mach, J. S. Mill, and Newton from the *Contributors.* Among the modern historians and philosophers of science, major consideration is given to Pierre Duhem, Philipp Frank, N. R. Hanson, Rom Harré, Mary Hesse, Ernest Nagel, Karl Popper, and William Whewell.

B92   Merton, R. K. Science, technology and society in seventeenth century England. *Osiris,* 1938, *4,* 603-632.

This is the classic study of the sociological factors at
work in the development of science of that time and in
that place. It has been seminal in producing a host of literature, pro and con. It is also noteworthy because of the way
it draws upon quantitative material in an ingenious fashion.

B93   Merz, J. *A history of European thought in the nineteenth
century.* Part 1. *Scientific thought.* (2 vols.) New York:
Dover, 1965. (1896, 1903).

A sweeping, panoramic view of scientific thought that
should be read in conjunction with its companion volumes
on philosophic thought (B112). That Merz wrote on both
science and philosophy enriched them both. After considering "the scientific spirit" in France, in Germany, and in
England, he turns to various views of nature, i.e., astro-
nomical, atomic, kinetic (mechanical), physical, morpho-
logical, genetic, vitalistic, psychophysical, and statistical,
and then he places mathematical thought in a context of
the general history of intellectual progress. Practically all
relevant European *Contributors* of that century are given
consideration in depth.

B94   Price, D. J. de S. *Little science, big science.* (2nd ed.) New
York: Columbia University Press, 1971. (1963)

From the one-man laboratory to the multi-manned
research team in three decades is the point meant to be
expressed in the title. More formally expressed, it is the
exponential growth of science and its effects on scientists
and on society, not discussed in terms of details of procedure, discovery, or theory, but in its "shape and size," in
terms of total number of journals, magnitude of scientific
manpower, and the like.

B95   Reichenbach, H. *The rise of scientific philosophy.* Berkeley,
Calif.: University of California Press, 1951.

Major topics Reichenbach considers are causality,
empiricism, induction-deduction, and rationalism through
a contrast of speculative philosophy and philosophy of
science. Hume and Kant receive relatively detailed treatment.

B96 Santillana, G. D., & Zilsel, E. *The development of rationalism and empiricism.* Chicago: University of Chicago Press, 1941.

The former author is concerned with the history of rationalism, the latter with that of empiricism. The essay on empiricism is especially valuable and pertinent. Sections devoted to psychology and the social sciences are included.

B97 Schofield, R. E. *Mechanism and materialism: British natural philosophy in an age of reason.* Princeton, N.J.: Princeton University Press, 1970.

A historical consideration of the impact of Newtonian science on selected facets of eighteenth-century British science is given. After an explication of the creed of Newtonian science, the author traces its ramifications for nineteenth-century physiology, i.e., for Hartley, M. Hall, and Whytt from the *Contributors* as well as for Hermann Boerhaave.

B98 Thorndike, L. *A history of magic and experimental science.* Vols. 7, 8. *The seventeenth century.* New York: Columbia University Press, 1958.

Thorndike interprets science and magic from the point of view of his day and proceeds to examine in assiduous detail the topics of astrology, alchemy, witchcraft, as well as those of the sciences, not only for individuals judged to be eminent at time of writing, but also for any and all individuals who concerned themselves with the relevant issues; e.g., the authors of doctoral dissertations from German universities during this century. Profuse detail makes this book partake of a being hardly more than a chronicle of events.

B99 Toulmin, S., & Goodfield, June. *The discovery of time.* New York: Harper & Row, 1965.

The view of the natural world that we have has the remarkable feature of being historical. How the present state of things came to be demands the study of time, which the authors proceed to do. Major themes are myths, scriptural authority, the view when natural philosophy was revived, the influence of civil history, geological findings, information about species, Darwinian evolution, progress, change, and the human sciences, and time and the physical world. From the *Contributors* Buffon, Cuvier, C. Darwin, Descartes, Kant, Lamarck, and Newton receive major consideration.

B100   Vucinich, A. *Science in Russian culture, 1861-1917.* Stanford, Calif.: Stanford University Press, 1963.

Many non-Russians are seen as influencing the history of Russian culture. Bernard, C. Darwin, DuBois-Reymond, Helmoltz, Kant, Ludwig, Marx, and Newton are the non-Russian *Contributors*, while Pavlov and Sechenov are among those from Russia itself.

B101   Wallace, W. A. *Causality and scientific explanation.* Vol. 1. *Medieval and early classical science.* Vol. 2. *Classical and contemporary science.* Ann Arbor, Mich.: University of Michigan Press, 1974.

The author relates the thinking of scientists of the period in question on casuality and scientific explanation to the work of modern philosophers of science. In Volume 1, he discusses Descartes, Galileo, Harvey, and Newton. In Volume 2, Bacon, Berkeley, Bernard, Bridgman, Comte, Descartes, Galileo, Hobbes, Hume, Kant, Kepler, Laplace, Leibniz, Locke, Mach, J. S. Mill, Newton, and Whitehead are considered. Against this background the work of contemporary historians and philosophers of science including Duhem, Koyré, Kuhn, and Madden is studied.

B102   Woolf, H. (Ed.), *Quantification: A history of the meaning of measurement in the natural and social sciences.* Indianapolis, Ind.: Bobbs-Merrill, 1961.

This is a collection of papers presented at a conference in 1959 on the history of the use of quantitative techniques in physics, chemistry, medicine, psychology, economics, and sociology. R. H. Shryrock, E. G. Boring, J. J. Spengler, and P. F. Lazarsfeld, respectively, prepared the papers for the four fields last mentioned.

PHILOSOPHY

General histories of modern philosophy, both introductory and advanced, are annotated. There are also a few references devoted to special periods such as the Enlightenment, the nineteenth century, and the contemporary scene and still other books stressing national developments in the United States, Britain, France, Germany, and Russia.

B103 Blau, J. L. *Men and movements in American philosophy.* New York: Prentice-Hall, 1952.

This is a textbook that covers ten major schools of American philosophy, illustrated by idealism, pragmatism, realism, and naturalism. Dewey, Edwards, James, Mead, Peirce, and Royce receive systematic treatment, while important background figures are Berkeley, Coleridge, Darwin, Descartes, Franklin, Kant, Locke, Newton, and Spencer.

B104 Boas, G. D. *Dominant themes of modern philosophy: A history.* New York: Ronald Press, 1957.

The chapter organization of this history of philosophy is conventional, i.e., "Descartes and the Cartesians," "The empirical tradition in England," "Les Philosophes," and, lastly, "The rise of existentialism." Nor, perhaps wisely, are the themes explicitly identified. The major index headings provide relevant information. These are animals, assumptions, causation, experience, freedom, God, ideas, insight, knowledge, man, matter, mind, nature, reason, soul, and truth. The major figures are those to be expected, including nearly all of the philosophers from the *Contributors.* Vico, Herder, and Condorcet are considered insofar as they are philosophers of history.

B105 Brehier, E. *The history of philosophy.* Vol. 4. *The seventeenth century.* Vol. 5. *The eighteenth century.* Vol. 6. *The nineteenth century: Period of systems, 1800-1850.* Vol. 7. *Contemporary philosophy — since 1850.* Trans. W. Baskin. Chicago: University of Chicago Press, 1966-1969. (1930-1938)

A seven-volume survey of the history of western philosophy from the Hellenic period to the twentieth century, of which the last four volumes are pertinent, with 50 *Contributors* being examined in this context. The development of French philosophy is given special consideration. Volumes 6 and 7, which deal with nineteenth and twentieth centuries, provide a rare survey (in English) of French philosophical thought. Maine de Biran, Brunschvicg, and Destutt de Tracey from the *Contributors,* as well as Charles Renouvier, Paul D. Holbach, and Theodore Jouffroy are considered, along with the more traditional topics of Anglo-American and German philosophy.

B106   Cassirer, E. The *Philosophy of the Enlightenment.* Trans. F.C.A. Koelln & J. P. Pettegrove. Princeton, N.J.: Princeton University Press, 1951.

    The Enlightenment in France, England and Germany is examined in terms of nature and natural science; psychology and epistemology, religion, historiography; law, state, and society and aesthetics. D'Alembert, Berkeley, Buffon, Condillac, Cordorcet, Descartes, Diderot, Goethe, Helvetius, Herder, Hobbes, Hume, Kant, LaMettrie, Leibniz, Lessing, Locke, Montesquieu, Newton, Pascal, Rousseau, Spinoza, Voltaire, and von Wolff from the *Contributors* are placed in the perspective of the theme of the book. Only Pierre Bayle, Bernard Fontennelle, Pierre L. M. de Maupertius, and Lord Shaftesbury receive comparable consideration.

B107   Copleston, F. *A history of philosophy.* Vol. 4. *Modern philosophy: Descartes to Leibniz.* Vol. 5. *Modern philosophy: The British philosophers.* Vol. 6. *Modern philosophy: The French Enlightenment and Kant.* Vol. 7. *Modern philosophy: Fichte to Nietzsche.* Vol. 8. *Modern philosophy: Bentham to Russell.* Westminster, Md.: Newman Press, 1959-1960. (Reprinted 1964-1967).

    Volumes 4 through 8 of this standard history of philosophy cover the period from Descartes through Bertrand Russell. A leisurely pace is maintained, and trends and individuals are examined in some depth. A short summarization is impossible, except to say that most relevant *Contributors* are considered.

B108   Farber, M. (Ed.), *Philosophic thought in France and the United States: Essays representing major trends in contemporary French and American philosophy.* Buffalo, N.Y.: University of Buffalo Press, 1950.

    This volume brings together the major philosophical trends of both countries in the first half of the twentieth century. The value of this volume is due to its variety of themes, extending from Bergsonianism and existentialism to the "Basic Issues in Logical Positivism." Many of the American selections are germane to the historian of the behavioral sciences.

B109   Fuller, B. A. G., & McMurrin, S. M. *A history of modern philosophy.* (3rd ed.) New York: Holt, Rinehart & Winston, 1955. (1938)

A standard introductory text is provided that is clear and relatively simple and yet does no great violence to what would be found in interpretations of greater depth. It uses both an individual and a theme approach. So many *Contributors* are mentioned that it is not feasible to list them. Along with those of Jones (B111) and O'Connor (B113), this book is recommended to the individual relatively unversed in philosophy.

Grundriss der Geschichte der Philosophie. F. Ueberweg. (A86)

B110   Höffding, H. *A history of modern philosophy.* (2 vols.) Trans. B. E. Meyer. New York: Humanities Press, 1950. (1894)

A classic in the history of philosophy, these volumes cover the period from Renaissance humanism to toward the end of the nineteenth century. A section on the discovery of humanistic man is followed by one on scientific developments, including the contributions arising from the work of Kepler, Galileo, and Bacon. "The Great Systems" of Descartes, Hobbes, Spinoza, and Leibniz are followed by "British Empirical Philosophy" in the persons of Locke, Berkeley, Hume, and their successors. The "Enlightenment in France," stressing the thinking of Voltaire, Montesquieu, Condillac, Helvetius, LaMettrie, Diderot, and Rousseau, closes Volume 1. The Germans come to the fore at the beginning of Volume 2 in Lessing and, above all, in Kant, followed by the Romantics, including Fichte, Schelling, Hegel, and Schopenhauer along with the undercurrent of the critical philosophy of Fries, Herbart, and Beneke; positivism is stressed first in the person of Comte, and then in that of J. S. Mill, followed by consideration of the philosophy of evolution through the work of Darwin and Spencer.

A relatively short closing section deals with later nineteenth-century philosophy in Germany involving Lotze, Fechner, and von Hartmann, among others.

B111   Jones, W. T. *A history of Western philosophy.* New York: Harcourt, Brace, 1952.

This standard authoritative introductory textbook devotes approximately half of its double-columned thousand pages to the modern period. After a prefatory chapter on science and the scientific method, consideration is given in separate chapters to Hobbes, Descartes, Spinoza, Leibniz, Locke, Berkeley, Hume, Kant, and the reactions to Kant on the part of Hegel and Schopenhauer. The focus then shifts to topical areas, namely social theory and social evolution, and the contemporary scene. Comte, Marx, and Nietzsche are stressed in the former, and Bergson, Dewey, Whitehead, and Russell in the latter.

B112   Merz, J. *A history of European thought in the nineteenth century.* Part 2. *Philosophical thought.* (2 vols.) New York: Dover, 1965. (1896, 1903)

Merz presents a sweeping panoramic view of philosophical thought, which should be read in conjunction with its companion volumes on scientific thought (B93). That Merz wrote on both, enriches both. After an introductory chapter, he considers the growth and diffusion of the critical spirit, the soul, knowledge, reality, nature, the beautiful, the good, the spirit, society, the unity of thought and the rationale of philosophical thought. Nearly all relevant European philosophic *Contributors* of that century are given consideration in depth.

B113   O'Connor, D. (Ed.), *A critical history of Western philosophy.* New York: Free Press, 1966.

This is a collection of 29 essays by different specialists on selected topics from the early Greeks to the present day. The psychologist will be more concerned with the later essays, e.g., "The Philosophy of Science 1850-1910," "Logical Positivism," and "Existentialism." It is highly recommended as a basic survey of the field.

B114   Passmore, J. *A hundred years of philosophy.* London: Duckworth, 1957.

An admittedly technical treatment of epistemology, logic, and metaphysics since J. S. Mill is provided. These topics allow the author to consider the works of Stout and Ward in England; Meinong, Mach, and Lotze in Germany; and James and Dewey in America. Also of interest are his chapters on logical positivism, on Wittgenstein, and on the philosophy of language.

B115   Randall, J. H., Jr. *The career of philosophy: From the Middle Ages to the Enlightenment.* New York: Columbia University Press, 1962.

Although the first section of this volume begins with a discussion of the great medieval philosophies of knowledge, it is pertinent to our concern with the modern period, because Randall is convinced and convincing about the essential continuity of the two periods. The second section is concerned with the coming of the new science and the rise of humanistic values, the third with the assimilation of science, and the fourth with reactions to the Newtonian science. Galileo, Descartes, Newton, Locke, Berkeley, and Hume, from among the *Contributors,* are given thoughtful treatment in a manner that relates their thinking to these themes.

B116   Randall, J. H., Jr. *The career of philosophy.* Vol. 2. *From the German Enlightenment to the age of Darwin.* New York: Columbia University Press, 1965.

A definitive modern history of philosophy, continuing the earlier volume (B115). German, French, and British philosophy are carried one by one to the middle of the nineteenth century. Mentioning only the most important of those "building the German tradition" involves Leibniz, Kant, Fichte, Hegel, and Marx, "integrating French culture" concerns the thinking of Condorcet, Maine de Biran, Claude-Henri de Sainte Simon, Fourier, and Comte, while tradition and individualism, the dual British problems, involved, among others, Coleridge, Reid, Stewart, T. Brown, Bentham, and James and John Stuart Mill.

B117   Schneider, H. W. *History of American philosophy.* (2nd ed.) New York: Columbia University Press, 1963. (1946)

This is the classic work on the history of American philosophy from the colonial era to the early twentieth century. Of special interest to the psychologist are Schneider's sections on orthodoxy and on evolution and human progress. In the former he describes the rise and purification of Scottish "Common Sense" philosophy in the hands of 19th-century American moral faculty philosophers. His treatment of evolution in America includes sections on Fiske, Wright, and James, as well as the evolutionary theology of McCosh and Hickock.

B118 Smith, J. E. *The spirit of American philosophy*. New York: Oxford University Press, 1963.

It is usual to regard American philosophical thought as coming of age in the late 19th century with Peirce, Royce; and James. This short but well-written work considers the contributions of these three men and of the twentieth-century philosophers Dewey and Whitehead. A good summary of the major postulates of each is presented.

B119 Tsanoff, R. A. *The great philosophers*. New York: Harper, 1953.

This volume, divided into four sections (antiquity, medieval, early modern, and the nineteenth and twentieth centuries), is a history of Western philosophy. The systems of the classical philosophers in each of these ages are considered within a biographical context. For the modern period, 44 of the *Contributors* are discussed.

Turner, M. B. *Philosophy and the science of behavior.* (E19)

PSYCHIATRY AND PSYCHOANALYSIS

Books devoted to the history of psychiatry and of psychoanalysis sometimes shade into one another. On other occasions, in a somewhat imperialistic vein, histories of "psychiatry" turn out to be accounts that begin with precursors to psychoanalytic thinking and then continue on to psychoanalysis itself. Others, while purporting to be general histories, resolutely shut their eyes to psychoanalytic developments. Still others concern themselves with special periods, a particular problem or disease, hypnosis, epilepsy, moral treatment, and the like, which may or may not call for narrowly psychiatric and psychoanalytic theories and findings to be utilized. Psychoanalysis is also a school of psychology, so some of the references are also cited in the earlier section devoted to the schools.

B120 Ackerknecht, E. H. *A short history of psychiatry.* (3rd ed.) Trans. Sula Wolff. New York: Hafner, 1968. (1959)

The author considers anthropological findings on mental disorder among primitives before turning to the history of psychiatry, beginning with the Greek and the Roman period and extending forward in time to the modern day. He sees the major modern emphasis to be on the empirical study of somatic conditions that give rise to psychiatric disorders. Considering the book's brevity, it is remarkable that he is able to give relatively thorough coverage to Charcot, Esquirol, Gall, Janet, Kraepelin, and Binet.

B121 Alexander, F. G., & Selesnick, S. T. *The history of psychiatry: An evaluation of psychiatric thought and practice from prehistoric times to the present.* New York: Harper & Row, 1966.

An account of the men, movements, and events that have influenced psychiatric thought from prehistoric times to the present, which is equated with Freudian developments. The book is composed of four parts: an introductory statement on the basic themes in psychiatry, the development of psychiatric thought from the ancients to a culmination in Freud, the Freudian age, and recent developments. From the list of *Contributors,* individuals emphasized are those consistent with its psychoanalytic orientation.

B122 Altschule, M. D. (collab. Evelyn R. Hegedue). *Roots of modern psychiatry: Essays in the history of psychiatry.* (2nd ed.) New York: Grune & Stratton, 1965.

This is a collection of rather miscellaneous essays on topics such as ideas about anxiety held by eighteenth-century British medical writers, the significance of the pineal gland, the concept of unconscious cerebration before 1890, and nineteenth-century eclecticism in the treatment of mental diseases.

B123   Bockoven, J. S. *Moral treatment in American psychiatry.*
New York: Springer, 1963.

The author is concerned with the successful use of
moral treatment in mental hospitals in the United States
from about 1830 to 1870, and the failure for it to be continued thereafter. This is sketched through hospital data,
information on the personality and scientific outlook of
the leading psychiatrists concerned, and the relationship
of moral treatment to the rise of scientific psychiatry.

B124   Burnham, J. C. *Psychoanalysis and American medicine:
1894-1918: Medicine, science, and culture.* New York: International Universities Press, 1967.

The impact of psychoanalysis upon American medicine during the period mentioned in the title is the major
theme of this book. The author begins with the impact,
favorable and unfavorable, of Freud on American psychiatry between 1894 and 1918; and then at the levels of
general, cultural, scientific, medical, and psychotherapeutic
forces that were at work; the various controversies in which
psychoanalysis became involved; the agents and agencies of
psychoanalysis; transmission, not only in the thinking of
Freud, but in that of others including Jung; Freud's writings and the misunderstandings of his views introduced
through the inelegant and erroneous Brill translations; the
influence of professional societies, textbooks, medical
schools, and hospital teaching; and the emergence of a
psychoanalytic movement. It continues with an over-all
evaluation of the many ways Freud's teaching intereacted
with the American scene, such as eclectic and piecemeal
use, redefinition of terms and concepts, the various misunderstandings that occurred, and the relating of his concepts
to social environmentalism.

B125   Deutsch, A. *The mentally ill in America: A history of their
care and treatment from colonial times.* (2nd ed.) Garden
City, N.Y.: Doubleday, 1949. (1937)

To be found in this book is a social history with a
broad sweep. The dominating individual figures at different
points in time were successively Rush, Dix, and Beers, but
throughout an account of the patients and the hospital
care given them receives the greatest emphasis.

B126   Caplan, Ruth B. (collab. G. Caplan) *Psychiatry and the community in nineteenth century America.* New York: Basic Books, 1969.

The nature of moral treatment in the early nineteenth century is examined and then the nature and reasons for change to custodial care that took place at mid-century. The effect of the reformers, their impact, and the revitalization of psychiatry at the turn of the century then follows. In an epilogue Gerald Caplan explores the implications of this historical background for community psychiatry.

B127   Dain, N. *Concepts of insanity in the United States, 1789-1865.* New Brunswick, N.J.: Rutgers University Press, 1964.

This is a thoroughly documented investigation of primary sources relevant to the topic. Beginning with the period when insanity was considered incurable, the author traces the developments, social and medical, that led to the triumph of moral management in institutions for mental patients. Dorothea Dix and Benjamin Rush played not inconsiderable parts, and the inspiration of Pinel was felt, but sharing the pages of this volume were also many individuals noted primarily for their contributions as superintendents of mental hospitals.

B128   Ellenberger, H. F. *The discovery of the unconscious: The history and evolution of dynamic psychiatry.* New York: Basic Books, 1970.

A history of dynamic psychiatry is presented, extending from primitive healing, through magnetism, hypnosis, and psychoanalysis to the newer dynamic schools of thought. Detailed analyses of the systems of Janet, Freud, Adler, and Jung are presented, each considered within their socioeconomic, political, and cultural background. The work is well documented and an invaluable reference source; the chapter on Freud, for example, contains over 500 references. Major attention is given to Adler, Bernheim, Bleuler, Breuer, Charcot, Flournoy, Forel, Jung, Nietzsche, Schopenhauer and, above all, to Freud and Janet. Some attention is given to many others.

B129   Ellenberger, H. F. Psychiatry from ancient to modern times. In S. Arieti (Ed.), *American handbook of psychiatry.*

Vol. 1. *The foundations of psychiatry.* (2nd ed.) New York: Basic Books, 1974, pp. 3-27.

A succinct introductory statement of the history of psychiatry by a senior historian of the field. The volume is divided into the conventional temporal periods.

B130 Foucault, M. *Madness and civilization: A history of insanity in the age of reason.* Trans. R. Howard. New York: Random House, 1965. (1961)

A panoramic history of mental illness and its treatment sweeps from the sixteenth through the eighteenth century. Based on original documents, the author has sought to recreate mental illnesses as they existed in that particular time, place, and social perspective. Special consideration is given to the social determinants of mental illness and its treatment. Consequently, only incidental mention is made of the physicians concerned with these problems during these centuries.

B131 Grob, G. N. *The state and the mentally ill: A history of Worcester State Hospital in Massachusetts, 1830-1920.* Chapel Hill, N.C.: University of North Carolina Press, 1966.

With Worcester State Hospital as the center of focus, the background of state and national policies receive considerable attention in this book. From among the *Contributors,* Dorothea Dix, Adolf Meyer, and Elmer E. Southard are seen as central.

B132 Hale, N. G., Jr. *Freud in America.* Vol. 1. *Freud and the Americans: The beginnings of psychoanalysis in the United States, 1876-1917.* New York: Oxford University Press, 1971.

The author begins with Freud's 1909 lectures at Clark University and then considers the professional and social forces that influenced the development of psychoanalysis in America. Beyond this, the author presents the specifically American interpretation of psychoanalysis, an account of early American analysts, and the then current popular responses to Freud's doctrines. Others from the *Contributors* who are placed in the context of the time of the volume are Bergson, Brill, Ellis, G. S. Hall, James, Janet, Jones,

Jung, Meyer, Prince, Sidis, White, and Woodworth. But equally prominent are Isidore Coriat, Horace W. Frink, August Hoch, Smith Ely Jeliffe, S. Weir Mitchell, James Jackson Putnam, and Bernard Sachs.

B133   Havens, L. L. *Approaches to the mind: Movement of the psychiatric schools from sects toward science.* Boston: Little, Brown, 1973.

This work is divided into three sections, the first two of which are historical in nature. In Part I, four schools of psychiatry are described: the objective-descriptive (e.g., Kraepelin, Janet); psychoanalysis (Freud); existentialism (e.g., Jaspers, Binswanger) and interpersonal psychiatry (Meyer, Sullivan). Case histories are used for illustrative purposes. Part II describes the similarities and differences between the schools, based on a number of psychiatric themes (e.g., development, relationship to patients). Part II is integrative, primarily a plea for a method of treatment to be based on the needs of the patients rather than on the therapist's theoretical position. Other *Contributors* given attention in depth are Bleuler and Charcot.

B134   Lewis, N. D. C. American psychiatry from its beginning to World War II. In S. Arieti (Ed.), *American handbook of psychiatry.* Vol. 1. *The foundations of psychiatry.* (2nd ed.) New York: Basic Books, 1974, pp. 28-42.

This article is particularly useful for its succinct account of early mental hospitals and administrators. Adolf Meyer, Emil Kraepelin, and Elmer E. Southard from the *Contributors* receive attention.

B135   Lowrey, L. G. The birth of orthopsychiatry. In L. G. Lowrey (Ed.), *Orthopsychiatry, 1923-1948: Retrospect and prospect.* New York: American Orthopsychiatric Association, 1948, pp. 190-216.

Very important for the dynamic tradition in psychiatry and psychology, and for collaborative work among psychiatrists, psychologists, and social workers, are the activities carried on by this association, the early history of which Lowrey traces. William Healy and Augusta Bronner, important figures whom Lowrey places in perspective, have in the same volume an article on the history of the child guidance clinic.

B136   Mora, G. History of psychiatry. In A. M. Freedman & H. I.
Kaplan (Eds.). *Comprehensive textbook of psychiatry.*
Baltimore, Md.: Williams & Wilkins, 1967, pp. 2-34.

An introductory history, covering the history of psychiatry from the period of primitive man to the early
1950s.

B137   Mora, G. Recent psychiatric developments (since 1939). In
S. Arieti (Ed.), *American handbook of psychiatry* (2nd
ed.) Vol. 1. *The foundations of psychiatry.* New York:
Basic Books, 1974, pp. 43-114.

A carefully prepared, detailed statement is given of
recent developments in psychiatric research and methodology; classification; psychopathology; the psychoanalytic
and other schools; new trends in ethology, general systems
theory, and the like; psychiatric treatment bearing the significant subtitle, "From hospital to community"; therapy,
both organic and psychological; psychiatric education; relation of American psychiatry to that of other countries;
and an epilogue on the social responsibility of psychiatry.
An extensive bibliography (with 621 citations) is provided.

B138   Munroe, Ruth L. *Schools of psychoanalytic thought: An
exposition, critique, and attempt at integration.* New York:
Dryden Press, 1955.

The author presents psychoanalysis, first in terms of
the orthodox view, then in that of Adler, Horney, Erich
Fromm, and Sullivan, examined, one by one, against the
framework of the themes of the organism, the milieu, the
genetic process, dynamics, and pathology and treatment.
After each exposition, Munroe stands aside and offers in
clearly demarcated sections her "critical comments." Jung
and Rank are then considered, each against a framework
unique to his particular view.

B139   Rapaport, D. A historical survey of psychoanalytic ego
psychology. (1958) Reprinted in M. M. Gill, (Ed.), *The
collected papers of David Rapaport.* New York: Basic
Books, 1967, pp. 745-757.

Four phases of psychoanalytic ego psychology are
sketched: the first three, in which Freud's thinking dominates, and the fourth through the writings of Anna Freud,
Hartmann, Erickson, Horney, Kardiner, and Sullivan, from

which the theory of object relations and its psychosocial implications are brought within the theoretical scope of psychoanalysis.

B140   Ridenour, Nina. *Mental health in the United States, a fifty-year history.* Cambridge: Harvard University Press, 1961.
The fifty years referred to begin with a meeting called by Beers that led to the first state society for mental hygiene; the book then proceeds to an account of the work of the laymen, psychiatrists, social workers, psychologists, and philanthropists important in the early mental health movement.

B141   Rosen, G. *Madness in society: Chapters in the historical sociology of mental illness.* Chicago: University of Chicago Press, 1968.
The author is concerned, he says, "with historical sociology," — the place of the mentally ill in society — "not with the history of psychiatry." The more specific topics include how the mentally ill were viewed in the ancient world, the present and contemporary problems of the psychopathology of aging, patterns of discovery and control today, and the relation between the public and mental health.

B142   Shakow, D., & Rapaport, D. *The influence of Freud on American psychology.* New York: International Universities Press, 1964
With a wealth of detail and an extensive bibliography, the authors first examine the background for Freud's reception in terms of comparing it with Darwin's, the working against the current of the emperimentalist approach epitomized by Helmholtz, the adjustments that psychoanalysis was called upon to make when Freudian ideas reached the United States during the first decades of the century, and the reactions not only from *academia,* but also in literary circles. This is followed by a more detailed examination of Freud's theories of the unconscious and motivation and their influence on psychology. Published appraisals and references to his work by psychologists in texts, histories, and the like are examined in some detail. An appraisal is given in the final chapter.

B143 Temkin, O. *The falling sickness: A history of epilepsy from the Greeks to the beginnings of modern neurology.* (2nd ed.) Baltimore, Md.: Johns Hopkins Press, 1971 (1945)

This is a study in depth of epilepsy, not only in its medical, but also in its social and philosophical aspects. From among the moderns, Hughlings-Jackson is the central figure. An extensive bibliography is given.

B144 Thompson, Clara. *Psychoanalysis: Evolution and development.* New York: Hermitage House, 1950.

A history of psychoanalysis that goes beyond classic psychoanalysis, with its emphasis upon the unconscious and the id, to emphasize ego psychology within this framework.

B145 Veith, Ilza. *Hysteria: The history of a disease.* Chicago: University of Chicago Press, 1965.

This is an important and thorough work concerned with the symptomatology and treatment of hysteria and the social circumstances in which it was found from Egyptian times to Freud. To quote the author, "Hysteria . . . has adapted its symptoms to the ideas and mores current in in each society; yet its predispositions and its basic features have remained more or less unchanged." The author notes that many of the characteristics of Freud's formulation were anticipated piecemeal by the ancients. Aside from Freud, among the *Contributors,* those receiving major attention are Breuer, Charcot, Harvey, Janet, Pinel, and Willis.

Whyte, L. L. *The unconscious before Freud.* (B55)

B146 Wyss, D. *Psychoanalytic schools from the beginning to the present.* Intro. L. L. Havens. New York: Aronson, 1973. (Originally published in English in 1966 as *Depth psychology: A critical history.*)

An evaluation of the central tenets and historical roots of depth psychology is presented. Lengthy consideration is given to the development of psychoanalysis and the Freudian school, along with the Neo-Freudians, Adler, Jung, and the Existentialists. The author also discusses whether psychoanalytic findings can lay claim to as great a validity as that attributed to those of the natural sciences. In addition to the individuals just mentioned, Abraham, Fenichel, Ferenczi, Horney, Jones, Klein, Kris, Rank, and Sullivan make their expected appearance. Less expected perhaps would be the emphasis upon Binswanger, Husserl, and Klages.

B147 Zilboorg, G., & Henry, G. W. *A history of medical psychology.* New York: Norton, 1941.
This volume is the classic psychoanalytically oriented work on the history of psychiatric thought from primitive times to the beginning of the twentieth century. Its culmination in the work of Freud, the aim from the very first pages steadfastly maintained throughout, results in omission of any matters that do not fit the design. It is so presentist as to epitomize this approach to history. Other *Contributors* are considered only in light of their relation to Freud.

PHYSIOLOGY, NEUROLOGY, AND ANATOMY

Included in this section are not only general histories of the fields just mentioned, but also histories of more specialized issues such as the electrical activity of the brain, neurophysiology, brain function and structure, and reflex action.

B148 Brazier, Mary A. B. *A history of the electrical activity of the brain: The first half-century.* London: Pitman, 1961.
A carefully documented history of this particular topic is presented. Many of the leading figures in this work are somewhat alien to the history of the behavioral sciences, but Bekhterev, DuBois-Reymond, Goltz, and Sechenov from the *Contributors* receive considerable attention.

B149 Brazier, Mary A. B. The historical development of neurophysiology. In J. Field (Ed.), *Handbook of physiology.* Section 1. *Neurophysiology.* Vol. 1. Washington, D.C.: American Physiological Society, 1959, pp. 1-58.
The author reviews the early concepts of nervous activity from the time of the Greeks; presents the theories of excitability and transmission in nerves since the eighteenth century, of reflex activity and of the spinal cord;

and considers the development of conceptions of the physiology of the brain.

B150 Brooks, C. McC., & Cranefeld, P. F. (Eds.), *The historical development of physiological thought*. New York: Hafner, 1959.

A collection of essays written by prominent scientists and historians of science that consider historical and philosophical issues related to physiology. Vitalism, the conservation of energy, and the biology of consciousness, for example, are relevant directly for the psychologist; there is also discussion of anatomical reasoning in physiological thought, the idea of the synapse, and more general papers on neurophysiology and the brain.

B151 Clarke, E., & Dewhurst, K. *An illustrated history of brain function*. Berkeley, Calif.: University of California Press, 1972.

Through its illustrations, this history comes alive. It gives a brief summarization of the views of antiquity and a lengthier account of medieval cell doctrine; shortly thereafter it turns to the very important sixteenth-, seventeenth-, and eighteenth-century studies, particularly in the persons of Willis and Descartes. Phrenology and the work in rebuttal that it stimulated, and thereafter the beginning of the history of cortical localization, and other major considerations, with modern aspects of cortical localization as the last topic treated.

B152 Fearing, F. *Reflex action: A study in the history of physiological psychology*. Baltimore, Md.: Williams & Wilkins, 1930. Reprinted 1964.

A history is given of the concept of reflex action from Descartes to the early twentieth-century work of Pavlov and Loeb. Other *Contributors* who receive major attention are Bell, Bowditch, Carpenter, Dodge, Flourens, Fulton, Golgi, Goltz, M. Hall, von Haller, Hartley, Harvey, Herrick, James, LaMettrie, Lewes, McDougall, J. Müller, Pflüger, Prochaska, Sherrington, Whytt, and Wundt. At a more general level, this classic volume traces the development of mechanical physiology, with special reference to the controversies that emerged from the concept of the reflex, e.g., the iatro-physicists versus the iatro-chemists, and the Pflüger-Lotze controversy.

B153   Hall, T. S. *Ideas of life and matter: Studies in the history of general physiology 600 B.C.-1900A.D.* Vol. 2. *From the Enlightenment to the end of the nineteenth century.* Chicago: University of Chicago Press, 1969.

Hall is concerned with three related questions: what is matter, what is life, and what configuration of matter makes life possible? In volume 2 he considers the period from 1750 to 1900. The emergence of the concepts of mechanism and vitalism are explicated and the pros and cons of each considered. From the *Contributors* Bonnet, Buffon, Diderot, Goethe, von Haller, La Mettrie, and Whytt are given consideration in depth for the period of the latter half of the eighteenth century. Pierre Louis M. de Maupertues, Gaub, and John Hunter also receive attention. There is somewhat less attention thereafter to individuals, but Bichet and Lamarck in the period at the turn of the century and the beginning of the next are given relatively extensive coverage.

Haymaker, W. *The founders of neurology.* (A167)

B154   Liddell, E. G. T. *The discovery of reflexes.* Oxford: Clarendon Press, 1960.

The first three chapters are concerned with the development of the requisite technological advances that opened up the nervous system to scientific study. The anatomy of nerve cells, the role of electricity in conduction, and some early experiments on the nervous system are dealt with in their historical context. Lastly, Sherrington's work is considered within the development of the "Neuron theory" in the late nineteenth century. Others of the *Contributors* who play a significant role in the development of the theme are Bell, Bernard, DuBois-Reymond, Flourens, Golgi, Goltz, M. Hall, Helmholtz, Magendie, J. Müller, Pflüger, Prochaska, and Whytt.

B155   McHenry, L. C. *Garrison's history of neurology, revised and enlarged with a bibliography of classical, original and standard works in neurology.* Foreword D. E. Denny-Brown. Springfield, Ill.: Thomas, 1969.

The first six chapters, Garrison's contribution for the most part, traces the development of neurology from the ancients through the eighteenth century. The last five chapters, primarily McHenry's work, along with the themes of neurophysiology from the previous chapters, deal with neurology in the nineteenth century and includes chapters devoted to neuroanatomy, neurophysiology, neurochemistry, neuropathology, clinical neurology, the neurological examination, and neurological diseases. From the *Contributors*, Babinski, Bell, Bernard, Brown-Séquard, Charcot, Flourens, Gall, M. Hall, von Haller, Hitzig, Jackson, Magendie, Meynert, Prochaska, Ramon y Cajal, Rolando, Sherrington, Spurzheim, and Whytt receive rather thorough consideration.

B156   Meyer, A. *Historical aspects of cerebral anatomy*. London: Oxford University Press, 1971.

A technical, detailed consideration of the development of neuroanatomy emerges in this work. The work is topic-oriented (e.g., the hypothalamus, the important olfactory pathways). The *Contributors* whose works are stressed are as follows: Bekhterev, Broca, Flechsig, Forel, Fulton, Gall, Golgi, von Haller, Herrick, Huxley, Jackson, Meynert, Monakow, Ramon y Cajal, and Spurzheim.

B157   Polyak, S. L. *The vertebrate visual system*. Ed. H. Klüver. Chicago: University of Chicago Press, 1957.

The first 200 pages are given over to the history of the investigation of the eye and visual pathways and visual brain centers.

B158   Riese, W. *A history of neurology*. New York: MD Publications, 1959.

The author covers a number of clinical topics (e.g., the history of diagnosis and prognosis in neurology) as well as the development of theoretical concepts such as the history of the nerve impulse, reflex action, and cerebral localization in relatively short compass, with Jackson receiving the most extensive consideration. One of the appendices is a chronological chart of important events in the history of neurology.

B159   Rothschuh, K. E. *History of physiology*. Ed. & trans. G. B. Risse. Huntington, N.Y.: Krieger, 1972. (1953)

The author traces the development of European physiology since the Middle Ages. His tratement of nineteenth-century German physiology, from the time of Johannes Müller, is especially extensive, tracing his teacher-pupil relationships throughout Germany. Bowditch, von Brücke, DuBois-Reymond, Ludwig, and von Helmholtz from the *Contributors* also receive major attention.

B160 Soury, J. *Le système nerveux central: Structure et fonctions: Histoire critique des théories et des doctrines.* Paris: Carré & Naud. 1899.

This is the most detailed history of neuroanatomy and neurophysiology extant, although its author was too close to the years 1870-1899 to give an accurate survey of this particular period.

B161 Walshe, F. *Further critical studies in neurology and other essays and addresses.* Baltimore, Md.: Williams & Wilkins, 1965.

A valuable historical supplement to Walshe's earlier work, *Critical Studies in Neurology* (1948), is supplied by this collection. A number of the essays are historical and/or deal with psychological problems. The psychologist may be particularly interested in the neurologist's thoughts on perception (VIII) and the mind-body problem (VII).

BIOLOGY

Some specialized aspects of biology were the basis for annotations in the previous section. More general histories of biology predominate here, some devoted to its entire span, others to specified centuries. Histories of genetics and of evolution are also included.

B162 Coleman, W. *Biology in the nineteenth century: Problems of form, function, transformation.* New York: Wiley, 1971.

The main theses of this monograph are given in the subtitle. "Form" of the plant or animal body is considered, first in terms of cell theory, then in that of individual development. The vital processes came to be studied in terms of "function." "Transformation" of plants and animals was also studied by those later to be called evolutionists.

In the final chapter, emphasizing events at the end of the century, the experimental investigation is shown to be the ideal toward which the biologists were striving in contrast to the seeking of historical explanations. Darwin naturally dominates throughout the book, but Bernard, Comte, Haeckel, Huxley, Lavoisier, Ludwig, Spencer, Wallace and, surprisingly perhaps, Durkheim are given prominent positions in the treatment of these themes.

B163 Dunn, L. C. *A short history of genetics: The development of some of the main lines of thought, 1864-1939.* New York: McGraw-Hill, 1965.

Mendel is the central figure in the history, but other *Contributors,* notably Darwin, DeVries, Fisher, Galton, and Pearson are also seen as important for the history of how the "riddle of heredity" became the science of genetics.

B164 Glass, B., Temkin, O., Straus, W. L., Jr. (Eds.), *Forerunners of Darwin, 1745-1859.* Baltimore, Md.: Johns Hopkins Press, 1959.

Darwin's centennial celebration supplies the content of this volume. It calls upon the skills of many senior scholars writing upon everything from fossils in relation to early cosmology to why the embryological theory of recapitulation, rejected before Darwin, was enthusiastically accepted after him. They stress the contributions of Agassiz, Bonnet, Buffon, Carpenter, Cuvier, C. Darwin, Descartes, Diderot, Goethe, Haeckel, Herder, Huxley, Lamarck, LaMettrie, Lavoisier, Leibniz, Newton, Spencer, Rousseau, and Voltaire from among the *Contributors.* Only K. E. von Baer, E. Guyenot, Baron Holbach, B. de Maillet, E. Rádl, and, above all, P. L. M. de Maupertuis are given comparable prominence.

Hall, T. S. *Ideas of life and matter.* (B153)

B165 Nordenskiold, E. *The history of biology: A survey.* Trans. L. B. Eyre. New York: Knopf, 1928. (1920-1924)

A standard history of biology from classical antiquity to the beginning of the present century is provided by the author. He uses a biographical approach, and, from among the numerous *Contributors* mentioned, Bacon, Bichat, Bonnet, Buffon, Comte, Cuvier, C. Darwin, DeVries, Descartes,

Galileo, Haeckel, Haller, Harvey, Humboldt, Huxley, Lamarck, LaMettrie, Linnaeus, J. Müller, Newton, and Swedenborg, receive the most emphasis. Scrutiny of these names will show that earlier rather than later modern history of biology is emphasized.

B166　Rádl, E. *The history of biological theories.* Trans. E. H. Hatfield. London: Oxford University Press, 1930. (1909)

This is primarily a history of evolution and genetics, despite its broader title. From the *Contributors,* Agassiz, Buffon, Cuvier, Erasmus Darwin, Driesch, Galton, Haeckel, Huxley, Lamarck, Preyer, Spencer, and Wallace are related in their thinking to that of Charles Darwin.

B167　Ritterbush, P. C. *Overtures to biology: The speculations of eighteenth-century naturalists.* New Haven, Conn.: Yale University Press, 1964.

A modern monographic treatment on the theme of the subtitle, with emphases on the use of analogy and the idea of scale of being. The works of Erasmus Darwin, Lamarck, and Linneaus receive special emphasis.

B168　Singer, C. J. *A history of biology to about the year 1900: A general introduction to the study of living things.* (3rd ed.) London: Abelard-Schuman, 1959. (1931)

A volume that in compact fashion manages to give a greater breadth to the history of biology than do many of the other histories. The author achieves this through shifts of perspective from chapter to chapter, e.g., the inductive philosophy, rise of classificatory systems, rise of the comparative method, distribution in space and time, and evolution form the themes of a central group of chapters. At about the turn of the century the history is brought to a close.

B169　Sirks, M. J., & Zirkle, C. *The evolution of biology.* New York: Ronald Press, 1964.

A survey of the phases through which biology passed, from its beginning in what was known about the distribution of plants, to Babylonian knowledge of pollination, and on to modern times.

B170　Young, R. M. *Mind, brain and adaptation in the nineteenth*

*century: Cerebral localization and its biological context
from Gall to Ferrier.* Oxford: Clarendon Press, 1970.

While written from the standpoint of investigating a
problem in biology, the author succeeds in drawing on the
literature from all relevant fields in a fashion that places
the problem squarely in the mainstream of the history of
science. Bain, Broca, Carpenter, Fritsch, Gall, Hitzig,
Hughlings Jackson, and Spencer of the *Contributors* receive
detailed consideration, as does David Ferrier. Young
describes the development of scientific thought in defining
the relation between the mind and its physical locus in the
brain, as well as the functional relations of the brain to en-
vironmental adaptation. The transformation of the philosophical conceptions of mind into biological concepts is
described within the context of research on cerebral localization of function. Overall, the book provides an illumin-
ating view of how philosophical presuppositions act to influence, and even determine, the course of physiological
inquiry.

B171 Zirkel, C. *Evolution, Marxian biology and the social scene.*
Philadelphia: University of Pennsylvania Press, 1959.

The incongruity of the Soviet Union's elimination of
genetics as a science for a period of years led Zirkle to examine in detail the peregrinations of Marxian biology in
relation to revolutions placed in the Russian social setting.
Naturally, the work of Darwin and Marx dominates, but
Ronald A. Fisher, Francis Galton, and Karl Pearson, also
from the *Contributors,* are given significant roles as well.

MEDICINE

Over the centuries probably more histories of medicine have been
published than in any other field except philosophy, yet relatively
few are annotated in this section. Several factors account for this:
the high percentage of amateur ventures — in the worst sense of
the term — that have appeared, the sheer unwieldiness of medicine
as a field, rendering it difficult to integrate the emphasis that
many medical historians place upon disease entities or upon institutional history, which are of less direct interest to the behavioral
scientist, and, most important of all, what I can only call a curious

imperviousness to the behavioral aspects of human disease on the part of historians of medicine. These factors, separately and in interaction, make it difficult to find very many relevant references to cite.

B172 Ackerknecht, E. H. *Medicine at the Paris Hospital, 1794-1848.* Baltimore, Md.: Johns Hopkins Press, 1967.

The period selected for study in depth in this book was an intensely active one, not only in medicine but also in politics, literature, and the other sciences. The medicine that emerged from work in this hospital, along with the surgery with which it was also united, was "hospital medicine" based on an integration of physical examination and pathological anatomy, on statistics, and on the concept of the lesion. Bichat, Cabanis, Magendie, and Pinel figure prominently.

B173 Ben-David, J. Scientific productivity and academic organization in nineteenth-century medicine. *Amer. soc. Rev.,* 1960, *25,* 828-843. Reprinted in B. Barber & W. Hirsch (Eds.), *The sociology of science.* New York: Free Press, 1962, pp. 305-328.

An account of medical discoveries in France, Britain, Germany, and the United States from 1800 to 1925 shows a variety of national changes over time. To illustrate, French supremacy in the beginning of the nineteenth century (with Britain a close second) gave way later in the century to an overwhelming preponderance of German discoveries. This and other findings were then interpreted, particularly in terms of difference in competitive decentralization of institutions of higher learning. Ingenious quantification of data and statistical manipulations were used in developing these hypotheses.

B174 Garrison, F. H. *An introduction to the history of medicine.* (4th ed.) Philadelphia: Saunders, 1929. (1913)

This history is most useful as a reference work, since it is somewhat disjointed as a narrative. Two thirds of this volume concern the modern period. Each of the centuries is considered in a separate chapter, with the subheads showing the synthesizing principle for the period. The seven-

teenth century is called "The Age of Individual Scientific
Endeavor"; the eighteenth, "The Age of Theories and
Systems"; the nineteenth, "The Beginnings of Organized
Advancement of Science"; and the twentieth, "The Beginnings of Organized Preventive Medicine," with a special
chapter on "Medicine in the World War and After." A
lengthy chronological appendix and bibliographies are included. Although thousands of individuals are mentioned,
understandably, relatively detailed attention can only be
given to very few.

B175   Puschmann, T., Neuburger, M., & Pagel, J. (Eds.), *Handbuch
der Geschichte der Medizin.* (Vols. 2, 3). Hildesheim: Olms,
1972. (1903-1905)
       A detailed factual account of thousands of individuals
who are judged to be prominent in the history of medicine,
most useful as a reference volume. All branches of medicine are presented in separate chapters, each prepared by a
specialist. Volume 2, which includes histories of anatomy
and physiology, gives some attention to Bell, Bernard,
Bichat, DuBois-Reymond, Brown-Séquard, Brücke, Charcot, von Frey, von Haller, Helmholtz, Ludwig, Magendie,
Meissner, J. Müller, Prochaska, Purkinje, Ramon y Cajal,
and Volkmann. Volume 3 includes the history of psychiatry and, aside from those of Beneke, Kraepelin,
Esquirol, and Pinel, one is struck by the plethora of what,
to this reader, are obscure names. In chapters devoted to
other topics, von Haller, Magendie, and Purkinje receive
consideration.

B176   Shyrock, R. H. *The development of modern medicine: An
interpretation of the social and scientific factors involved.*
London: Gollancz, 1948. (1936)
       The background suggested by the subtitle is stressed
and the conclusion defended that increased investigation
of quantitative measures and experimentation were the
prime basis for advance. Relatively little emphasis is placed
upon individual *Contributors* by name.

B177   Sigerist, H. E. *The great doctors: A biographical history of
medicine.* (2nd ed.) Trans. E. & C. Paul. New York: Norton, 1933 (1932) Reprinted Freeport, N.Y.: Books for
Libraries Press, 1971.

Short biographical accounts are provided. From among the *Contributors,* the volume includes those for Bichat, von Helmholtz, von Haller, and J. Müller.

B178   Singer, C., & Underwood, E. A. *A short history of medicine.* (2nd ed.) Oxford: Oxford University Press, 1962. (1928)'

In this revision, Underwood entirely rewrote that portion of the text dealing with the nineteenth and twentieth centuries. Although there is some space devoted to the period opening with the time of Leonardo da Vinci, the broad subdivisions under which the material is grouped are the rebirth of science, the period of consolidation, and the period of scientific subdivision, the last being by far the longest. About 1600 individuals are referred to briefly.

B179   Underwood, E. A. (Ed.), *Science, medicine and history: Essays on the evolution of scientific thought and medical practice written in honour of Charles Singer.* (2 vols.) London: Oxford University Press, 1953.

A miscellany of 90 papers by 95 authors, many of considerable stature, divided into eight books, "the first seven of which treat the history of science and medicine as it unfolds itself in chronological periods." The eighth book includes those papers that would not permit such chronological placement. It is the sort of volume most properly used by someone already generally familiar with its contents who turns to it when a specific need arises. The topics defy summarization other than by listing the names of the *Contributors* receiving treatment of article length. They are Bacon, Descartes, Flourens, Gall, M. Hall, Rush, Schopenhauer, Spurzheim, and Young.

ANTHROPOLOGY

Anthropology is a field of broad scope, only certain aspects of which are of direct interest to the historian of the behavioral sciences. For this reason, physical anthropology is hardly touched upon in the annotations that follow. Social anthropology or ethnology form the focus of interest.

B180   Bender, D. The development of French anthropology. *J. Hist. behav. Sci.*, 1965, *1*, 139-151.

This article gives special emphasis to the ways in which French anthropology differed in its development from its English-speaking counterpart. Broca, Durkheim, and Levy-Bruhl from the *Contributors* and Claude Lévi-Strauss figure prominently in the account.

B181   Harris, M. *The rise of anthropological theory: A history of theories of culture.* New York: Crowell, 1968.

This, the most detailed of available histories of cultural anthropology, opens with the Enlightenment and the beginnings of the concept of culture. Major themes of subsequent chapters are racial determinism, evolutionism, particularism, culture and personality, structuralism, the nomothetic revival, and cultural materialism. From the *Contributors,* Benedict, Boas, Comte, Darwin, Durkheim, Hegel, Kardiner, Lamarck, Malinowski, Malthus, Marx, Nietzsche, Róheim, Quételet, Rivers, Sapir, Spencer, Tylor, and Wissler are placed in perspective.

B182   Hodgen, Margaret T. *Early anthropology in the sixteenth and seventeenth centuries.* Philadelphia: University of Pennsylvania Press, 1964.

An examination is provided of the literature of the period, which laid the foundation for modern anthropology.

B183   Kardiner, A., & Preble, E. *They studied man.* Cleveland, Ohio: World Publishing, 1961.

The first section is organized around the dimension of "cultural" anthropology through the contributions in chronological sequence of Charles Darwin, Spencer, Tylor, Frazer, Durkheim, Boas, Malinowski, Kroeber and Ruth Benedict; the second section has the new dimension "Man" with Freud as the overpowering central figure.

B184   De Laguna, Frederica (Ed.), *Selected papers from the American Anthropologist, 1888-1920.* Evanston, Ill.: Row, Peterson, 1960.

This volume opens with a relatively lengthy history of anthropology in America prepared especially for the volume by A. I. Hallowell. The first section of papers is the most general, characteristically coming from publications of the early decades of the century, and concern the World's Fair anthropological exhibit, John Wesley Powell, and the like. The other sections may be described more succinctly and are devoted to reports on American Indian origin, archaeology, physical anthropology, language, etnography, and method and theory.

B185 Lowie, R. H. *The history of ethnological theory.* New York: Farrar & Rhinehart, 1937.

After introductory chapters, including one devoted to Adolf Bastian and others to Lewis H. Morgan and E. B. Tylor, there is a discussion of the various fields and concepts that formed a background for further advances. A relatively thorough disucssion of Franz Boas, conceived as being comparable to Tylor in his influence, follows. Chapters on the diffusionists, both British and German, on French sociology, and on the functionalists follow. The book closes on the theme that the universalist and objective approach of Tylor and Boas should be maintained. Other *Contributors* receiving attention are Benedict, Durkheim, Galton, Lévy-Bruhl, Lubbock, Malinowski, Rivers, Tarde, and Wissler. J. J. Bachoven, G. Klemm, A. L. Kroeber, L. H. Morgan, G. E. Smith, and R. Thurnwald are also discussed at equal depth.

B186 Penniman, T. K. (Contrib. Beatrice Blackwood & J. S. Weiner.) *A hundred years of anthropology.* (3rd rev. ed.) New York: International Universities Press, 1970. (1935)

A general history of anthropology that, throughout the first fifty years of its coverage, shows relatively little national insularity in the topics and men selected for exposition. In the last half of the century, greater coverage of the British scene, as contrasted to the American, may be discerned. The views of the more-or-less expected *Contributors,* Benedict, Bentham, Boas, Broca, Darwin, Freud, Huxley, Lamarck, Malinowski, McDougall, Pearson, Rivers, and Tylor are to be found. Given about equal prominence are J. J. Bachofen, L. H. D. Buxton, Sir J. G. Frazer, A. C. Haddon, Sir Arthur Keith, R. R. Marett, and J. L. Myers.

B187 Stocking, G. W., Jr. *Race, culture and evolution: Essays in the history of anthropology.* New York: Free Press, 1968.

        While the problem of race in professional-historical
context is the central theme, methodological considerations
are very evident, never more prominently than the first
article on "presentism" and "historicism" cited elsewhere
(C21). Baldwin, Boas (especially), Broca, Darwin, Galton,
Lamarck, Spencer, and Tylor from among the *Contributors,*
as well as A. L. Kroeber, W. I. Thomas, and L. F. Ward
receive major consideration.

SOCIOLOGY

General histories of sociology predominate among the annotations
that follow. The approaches, however, are diverse: the individuals
concerned, the institutions involved, the guiding concepts, the research techniques adopted, the influence of social factors expressed
are only some of the themes considered central by different writers.

B188   Aron, R. *Main currents in sociological thought.* (2 vols.)
        Trans. R. Howard & Helen Weaver. New York: Basic Books,
        1965-1967.
        This is a two-volume historical introduction to classi-
        cal sociological thought. The author adopts the "Great
        Man" approach. Volume 1 considers Montesquieu, Comte,
        Marx, de Tocqueville and the sociologists of the Revolution
        of 1848; Volume 2 centers upon M. Weber, Pareto, and
        Durkheim.

B189   Barnes, H. E. (Ed.), *An introduction to the history of
        sociology.* Chicago: University of Chicago Press, 1948.
        From among the *Contributors* Comte, Cooley, Durk-
        heim, Hobhouse, LeBon, Ross, Tarde, Max Weber, and
        Wundt receive either biographical exposition, critical
        analysis, or both, in some of the 47 articles that are in-
        cluded.

B190   Becker, H., & Barnes, H. E. *Social thought from lore to
        science.* (3rd ed.) (3 vols.) New York: Dover, 1971. (1938)
        This comprehensive three-volume history of sociolog-
        ical thought is so detailed as to cause one to lose the thread
        of continuity, but it is well worth reading. Volume 2 opens

the account of the modern period. Successive chapters concern man in the state of nature, progress, forms of sociological differentiation, objectivity and Comte, social reform, Marxism, positivism and evolutionism, social Darwinism, and the deflation of social evolutionism. Volume 3 is concerned with still later developments and is organized around trends in different countries. Within each country the men, the movements, and the central problems are reviewed.

B191 Coser, L. A. *Masters of sociological thought: Ideas in historical and social context.* New York: Harcourt, Brace & Jovanovich, 1971.

Coser approaches the history of sociological theory through exposition of the thinking of each of twelve of its leaders in terms of his orientation and ideas, his life, his position in intellectual history and, lastly, the sociological questions that his life and opinions reflect. Six are from among the *Contributors:* Comte, Cooley, Durkheim, Marx, Spencer, and Weber. Others discussed include Robert Park and Karl Mannheim.

B192 Faris, R. E. L. *Chicago sociology, 1920-1932.* San Francisco, Calif.: Chandler, 1967.

After depicting the historical milieu from which the Chicago school of sociology emerged, consideration is given to the men and research that made the University of Chicago a dominant force in the development of American sociology. Major figures are Ernest W. Burgess, Ellsworth Faris, Franklin H. Giddings, Everett C. Hughes, William F. Ogburn, Robert E. Park, Albion W. Small, William I. Thomas, and Louis Wirth; and, from the *Contributors,* Cooley, Dewey, Mead, and Ross.

B193 Fletcher, R. (Ed.), *The making of sociology: A study of sociological theory.* Vol. 1: *Beginnings and foundations.* Vol. 2: *Developments.* London: Joseph, 1971.

The author believed that in organizing a book about its history, he could demonstrate the continuity that might otherwise not be apparent in the amorphous field of sociology. He also had the subsidiary aim of integrating British sociology into the framework now dominated by

American contributions. From among the *Contributors,* those receiving detailed attention in one or both volumes are Comte, Cooley, Durkheim, Freud, Hegel, Hobbes, Hobhouse, Hume, Kant, Malinowski, Marx, McDougall, Mead, J. S. Mill, Montesquieu, A. Smith, Spencer, Tylor, and M. Weber. Others receiving comparable discussion are F. H. Giddings, Le Play, V. Pareto, T. Parsons, G. Simmel, W. G. Sumner, F. S. Tonnies, L. F. Ward, and E. A. Westermarck.

B194 Glazer, N. The rise of social research in Europe. In D. Lerner (Ed.), *The human meaning of the social sciences.* New York: Meridian Books, 1959, pp. 43-72.

This essay traces the contributions of the nineteenth-century European social scientist, Frederic Leplay, and, from the *Contributors,* the statistician, Quételet, who collected social statistics in a systematic fashion. The author then considers the further development of empirical sociology and its influence on early twentieth-century sociology.

B195 Gouldner, A. W. *The coming crisis of Western sociology.* New York: Basic Books, 1970.

This is a critical, original interpretation of the historical roots of contemporary sociological doctrines. After presenting as the setting the contradictions in contemporary society between theory and practice, Gouldner examines what happens in sociology, moving from the sociological positivism of Henri Saint-Simon and Comte, to Marxism then to the classical sociology of Weber, Durkheim, and Pareto and on to the structural-functionalism of Talcott Parsons and his students.

B196 Hinkle, R. C., Jr., & Hinkle, Gisela J. *The development of modern sociology: Its nature and growth in the United States.* New York: Random House, 1954.

This short introductory work is primarily concerned with the development of American sociology. Its three chapters cover three periods (1905-1918, 1918-1935 and 1935-1954) in American sociological thought, emphasizing the development of increasingly sophisticated research techniques and theories. From among the *Contributors,*

Baldwin, Comte, Cooley, Durkheim, Freud, Ross, Spencer, and M. Weber are given major emphasis, but the same degree of attention is devoted to Howard Becker, Robert Mac Iver, Robert K. Merton, William F. Ogburn, Vilfredo Pareto, Talcott Parsons, Albion W. Small, William Graham Sumner, William I. Thomas, and Lester F. Ward.

B197 Madge, J. *The origins of scientific sociology.* New York: Free Press, 1962.

After an introductory chapter on Durkheim's contributions, the author traces the development of scientific sociology in America. The emergence of the Chicago school, with the rise of urbanization and of an industrial working class in America, is given detailed consideration. The topics of subcultures, race, sexual behavior, social science and the soldier, fascism, and group dynamics are then surveyed from an historical viewpoint. Because of the nature of the problems evaluated, a somewhat idiosyncratic selection from the *Contributors* emerges in the persons of Frenkel-Brunswik, Kinsey, Lewin, Mayo, and Stouffer. Some other individuals receiving major consideration are R. F. Bales, W. J. Dickson, L. Festinger, H. H. Hyman, H. H. Kelley, P. F. Lazarsfeld, R. S. Lynd, R. K. Merton, E. A. Shills, W. I. Thomas, and Florian Znaniecki.

B198 Odum, H. W. *American sociology: The story of sociology in the United States to 1950.* New York: Longmans, Green, 1951.

After a short treatment of the origins of American sociological thought in European and American culture, the author considers the works of the presidents of the American Sociological Society from 1906 to 1950. This includes only Cooley and Ross from the *Contributors.* The author then reviews the major sociological texts in a number of specialized areas, e.g., the family, social problems, demography. The book concludes with an analysis of modern trends in sociology. C. Darwin, Durkheim, Hobhouse, Spencer, Stouffer, and M. Weber from the *Contributors* receive attention in these later sections. However, greater emphasis is given to some thirty others such as Emory S. Bogardus, Ernest W. Burgess, Ellsworth Faris, Franklin Henry Giddings, Robert K. Merton, Howard W.

Odum, William F. Ogburn, Robert E. Park, Talcott Parsons, Albion Woodbury Small, William Graham Sumner, William I. Thomas, and Lester F. Ward.

B199   Raison, T. (Ed.), *The founding fathers of social science.* Baltimore, Md.: Penguin Books, 1969.

This is a collection of 24 essays, each on an important figure in the history of sociology. The essays are biographically oriented as well as summarizations of that person's contribution to the development of social thought. Nine are from the *Contributors.* Other individuals covered include Saint-Simon and Robert E. Park.

B200   Zeitlin, I. M. *Ideology and the development of sociological theory.* Englewood Cliffs, N.J.: Prentice-Hall, 1968.

The historical survey of the origins of classical sociology begins with the Enlightenment, since Zeitlin argues that a rational criticism of social institutions was initiated during the period. Then the romantic and conservative responses to the French revolution are considered, along with the development and influence of Marx's ideas in the nineteenth and twentieth centuries. Aside from Marx, other *Contributors* considered in some depth are Comte, Durkheim, Hegel, Rousseau, and M. Weber. Louis de Bonald, Joseph de Maistre, and Henri de Saint-Simon are other major figures placed in context.

EDUCATION

Histories of education in the United States and in the Western world are annotated. Many books on history of education in the United States have settled into certain well-worn grooves, exemplified by the particular individuals who receive central attention. From among the *Eminent contributors to psychology,* Dewey, Franklin, Froebel, Hall, Herbart, Locke, Pestalozzi, and Rousseau almost always receive major consideration, while Jonathan Edwards and Samuel Johnson receive somewhat less. Others apt to be placed in historical perspective are Henry Barnard, Nicholas Murray Butler, Thomas Jefferson, and Horace Mann. There is somewhat less tendency to include Charles W. Eliot, Frances W. Parker, and Joseph Mayer Rice.

B201 Bayles, E. E. & Hood, B. L. *Growth of American educational thought and practice.* New York: Harper & Row, 1966.

As the title suggests, a history of education in the United States is provided. The European influence of Comenius, Locke, Rousseau, Pestalozzi, Herbart, and Froebel are placed in that perspective. Thorndike and Dewey are central for later chapters.

B202 Butts, R. F., & Cremin, L. A. *A history of education in American culture.* New York: Holt, Rinehart & Winston, 1953.

A cultural approach to the history of American education devoting attention to those individuals mentioned in the section introduction is given in this survey.

B203 Cremin, L. A. *The transformation of the school: Progressivism in American education, 1876-1957.* New York: Knopf, 1961. (Reprinted New York: Vintage, 1964)

The origins of progressive education are found by Cremin in the post-Civil-War period and traced to its collapse in the post-World-War-II period. John Dewey is a central figure, while Hall, James, Spencer, and Thorndike played less important roles.

B204 Cubberley, E. P. *The history of education: Educational practice and progress considered as a phase of the development and spread of Western civilization.* Boston: Houghton Mifflin, 1948. (1920)

This 850-page classic of the twenties is still valuable today. Modern educational history takes up the second half, with due attention to national education in various countries. The usual array of individuals is present, but they are submerged beneath consideration of practice and organization in education.

B205 Curti, M. *The social ideas of American educators.* New York: Scribner's, 1935.

Social ideas having to do with elementary and secondary education receive emphasis in this book. From the *Contributors* Hall, James, Thorndike, and Dewey receive full discussion, as do Henry Barnard, William T. Harris,

Horace Mann, John L. Spalding, Francis W. Parker, and
Booker T. Washington.

B206   Good, H. G. *A history of American education.* (2nd ed.)
New York: Macmillan, 1962.
        In addition to the expected figures in the history of
education, a nicely balanced view of internal growth and
external pressure upon education are given. William C.
Woodbridge does receive considerable attention.

B207   Good, H. G., & Teller, J. D. *A history of Western education.* (3rd ed.) London: Macmillan, 1969. (1947)
        As the title implies, this survey is not limited to one
country. About one half of the book takes the history of
education through Pestalozzi, Froebel, and Herbart, with
one unusual chapter devoted to Johann Bernhard Basedow.
The rest of the book involves national trends in education
in France, Germany, Russia, England, and the United
States, each taken from their beginnings to the present.

B208   Nash, P., Kazamias, A. M., & Perkinson, H. J. (Eds.), *The
educated man: Studies in the history of educational
thought:* New York: Wiley, 1965.
        The theme of the educated man is related to the work
of a specific individual, each chapter prepared by a specialist. From among the *Contributors,* Locke, Rousseau, Huxley, Marx, and Dewey each receive a chapter. For before
the modern period, there are chapters on Plato, Augustine,
Aquinas, and Erasmus; contemporaries represented are
T. S. Eliot, M. Buber, and B. F. Skinner.

B209   Rippa, S. A. *Education in free society: An American his-
tory.* New York: McKay, 1967.
        This book is written in the form of a social history of
American education. Other than the usual cast of characters,
Bacon, Montessori, Spencer, and Thorndike are considered.

B210   Rusk, R. R. *The doctrines of the great educators.* (4th ed.)
New York: St. Martin's Press, 1969. (1918)
        This volume is organized around the teachings of edu-
cators extending from Plato to the modern times. For the
modern period, all chapters with the exception of one con-

cern *Contributors,* namely, Comenius, Locke, Rousseau, Pestalozzi, Herbart, Froebel, Montessori, Dewey, and Whitehead.

B211 Thayer, Vivian T. *Formative ideas in American education: From the colonial period to the present.* New York: Dodd, Mead, 1965.

A history of educational philosophy as related to practice is the theme of this book. Along with the conventional array of leaders of education mentioned in the introduction to this section, James, Thorndike, and Watson also receive attention.

READINGS

A search of the relevant literature on the history of the behavioral sciences showed that 95 books of readings in English contained excerpts from at least five of the *Eminent contributors to psychology.* Only a severely limited number can be reported here. Selected for inclusion because of sheer breadth of coverage and depth of scholarship were those edited by Clarke and O'Malley (B213), Dennis (B215), Diamond (B216), Herrnstein and Boring (B218), and Rand (B227). The last four of these are primarily selections from the history of psychology, while the first is more concerned with physiology and anatomy. To extend coverage to other fields, others cited are Beardslee and Wertheimer (B212) for perception; Coser and Rosenberg (B214) for sociology, Gardiner (E24) for philosophy of history, Hall (B217) for biology, Hunter and Macalpine (B219) for psychiatry, Kessen (B220) for child psychology, Lindzey and Hall (B222) for personality, both Kockelmans (B221) and Madden (B223) for philosophy of science, Mandler and Mandler (B224) for thinking, Miller (B225) for mathematics and quantitative measurement, Rand (B226) for philosophy, Rapaport (B228) for pathology of thinking, Russell (B229) for motivation, and Ulich (B230) for education.

Although it might be too strained to include as a "book of readings" in the sense intended here the 54 volumes edited by R. M. Hutchins, *Great Books of the Western World* (Chicago: Encyclopaedia Britannica, 1952) must be mentioned. The series contains complete works by Bacon, Berkeley, C. Darwin, Descartes, Faraday, Freud, Galileo, Goethe, Harvey, Hegel, Hobbes, Hume,

Huygens, James, Kant, Kepler, Lavoisier, Locke, Marx, J. S. Mill, Montesquieu, Newton, Rousseau, Smith, and Spinoza from the *Eminent contributors to psychology*. Moreover, the most modern works included in the series are those by James and Freud. The heritage with which the historian of the behavioral sciences works is not an inconsiderable one.

Each cited book of readings contains excerpts from among among the *Eminent contributors*. In all, 226 of the 538 *Contributors* are represented by at least one selection. Pride of place goes, however, to Descartes, since eight of the 20 books of readings include something from his writings.

B212   Beardslee, D. C., & Wertheimer, M. (Eds.), *Readings in perception*. Princeton, N.J.: Van Nostrand, 1958.

B213   Clarke, E., & O'Malley, C. D. (Eds.), *The human brain and spinal cord: A historical study illustrated by writings from antiquity to the twentieth century*. Berkeley, Calif.: University of California Press, 1968.

B214   Coser, L. A., & Rosenberg, B. (Eds.), *Sociological theory: A book of readings*. New York: Macmillan, 1957.

B215   Dennis, W. (Ed.), *Readings in the history of psychology*. New York: Appleton-Century-Crofts, 1948.

B216   Diamond, S. (Ed.), *The roots of psychology: A sourcebook in the history of ideas*. New York: Basic Books, 1974.

Gardiner, P. (Ed.), *Theories of history*. (E24)

B217   Hall, T. S. (Ed.), *A source book in animal biology*. New York: McGraw-Hill, 1951.

B218   Herrnstein, R. J., & Boring, E. G. (Eds.), *A source book in the history of psychology*. Cambridge: Harvard University Press, 1965.

B219   Hunter, R., & Macalpine, Ida (Eds.), *Three hundred years of psychiatry 1535-1860: A history presented in selected English texts*. London: Oxford University Press, 1963.

B220 Kessen, W. (Ed.), *The child.* New York: Wiley, 1956.

B221 Kockelmans, J. J. (Ed.), *Philosophy of science: The historical background.* New York: Free Press, 1968.

B222 Lindzey, G., & Hall, C. S. (Eds.), *Theories of personality: Primary sources and research.* New York: Wiley, 1965.

B223 Madden, E. H. (Ed.), *The structure of scientific thought: An introduction to the philosophy of science.* Boston: Houghton Mifflin, 1960.

B224 Mandler, Jean M., & Mandler, G. (Eds.), *Thinking: From association to Gestalt.* Boston: Houghton Mifflin, 1960.

B225 Miller, G. A. (Ed.), *Mathematics and psychology.* New York: Wiley, 1964.

B226 Rand, B. (Ed.), *Modern classical philosophers: Selections illustrating modern philosophy from Bruno to Bergson.* (2nd ed.) Boston: Houghton Mifflin, 1924.

B227 Rand, B. (Ed.), *The classical psychologists: Selections illustrating psychology from Anaxagoras to Wundt.* Boston: Houghton Mifflin, 1912.

B228 Rapaport, D. (Ed.), *Organization and pathology of thought: Selected sources.* New York: Columbia University Press, 1951.

B229 Russell, W. A. (Ed.), *Milestones in motivation: Contributions to the psychology of drive and purpose.* New York: Appleton-Century-Crofts, 1970.

B230 Ulich, R. (Ed.), *Three thousand years of educational wisdom: Selections from great documents.* Cambridge: Harvard University Press, 1947.

C. METHODS OF HISTORICAL RESEARCH

The first major topic in this section concerns the way the historian analyzes his material and prepares his narrative, while the second is that of the application of quantitative methods to documents.

CRITICAL ANALYSIS: NARRATIVE METHODS

The importance attributed to this combined task by many historians can hardly by overemphasized. Many historians see it as the only important methodological skill necessary. The use of terms such as "guide," "historian's craft," "primer," and "method" in the titles that follow are indicative of this, since most of their pages are devoted to a consideration of writing the narrative. One or another of the books annotated is apt to be used in graduate history departments as the basic textbook for courses in historical methodology. It behooves historians of the behavioral sciences who have not been trained in these departments to become familiar with them.

The narrative form adopted in historical works would seem to call primarily for skill in the art of writing that narrative. The critical analysis of the primary and secondary material dealing with whatever topic is in question is performed with the narrative-to-be in mind. As is the case in any artistic endeavor, the would-be historian is expected to experience examples of the art, in this case through reading and more reading of history, through some personal critical interaction with more experienced practitioners in the field, and through reading what others have to say about the art of critically analyzing the material and preparing the narrative. The books and articles that follow supply a sample of the last form of experience mentioned. Narrative problems involved with biography, the use of sympathetic understanding in approaching the raw materials that are to become the narrative, the question of methodological objectivity and related attitudes in preparing the narrative are taken up in later, more specific sections.

C1   Barzun, J., & Graff, H. F. *The modern researcher.* (3rd ed.)
      New York: Harcourt, 1977. (1957)
          This book manages to include so many topics that it
      was difficult to place it into the proper category. The sparse
      treatment of "finding the facts" rules it out as a "guide" in
      the sense in which the word was used to describe the first
      section. Causality, laws (which in the opinion of the
      authors are of very little use), the great philosophies of his-
      tory, historiography in Europe and America, and the rela-
      tion of history to other fields also receive cursory treat-
      ment; but, despite the value and even the brilliance with
      which these topics are discussed, none is the major topic.
      Since roughly one third of the book is devoted to "Writ-
      ing," it has been included here because of its contribution
      to the preparation of narrative accounts of history. The
      authors make an attempt to demonstrate that the writing
      of 'straight history' has many points of similarity, if not
      identity, with literary writing. The tasks common to them
      are care in the verification of the points made, correct ways
      of shaping of sentences and chapters, and proper citing of
      authorities.

      Berkhofer, R. K. *A behavioral approach to historical
      analysis.* (D117)

C2   Bloch, M. *The historian's craft.* Trans. P. Putnam. New
      York: Knopf, 1953.
          The nature of history, the place to be accorded to
      accounts by observers, the appreciation of criticism, and
      the nature of historical change and causation are the major
      topics in this temperate, thoughtful account. The author
      argues that historical facts essentially are psychological
      facts.

      Brickman, W. W. *Guide to research in educational history.*
      (A2)

      Danto, A. C. *Analytical philosophy of history* (E4)

C3   Fischer, D. H. *Historians' fallacies: Toward a logic of his-
      torical thought.* New York: Harper & Row, 1970.
          This book classifies and exemplifies fallacies commit-

ted by historians in making narrative statements. Although based on the narrative, it is essentially the critical analysis phase that was carried on in such fashion as to result in fallacies in the narratives. The author offers a plea for reason in the more limited form of logic in thinking and writing about history. In an engaging manner, he lays bare some of the fallacies involved in inquiry (question-framing, factual verification, and factual significance); in explanation (generalization, causality, motivation, composition, and false analogy); and in argument (semantical distortion and substantive distraction). Specific and numerous illustrations of each of the fallacies, drawn primarily from the writings of competent contemporary historians, lend vivid point to his arguments.

Gallie, W. B. *Philosophy and the historical understanding.* (D71)

C4   Garraghan, G. J. *A guide to historical method.* New York: Fordham University Press, 1946.

   After introductory chapters on meanings, methods, and nature of certainty in history and of the fields auxiliary to history, the remainder of the book is divided into three major segments—a relatively short one on finding the sources, one devoted to criticism in appraising the sources for the narrative with special emphasis upon credibility, and, lastly, synthesis or presentation of the resulting narrative.

C5   Gottschalk, L. *Understanding history: A primer of historical method.* New York: Knopf, 1950.

   The book does not fill the role of being a guide, as the term is used in this volume, because it does not include the characteristic information on bibliographic sources. However, in another sense it is a guide—a guide to the *writing* of history. It was prepared to show how the historian works and how history is written, in terms of collecting historical materials and then fashioning them into an historical narrative. It is one of the most widely used texts in the field. Along with the methodological discussion, the author includes chapters devoted to "cause, motive and influence" and "problems of the present," where general-

ization is the major theme. Objective relativism, also discussed, is his way of denying a belief in absolute principles
or of a single principle of the dynamics of history.

C6   Mora, G., & Brand, Jeanne L. (Eds.) *Psychiatry and its
history: Methodological problems in research.* Springfield,
Ill.: Thomas, 1970.
    Participants of the symposium may not have intended
primarily to discuss the analytic narrative method. Nevertheless, although several articles from this collection are
cited in other sections, mention of the volume as a whole
is most appropriate to this section. If read with this conscious set, many of the articles, especially the first three
papers by Mora, Ellenberger, and Cranefield, can be recognized as valuable in offering suggestions on how to proceed
with analysis and how to prepare the narrative.

C7   Nevins, A. *The gateway to history.* (Rev. ed.) Garden City,
N.Y.: Doubleday, 1962. (1938)
    In this work, various approaches to history are
sketched, along with comments on the way documents are
utilized, on the criteria for valid evidence, on the importance in history of accepting guiding thematic ideas supplied
by either the historical figures or by the historians themselves, on the influence of geography, sociology, and economics upon history, on the relation of biography to history, and on the problem of the writing of history in relation to criteria of literary merit. The importance of ideas
or concepts as dynamic in history is defined very ably.

BIOGRAPHY AS NARRATIVE

The methodological literature on the preparation of biographies
tends to stress the narrative rather than the quantitative method,
so that most references are more appropriately seen as forming a
subdivision of the analytic-narrative literature. However, some
quantitatively methodological references cited later refer specifically to biographies.

C8   Allport, G. W. *The use of personal documents in psycholo-*

gical science. New York: Social Science Research Council, 1942.

Although biographies and autobiographies are among the documents that Allport does discuss, the very title correctly suggests broader usage. In view of its intent to relate documents to psychological science in general, Allport was not under the historian's limitation to deal with documents, over the composition of which he had no control. Naturally, then, questionnaires and the like, relevant to the volume but somewhat irrelevant to the task of the historian, are included. Even if they are omitted from consideration, the documents still left are very rich material for the historian. There are three major sections; the use of personal documents, their forms, and, lastly, their value, including a chapter each on the case for and the case against the use of personal documents.

C9   Bermann, M. S. Limitations of method in psychoanalytic biography: A historical inquiry. *J. Amer. psychoanal. Ass.,* 1973, *21,* 833-850.

       This is the latest in a series of five methodological review articles in the same journal (which Bermann cites) extending back to 1960. Taken together, they give an excellent picture of psychoanalytic method applied to biography. Of the other four, that by Mack (1971, *19,* 143-179) is expecially recommended.

C10   Garraty, J. A. The interrelations of psychology and biography. *Psychol. Bull.,* 1954, *51,* 569-582.

       There is a reciprocal relationship not only between psychology and biography, but also between psychology and history and between history and biography. This article is a plea for greater use of the methods of the one field by representatives of the other. The author proceeds to give an account of how a historian uses the methods of the psychologist and how these interrelate with the writing of biography. In view of the scope of the article, it is hardly surprising that he does mention some quantitative methods, particularly content analysis, but reliance upon the nartive approach is paramount.

C11   Garraty, J. A. *The nature of biography.* New York: Knopf, 1957.

This is the most psychologically oriented book on biographical methodology available today. It is a history of biography as well as a statement of methodology and includes an informative essay on sources. The nature of biography and its historical development is followed in the last half of the book, with the method of its study expressed in choosing a subject, its materials, the problem of personality, and the task of writing the biographical narrative.

C12   Helm, June (Ed.), *Pioneers of American anthropology: The uses of biography.* Seattle, Wash.: University of Washington Press, 1966.

How biography may be used as a technique in anthropological research is the theme of these collected papers.

Langer, W. L. *The mind of Adolf Hitler.* (D92)

C13   Shapin, S., & Thackray, A. Prosopography as a research tool in history of science: The British scientific community 1700-1900. *Hist. Sci.,* 1974, *12,* 1-28.

Prosopography, rather than collective biography, was the term of choice used by the authors to signalize the fact that they are dealing with a coherently organized technique with well-developed rules of procedure; these are described in the book.

C14   Stone, L. Prosopography. In F. Gilbert & S. R. Graubard (Eds.), *Historical studies today.* New York: Norton, 1972, pp. 107-140.

The technique of collective biography is described and evaluated.

THE NARRATIVE AND VERSTEHEN

Verstehen, and sympathetic understanding or imaginative reconstruction, the position of Collingwood, are perhaps the best known of the several terms that apply to this attitude as the heart of the phase preliminary to writing the narrative. The intent of the method to be discussed calls for the historian to immerse himself in the events he intends to write about, so that he integrates understanding and feeling in a unified whole by placing himself in the position of the individual about whom he is writing.

C15   Abel, T. The operation called *Verstehen. Amer. J. Sociol.*,
       1948, *54*, 211-218. Reprinted in H. Feigl & May Brodbeck
       (Eds.), *Readings in the philosophy of science.* New York:
       Appleton-Century-Crofts, 1953, pp. 677-687.

       An attempt to describe *Verstehen* as a method, not
       merely as a rather hazy point of view. The topic is illus-
       trated and evaluated from a sociological perspective, but
       no trouble should be experienced in transferring what he
       says to historical issues.

C16   Beer, S. H. Causal explanation and imaginative reenactment.
       Hist. Theory, 1963, *3*, 6-29.

       A protagonist for *Verstehen* argues for the desirability,
       even the necessity, of this approach in the analytic phase
       of narrative preparation.

       Collingwood, R. G. *The idea of history.* (E23)

C17   McCarthy, T. The operation called *Verstehen*: Towards a
       redefinition of the problem. In K. F. Schaffner & R. S.
       Cohen (Eds.), *Boston studies in the philosophy of science.*
       Vol. 20 *Proceedings of the 1972 biennial meeting, Philo-
       sophy of Science Association,* Ed. K. F. Schaffner & R. S.
       Cohen. Dordrecht: Reidel, 1974, pp. 167-193.

       McCarthy calls for an extension of *Verstehen,* beyond
       an explanation of individual actions through their motives,
       by reviewing the work of others who had already done so,
       and he presents his own views about the extenstion.

       Nagel, E. *The structure of science.* (E12)

       Schutz, A. Concept and theory formation in the social
       sciences. (D133)

METHODOLOGICAL OBJECTIVITY,
AND THE PRESENTIST AND HISTORICIST ATTITUDES
IN WRITING THE NARRATIVE

History is always written from a point of view—it can never be im-
personal, written from no one's point of view. History, then, reflects the attitudes of the historian. What attitudes make for
objectivity, and what do not? Two major competing theories seem

to dominate current thinking: the correspondence theory of truth, namely, in baldest terms, that truth is what corresponds to facts, and the coherence theory, which demands not a correspondence between fact and statement but between statement and statement.

Moreover, history may be written for the sake of depicting the past or for the sake of understanding the present—the historicist and presentist attitudes, respectively, to use Stocking's terms.

An awareness of the immersion of the historian into his own culture, his own involvement in the situation, his position as a participant observer had led to a considerable discussion of relativism. Paradoxically, this may mean that involvement implies the impossibility of total objectivity.

It is debatable whether or not the issues now to be considered are primarily theoretical, contentual (in the sense of being concerned with history as a field), or methodological in import. Part of this confusion comes about because the locus of objectivity (or the correlative subjectivity) is found sometimes to reside in the very materials of history (contentual objectivity or subjectivity), sometimes in the methods used (methodological objectivity or subjectivity), and sometimes in the historian himself (personal objectivity or subjectivity). A case could be made then for citing some of the annotations that follow in a category under history as a field and others under objectivity as a theoretical issue. The decision to consider most references to objectivity as a methodological issue related to the way the narrative is prepared primarily because many historians tend to consider it in this fashion. References to objectivity clearly related to history as a field, therefore a re-citation of Nagel (E12) as well as a reference by Popper (E15) are to be found in a later section.

C18   Aron, E. Relativism in history. In H. Meyerhoff (Ed.), *The philosophy of history in our time*, pp. 153-161. (D10)
        A case for a form of relativism in terms of perspectives toward historical events, along with severe criticism of "vulgar" relativism.

C19   Blake, C. Can history be objective? *Mind,* 1955, *64,* 61-78. Reprinted in P. Gardiner (Ed.), *Theories of history,* pp. 329-343. (E24)
        Blake considers the question of what kind of objectivity can be expected of the historian and why this issue

of objectivity has been a problem to many philosophers and historians. He relates some of its difficulties to acceptance of the correspondence theory of truth such as that advocated by Mandelbaum.

C20   Butterfield, H. *The Whig interpretation of history.* London: Bell, 1931.
To quote from the preface, "What is discussed is the tendency of many historians to write on the side of the Protestants and Whigs, to praise revolutions provided they have been successful, to emphasize certain principles of progress in the past and to produce a story which is the ratification if not the glorification of the present" (p.v.). The happily chosen phrase, "the Whig interpretation of history" is a prominent example of the theme of the book, but the author goes on to many others that show how personal predilection may influence the selection and interpretation of historical material. From the present perspective he is calling attention to the ways in which a historian may be beguiled into a lack of objectivity by accepting those convictions of the past that coincide with one's own. This view, which he criticizes, is "presentism" in Stocking's sense of the term (C21). Butterfield himself sees the task of the historian not as offering solutions for the problems of the present but as the depiction of the past.

Mandelbaum, M. Concerning recent trends in the theory of historiography. (D9)

Mandelbaum, M. *The problem of historical knowledge.* (E28)

Nagel, E. *Structure of science.* (E12)

C21   Stocking, G. W., Jr. Editorial: On the limits of 'presentism' and 'historicism' in the historiography of the behavioral sciences. *J. Hist. behav. Sci.,* 1965, *1,* 211-218.
This is one of the few papers addressed directly to the historiography of the behavioral sciences, although it is of wider significance. It is concerned with two alternative

orientations the historian may take. The formulation of
these he credits to Butterfield, but he identifies them as
'historicism' and 'presentism.' To summarize baldly the
two orientations, they are "to understand the past for the
sake of the past, . . . or to characterize the study of the
past for the sake of the present."–in Butterfield's terminology. The paper is directed to the historian of behavioral
science, who comes into history from one of these sciences
—rather than directly from history—because he fears he
would tend to be "presentist" in his orientation. "Historicism" is perhaps an unfortunate choice of term because of
the well-known ambiguities that cling to it. If his definition
be adhered to and used in contrast to presentism then the
ambiguity might be alleviated.

Walsh, W. H. *Philosophy of history.* (E19a)

Weber, M. *The methodology of the social sciences.* (E102)

C22   White, M. Can history be objective? (1949) Reprinted in
       H. Meyerhoff (Ed.), *The philosophy of history in our time,*
       pp. 188-202. (D10)
           As the author sees it, there has been a confusion be-
       tween the psychology of historical interpretation and its
       logic. There is, in fact, a fundamental difference between
       discovery and justification; in the case of the latter, the his-
       torian is a scientist, and just as any other scientist he must
       submit findings to objective tests. Beard's work is the
       major source for his discussion of what he means by "ob-
       jective" tests.

C23   Wyatt, R. The reconstruction of the individual and of the
       collective past. In R. W. White (Ed.), *The study of lives:
       Essays in personality in honor of Henry A. Murray.* New
       York: Atherton Press, 1963, pp. 304-320.
           The purpose of this essay is to examine the logic of
       the reconstructions of both history and psychology and
       their ultimate validity. The author argues that there is
       no authentic past to be retrieved, since the historical par-
       ticipants could not understand the event as it occurred as
       we can with modern theory and technique. Thus the his-
       torian uses his own context, which integrates all relevant

data. Hence, this is a defense of presentism in Stocking's sense of the term (C21).

QUANTITATIVE METHODS IN GENERAL

There has been a marked recent increase in interest in the use of quantitative methods to supplement the critical-analysis narrative approach in the writing of history. This interest can be so keen that occasionally some protagonist for quantitativism becomes so stirred by the advantages he sees in quantification that he writes as if this could supplant the narrative. In more cautious moments, it is doubtful that anyone would try to act from this extreme position. Quantitative techniques can supplement, but they cannot supplant, the narrative.

Citations in this section are to discussions of the value of quantitative methods in historical research and how, when, and to what extent to use them, to graphic presentations, and to general guides to quantitative methods and computors for those desiring to learn statistical and research design techniques.

Annotations of references more specifically concerned with content analysis, citation indexes, and application of other quantitative documentary techniques follow in later sections.

C24   Aydelotte, W. O. *Quantification in history*. Reading, Mass.: Addison-Wesley, 1971.

This volume is probably the best introduction for students and for historians unfamiliar with, and perhaps skeptical of, quantification in history. With common sense, good humor, and tolerance for other views, Aydelotte quietly but (in the opinion of this writer) effectively disposes of the various arguments advanced by opponents to the use of quantitative methods in history.

C25   Crowley, T. H. *Understanding computers*. New York: McGraw-Hill, 1967.

This is not an attempt to teach programming, but, rather, to explain what programmers do. The computer must not be viewed merely as a new impressive numerical calculator but as relevant to the historian, since it can sort, match, and group nonnumerical materials.

C26   Dollar, C. M., & Jensen, R. J. *Historian's guide to statistics: Quantitative analysis and historical research.* New York: Holt, Rinehart & Winston, 1971.

This is an introductory guide to statistical technique in historical research. A general statement of the purposes and methods of quantitative research is followed by three chapters devoted to statistical techniques. The next two chapters explain electronic data processing. What is probably the most extensive selected bibliography of references to quantitative historical research available at the present time closes the volume.

C27   Floud, R. *An introduction to quantitative methods for historians.* Princeton, N.J.: Princeton University Press, 1973.

Floud first considers the classification and arrangement of historical data for statistical manipulation. The volume thereafter can be characterized as an introduction to statistics for historians. Frequency distributions, measures of central tendency, and correlation are discussed. The author also describes the analyses of time series and some of the problems faced when either too much or too little data is available, and, lastly, he presents a chapter on the use of computers in historical research.

C28   McQuitty, L. L. Elementary factor analysis. *Psychol. Rep.,* 1961, *9,* 71-78.

The best introduction to factor analysis known to the writer, although not specifically addressed to the historian.

C29   Price, D. J. Quantitative measures of the development of science. *Actes du VI congres int. d'hist. sci.,* 1950, *6,* 413-421.

Although this is an early paper by Price, its short compass makes it possible to grasp the essentials of how he would apply quantitative measures to studies of the development of science.

C30   Rothschuh, K. E. The graphic presentation of data and relationships in medicine. In E. Clarke (Ed.), *Modern methods in the history of medicine.* London: Athlone, 1971, pp. 314-334.

Although this book is specifically directed to the historians of medicine, the author's account of the use of diagrams and graphs for depicting relationships among data can readily be adapted to other fields.

C31   Rowney, D. K., & Graham, J. Q. (Eds.), *Quantitative history: Selected readings in the quantitative analysis of historical data.* Homewood, Ill.: Dorsey Press, 1969.

This is a collection of papers discussing or exemplifying quantitative studies of history. Some of the papers in the first section are very important. William Aydelotte, a pioneer leader in the judicious use of quantitative methods, answers some of the standard objections to their use. Lee Benson suggests an approach for the study of public opinion of the past. Robert A. Kann approaches the same problem with a plea that if the technique be used, one should learn how it has been done by the specialist before plunging in; to this end he traces explicitly the major steps in this undertaking. Later sections, each with several papers, are devoted to applications of quantitative methods to political history, historical demography, economic history, and voting behavior.

C32   Schlesinger, A. Jr., The humanist looks at empirical social research. In R. P. Swierenga (Ed.), *Quantification in American history: Theory and research.* New York: Atheneum, 1970, pp. 30-35.

A humanistic critique directed against quantitative history. The author contends that the most important questions in history are not amenable to quantitative answers.

C33   Siegel, S. *Nonparametric statistics for the behavioral sciences.* New York: McGraw-Hill, 1956.

A text devoted to the statistical procedures indicated when the sample of the population data that one is using does not conform to the requirements for a so-called normal distribution, i.e., the sample is biased in some fashion. Many samples of data the historian uses call for nonparametric statistical measures.

C34   Smelser, M., & Davidson, W. I. The historian and the computer: A simple introduction to complex computation. In

R. P. Swierenga (Ed.), *Quantification in American history: Theory and research.* New York: Atheneum, 1970, pp. 53-74.

The theme given in the title is illustrated by examples.

CONTENT ANALYSIS

The theme for this section is content analysis as a technique for research with documents. Included among the items annotated are several describing the nature of content analysis itself, others concerning the development of coding categories for use in content analysis, and still others on the measurement of reliability and validity of the categories developed. Particular applications to biography are also cited. Introductions to computer analysis have been cited in the previous section on quantitative methods; content analysis using the computer concerns us here. It is important to keep in mind that computers were built originally to be used with numbers and for operations on numbers. Computer analysis of natural language (words) is a much newer and less well-developed usage.

Some of the references that are reported use documents for nonhistorical problems. They are reported for their value for possible application to historical documents. For example, the analysis of therapeutic records from the province of the psychiatrist or clinical psychologist may offer approaches that suggest application to problems in the history of the behavioral sciences. Moreover, in the emerging field, the psychology of science as well as the better established sociology of science offer techniques capable of transfer. Terms, such as "illustrative" and "suggestive" and mention of specific kinds of "nonhistorical" samples serve to distinguish these references from the others.

C35   Baldwin, A. Personal structure analysis: A statistical method for investigating the single personality. *J. abnorm. soc. Psychol.,* 1942, *37,* 163-183.

This article describes a personally developed method for the content analysis of documents, with the intent of bringing out the personality structure of the individuals who wrote the documents. Illustrations of its application suggestive of its value in historical research are offered.

C36 Beach, F. A. The snark was a boojum. *Amer. Psychologist*, 1950, *5*, 115-124.

A simple, yet convincing demonstration using as content categories the percentage of articles devoted to various phyla, classes, or species and to various psychological functions, demonstrating that certain trends did, in fact, occur in the fields of comparative and experimental psychology between 1911 and 1948.

C37 Bellak, L. Somerset Maugham: A thematic analysis of ten short stories. In R. W. White (Ed.), *The study of lives*. New York: Atherton Press, 1963, pp. 143-159.

Short stories analyzed by a modification of the scoring of Murray's Thematic Apperception Test, on the basic assumption that stories, just as other actions, are the product of the person and, consequently, must bear some significant relationship to the personality of the author. The particular approach developed by Bellak is presented in convincing detail.

C38 Berelson, B. *Content analysis in communication research*. Glencoe, Ill.: Free Press, 1952.

Although more than 20 years have elapsed since publication of this book, it is still well worth reading, provided one remembers that in the intervening years content analysis has become bolder in its aspirations, more optimistic in outlook, deeper in its probing, and broader in its scope. A bibliography is included that "probably contains most of the content analyses published through 1950."

C39 Cardno, J. A. Victorian psychology: A biographical approach. *J. Hist. behav. Sci.*, 1965, *1*, 165-177.

The author describes a quantitative technique for isolating contributors to psychology of a certain temporal period, in this case the Victorian. He does this by consulting standard biographical sources to select the individuals in question, following a specified procedure. He then concentrates on a concept or concepts used in their writing by content analysis of their works. Extension of the same method to a comparison to pre-Victorian authors and works is also illustrated.

C40 Child, I. L., Potter, E. H., & Levine, Estelle, M. Children's

textbooks and personality development: An exploration in
the social psychology of education. *Psychol. Monogr.,* 1946,
No. 279.

A research study of the content of all children's third-
grade textbooks published between 1930 and about 1945,
limited to stories only and not including poems and the
like. Content analysis categories derived from these were
then applied in order to ascertain the values implicit in
them; this is a study suggestive of extension to other historical documents.

C41   Combs, A. W. A method of analysis for the Thematic Apperception Test and autobiography. *J. clin. Psychol.,* 1946,
2, 167-174.

The first of a series of papers published in the same
journal, describing a method originating from the scoring
of the TAT but applied to 1500 pages of autobiographical
material (otherwise unidentified). Application to other
historical documents would seem useful with this method
of content analysis as a suggestive beginning.

Garraty, J. A. The interrelations of psychology and biography. (C10)

C42   Gerbner, G., Holsti, O. R., Krippendorff, K., Paisley, W. J.,
& Stone, P. J., (Eds.), *The analysis of communication content: Developments in scientific theories and computer
techniques.* New York: Wiley, 1969.

Papers given at a conference held in 1967 but subsequently revised and updated to take into account pertinent
material brought out at the conference and then carefully
edited so as to fill the gaps that had become obvious. An
important volume is the result. One section is devoted to
theories and constructs for content analysis, including
systematic views, conceptual categories, linguistic foundations, and kinds of messages found. A second section considers the problem of inferring from content data, including
an important paper on contextual similarity as the basis
for doing so. A third section is devoted to recording and
notation in content analysis. The last section relates computer techniques and computational techniques to content
analysis. A lengthy general bibliography of the relevant
literature is appended.

C43 Gottschalk, L. A. & Gleser, Goldine, C. *The measurement of psychological states through the content analysis of verbal behavior.* Berkeley, Calif.: University of California Press, 1969.

Although their research involved patient populations, the authors' approach is suggestive of applications to historical documents. A *Manual of Instructions* is also available.

C44 Holsti, O. R. *Content analysis for the social sciences and humanities.* Reading, Mass.: Addison-Wesley, 1969.

Probably the best guide to content analysis as a method of documentary research is to be found in this volume. An introduction is followed by chapters devoted to research designs; their uses in describing the characteristics of communication and in making inferences about causes and effects of communication; coding; sampling, reliability, and validity; and handling the various problems raised through the use of computers. Extensive references are provided.

C45 Iker, H. P., & Klein, R. H. WORDS: A computer system for the analysis of content. *Behav. Res. Meth. Instrum.,* 1974, *6,* 430-438.

The article leads one back through ten years of research on the authors' computer system, which possesses the considerable advantage of not requiring an a priori categorization system to find themes, since the word itself is the unit of information. Temporal association by and between words generates the content themes.

C46 McClelland, D. C. The use of measures of human motivation in the study of society. In J. W. Atkinson, (Ed.), *Motives in fantasy, action and society.* Princeton, N.J.: Van Nostrand, 1958, pp. 518-554.

The measurement of motivational status has occupied McClelland and his students for two decades, including those reported in *The Achieving Society* (000). Various historical time periods have been investigated in the course of these studies. In this 1958 article, the author argues that coding historical documents for motivational variables provides a method for estimating their strength at critical periods in history.

C47 McClelland, D. C. Coding historical source materials for

motivational variables. In *Power: The inner experience.*
New York: Wiley, 1975, pp. 395-410.

This is a 1971 follow-up and extension of the 1958
paper previously cited, with motivational variables applied
not only to need for achievement, but also to affiliation
and to power. The author gives a detailed illustration of
the method applied to English history between 1500 and
1800 and then summarizes the steps in the procedure to be
followed in coding.

C48   McClelland, D. C., Davis, W., Wanner, E., & Kalin, R. A
cross-cultural study of folk-tale content and drinking.
Sociometry, 1966. *29,* 308-333.

For studying the topics of the title, the authors used
the computer-based General Inquirer System for coding
content. They were able to demonstrate various intricate
relationships.

C49   Mosteller, F., & Wallace, D. L. *Inference and disputed
authorship: The Federalist.* Reading, Mass.: Addison-Wesley,
1964.

This book illustrates what may be done in applying
sophisticated content techniques as a supplement to the
usual historical narrative. The source of material was certain
works in the *Federalist Papers,* about which it was known
only that they had been written either by Alexander Ham-
ilton or by James Madison. Much of the uncertainty about
the writer of the disputed papers was removed through a
content analysis of the frequency of usage of certain words.

C50   North, R. C., et al. *Content analysis: A handbook with applications for the study of international cases.* Evanston,
Ill.: Northwestern University Press, 1963.

A general introduction to content analysis with chapters devoted to purpose and assumptions, data preparation,
and modes of analysis. There is a selected bibliography.

C51   Pool, I. De S., et al. *Symbols of democracy.* Stanford,
Calif.: Hoover Institute Studies, Stanford University Press,
1952.

This is an illustrative content analysis study of historical changes in democracy as a symbol, that is, how the

meaning and popularity of democracy changed in the United States and in the Soviet Union.

C52   Pool, I. De S. (Ed.), *Trends in content analysis.* Urbana, Ill.: University of Illinois Press, 1959.

    The book contains papers given at a 1955 conference on content analysis; it includes both quantitative and non-quantitative approaches and various methods of study—evaluative, assertion analysis, contingency analysis and "cloze" procedure, the exploration of emotional states in psychotherapeutic sessions using an instrumental model, the interrelation of linguistics and content analysis, content analysis applied to folklore texts, and the application of content analysis to biography and history. The editor prepared a summary chapter. The bibliography provided is highly selective but good.

C53   Rokeach, M., Homant, R., & Penner, L. A value analysis of the disputed Federalist papers. *J. Pers. soc. Psychol.,* 1970, *16,* 245-250.

    A markedly different content analysis approach to the documents examined in the Mosteller and Wallace study (C49). The latter had used frequency of occurrence of words; here it was the values sought, such as equality or social recognition, and the instrumentalities used to attain them, such as being honest or responsible, that were the bases for the content categories. Their positive results led the authors to suggest that further historical documentary studies be made using their procedure.

C54   Schutz, W. C. On categorizing qualitative data in content analysis. *Publ. Opin. Quart.,* 1958-1959, *22,* 503-515.

    A step-by-step procedure for content analysis that has much to recommend it.

C55   Stephenson, W. Critique of content analysis. *Psychol. Rec.,* 1963, *13,* 155-162.

    This critique is concerned, not with technical matters, but with more general issues, particularly the relative lack of a theoretical basis to content analysis.

C56   Stone, P. J., Dunphy, D. C., Smith, M. S., & Ogilivie, D. M.

The general inquirer: A computer approach to content analysis. Cambridge: M.I.T. Press, 1966.

The volume describes a flexible computer-based system of content analysis, which has already been used under a wide variety of circumstances. It is applied to the actual text to be analyzed using a specially prepared dictionary. A *User's Manual* is also available.

C57   White, R. K. Black boy: A value analysis. *J. abnorm. soc. Psychol.,* 1947, *42,* 440-461.

A content analysis study of an autobiography, using categorization of the values held by its writer is the means of analysis.

CITATION INDEXES

The citation index is a tool for research as well as a means of retrieval of bibliographic information. It is the former literature that is now to be annotated.

Garfield, E. Citation Indexing: A natural science literature retrieval system for the social sciences. (A66)

C58   Garfield, E. Historiographs, librarianship and the history of science. In C. H. Rawski (Ed.), *Toward a theory of librarianship: Papers in honor of Jesse Hauk Shera.* Metuchen, N.J.: Scarecrow Press, 1973, pp. 380-402. (Reprinted in *Current Contents* 1974, No. 38. p. RL-R15.)

The paper explains and illustrates the historiograph, a graphic display of citation data for key scientific events in terms of their chronology and interrelationships.

C59   Krantz, D. L. The separate worlds of operant and non-operant psychology. *J. appl. behav. Anal.,* 1971, *4,* 61-70.

An ingenious study, depending in part upon the frequency of self-citation within one "operant" psychology journal as compared to frequency in another "nonoperant" journal, to bring out the degree of isolation of the literature in the first journal from sources other than itself.

C60   Meadows, A. J., & O'Connor, J. G. Bibliographical statistics as a guide to growth points in science. *Sci. Stud.,* 1971, *1,* 95-99.

While the content of this research, the identification of new growth points in astronomy by citation analysis, is not very relevant, the transfer of the method to other contents may prove not too difficult.

C61   Ruja, H. Productive psychologists. *Amer. Psychologist,* 1956, *11,* 148-149.

Using the issues of three psychological journals between specified years, the investigator calculated the number of cited papers by specific writers to arrive at indicators of the names of the psychologists who were most productive during this period.

C62   Small, H., & Griffith, B. C. The structure of scientific literatures. I: Identifying and graphing specialties. *Sci. Stud.,* 1974, *4,* 17-40.

The use of cocitation as a means of studying the structure of research specialties is the theme of this paper. While none of the various clusters that emerged are too closely related to present interests, the transfer value of this procedure to other specialties is apparent.

Science citation index. (A131)

Social sciences citation index. (A133)

C63   Weinstock, M. Citation indexes. In *Encyclopedia of library and information science.* Vol. 5. New York: Dekker, 1971, pp. 16-40.

A general, authoritative account with a well-selected bibliography.

C63a   Xhignesse, L. V., & Osgood, C. E. Bibliographical citation characteristic of the psychological journal networks in 1950 and 1960. *Amer. Psychologist,* 1967, *22,* 778-779.

A network of 21 journals yielded a pattern of reciprocal citation for the literature of 1950 and 1960. A variety of measures were derived and interpreted. To mention but one result, the high "self-feeding" (citation within a journal being high to that same journal) may be symptomatic of the development of potentially independent disciplines.

ILLUSTRATIONS OF APPLICATIONS OF OTHER QUANTITATIVE TECHNIQUES

The contents of this section are partially defined by exclusion: while using quantitative techniques, the references that follow concern neither content analysis nor citation indexes. All references have the positive characteristics of thoughtful use of data sources and appropriate statistical manipulation for the problems under investigation, of relevance for the historian, and of a technique that has been applied to documents or seems capable of being so used.

Allport, G. W. *The use of personal documents in psychological science.* (C8)

C64   Annin, Edith L., Boring, E. G., & Watson, R. I. Important psychologists, 1600-1967. *J. Hist. behav. Sci.,* 1968, *4,* 303-315.

   The authors describe the use of a panel technique to select deceased individuals eminent for their contributions to the history of psychology.

Ben-David, J. Scientific productivity and academic organization in nineteenth-century medicine. (B173)

Ben-David, J., & Collins, R. Social factors in the origins of a new science. (B56)

C65   Bullough, Bonnie, & Bullough, V. Intellectual achievers: a study of eighteenth-century Scotland. *Amer. J. Sociol.,* 1970-1971, *76,* 1048-1063.

   A study using biographies for individuals selected by a survey of standard reference works, checked against the *Dictionary of National Biography* (eliminating most military leaders and clergymen) and biographical material found, including parish of birth, education, length of life, etc. The study led to the conclusions that education was the key to achievement, that more achievers came from urban areas, and that they lived longer than the average person. "Collective biography" is an approach deserving much wider use by historians.

C66 Fernberger, S. W. Statistical analysis of the members & associates of the American Psychological Association, Inc. in 1928. *Psychol. Rev.*, 1928, *35*, 447-465.

One of the series of papers by the same author, using available material about members of the American Psychological Association for arriving at various findings—geographical distribution, academic background, university departments and nonacademic positions, subjects of instruction, and fields of research. Division into categories of men and women routinely followed for the results he presented.

Fuchs, A. H., & Kawash, G. F. Prescriptive dimensions for five schools of psychology. (E46)

Garraty, J. A. The interrelations of psychology and biography. (C10)

C67 Gilbert, G. N., & Woolgar, S. (Essay Review) The quantitative study of science: An examination of the literature. *Sci. Stud.*, 1974, *4*, 279-294.

The literature being examined is confined to studies of patterns of scientific growth. The work of Price and his critics dominates. This is a convenient source for references to this literature.

C68 Horrocks, J. E., & Hogan, J. D. A survey and interpretation of article characteristics: *The Journal of Genetic Psychology*, 1945-1969. *Genet. Psychol. Monogr.*, 1973, *87*, 3-31.

A study of the contents of the *Journal of Genetic Psychology* for the years 1945-1969, with emphasis both on describing its characteristics and noting changes with time. Several methods were used, including content analysis. Data analyzed include general characteristics (e.g., number of articles and book reviews), authorships (e.g., sex of authors, single or multiple authorships), institutional affiliation, extent and basis of research support, categorization of content, the most frequently cited authors, and the like.

C69 Jensen, R. Quantitative collective biography: An application to metropolitan elites. In R. Swierenga (Ed.), *Quantification in American history: Theory and research.* New York: Atheneum, 1970, pp. 389-405.

A thorough study using multivariate analysis carried out by computer, with sufficient attention to method to be pertinent.

Kawash, G., & Fuchs, A. H. A factor analysis of ratings of five schools of psychology on prescriptive dimensions. (E55)

C70   Knapp, R. H., & Goodrich, H. G. *Origins of American scientists.* Chicago: University of Chicago Press, 1952.

This volume includes a report of a study identifying institutions with an appreciable number of graduates between 1924 and 1934 who became scientists, identified as such by a particular edition of the *American Men of Science.* College records were the source of data.

C71   Lehman, H. C. *Age and achievement.* Princeton, N.J.: Princeton University Press, 1953.

A summarization of Lehman's many years of research on the problem of psychology of science (and art), with an emphasis upon the relation of age to creativity. Data utilized in the studies that permitted quantitative manipulation were birth and death dates, dates of publication, dates of patents, consensus ratings, income, positions held, and the like. These measures were applied to individuals in various fields such as science, medicine, and philosophy.

C72   Mullins, N. C. The development of specialties in social science: The case of ethnomethodology. *Sci. Stud.,* 1973, *3,* 245-273.

Prior to the study itself, Mullins cites literature on earlier studies concerning the theoretical orientation of scientific disciplines developing within the boundaries of definite social groups. He then develops information about ethnomethodology in terms of giving properties by years and identifying the key individuals.

C73   Wrigley, E. A. (Ed.), *Nineteenth-century society: Essays in the use of quantitative methods for the study of social data.* Cambridge: Cambridge University Press, 1972.

Sources and methods of research using English census data derived from printed census volumes and enumerators' work books is the theme of this collection of papers. Aside from methodological studies in accuracy and sampling, research content studies on family structures, occupation, migration, crime, and education are also included.

D. HISTORIOGRAPHIC FIELDS

Attention is directed to writings of practitioners who consider the nature of their fields and their relationship to other fields. Historiographic field categories are grouped under somewhat different headings than was the case with the substantive field categories of Section B. Historiographic contributions are grouped by the particular field orientation adopted by their authors. For example, books in child psychology earlier grouped together because of content, may have included contributions by both psychologists and psychohistorians; if these same authors were to choose to write on their respective fields, some might be grouped under psychology, others would be grouped under psychohistory. Moreover, while the substantive histories cited earlier show enough commonality to embrace psychiatry and psychoanalysis under one rubric, this is no longer the case when we turn to them as historiographic fields of endeavor.

The new first section contains annotations devoted to history in general. Psychology, instead of having several subdivisions, is annotated under one heading. New fields are added: the historiography of the behavioral sciences and intellectual history. The social sciences are combined with sociology. Psychiatry and psychoanalysis, formerly grouped together, are now separated, and psychohistory is added to the latter.

Another aspect of the historiography of these fields annotated here is training in the discipline, including methods of teaching either practiced or suggested.

The relation between the literature analyzing a field of endeavor, the present concern, and the theories of historiography, the next major topic, is very close. Some writers chose to describe the field in terms of theories espoused. How one views explanation is intimately related to how one views the nature of history. So what is emphasized here—the field in question—under a different focus of interest may be seen as relevant to theory.

In the present section, more or less contemporaneous views about the fields of history are presented. Papers or books concerned with the "nature of historical knowledge," reported in a later section "Speculative Theories of History, and the Nineteenth-Century Reaction," concern older views about the nature of history as a field and should be consulted when pertinent.

GENERAL HISTORY

D1   Becker, C. L. *Detachment and the writing of history: Essays and letters of Carl L. Becker.* Ed. P. L. Snyder. Ithaca, N.Y.: Cornell University Press, 1958.

A collection of essays on the perennial problems in history, including many that emphasize the author's particular approach to history.

D2   Benson, L. *Toward the scientific study of history: Selected essays.* Philadelphia: Lippincott, 1972.

The theme of how the author would define history dominates this collection. History is not only the scientific study of past human behavior, but also a key to the scientific study of present human behavior. The author submits as evidence a variety of his papers typically concerned with the topic of the causes of the Civil War. Objectivity, the finding of general laws, and many criticisms of what he considers to be traditional historical writing also appear as themes throughout the essays.

D3   Butterfield, H. *Man on his past: The study of the history of historical scholarship.* London: Cambridge University Press, 1955.

In this volume Butterfield relates the rise of the German historical school to the subsequent work of Lord Acton, leader of the nineteenth-century historical movement in Britain, and that of Ranke, the preeminent German historian of the century; he goes on to explicate his own approach, crediting these men for being his intellectual forebears.

D4   Curti, M. *Human nature in American historical thought.* Columbus, Mo.: University of Missouri Press, 1968.

How assumptions about the limits and potentialities of human nature influenced the thinking and writing of

Francis Parkman, Reinhold Niebuhr, Charles Beard, Carl Becker, Harry Elmer Barnes, and others, including some psychohistorians, is the theme of this book. Titles of three of the essays give a concise summarization of the content: "The limitations of man's capacities," "Emphasis on man's potentialities," and "The commitment to scientific explanation."

Collingwood, R. G. *The idea of history.* (E23)

D5   Engel-Jànosi, F. *The growth of German historicism.* Baltimore, Md.: Johns Hopkins Press, 1944.

The 'historicism' of the title refers to the German school whose members saw history as unique and important, from their point of view, and permeating all aspects of theoretical life. Its historiography is presented in terms of those who have influenced its point of view: Lord Acton, Jacob Buckhardt, Barthold G. Niebuhr, and Leopold von Ranke. From among the *Contributors,* Condorcet, Goethe, Hegel, Herder, von Humboldt, Marx, Schopenhauer, and Voltaire are discussed extensively in terms of their influence on this school.

D6   Higham, J. (with L. Krieger & F. Gilbert). *History.* Englewood Cliffs, N.J.: Prentice-Hall, 1965.

As one of a series on *Humanistic Scholarship in America,* this volume examines history as a profession, the basic theories behind successive stages of American historiography, American history as such, the study of European history in America, and European and American historiography. In relatively short compass, the contents capture the essentials of the view of a considerable number of historians. Of these, those most relevant to present concerns are Harry Elmer Barnes, Carl Becker, Marc Bloch, Daniel Boorstin, Crane Brinton, Benedetto Croce, Merle Curti, John Dewey, William A. Dunning, Lucien Febvre, Richard Hofstadter, William L. Langer, Vernon L. Parrington, Leopold von Ranke, James Harvey Robinson, and Lynn Thorndike.

D7   Hughes, H. S. *History as art and as science: Twin vistas on the past.* New York: Harper & Row, 1964.

The complementarity of art and science in the study
of the writings of history is a general theme of this collection of essays. More specifically the author considers the
relationship between history and anthropology and between
history and psychoanalysis, from whence comes the explanation of human motives, defends the narrative as central
to integrating the findings from the social sciences with the
materials of history, and evaluates the writing of "contemporary" history. He envisions a broadening of the historical
definition of human motivation as a result of the historian's
increasing contact with anthropology, biology, the humanities, psychology, and psychoanalysis.

D8   International Social Science Council, Akademiya Nauk
      SSSR. *Social sciences in the USSR.* Paris: Mouton, 1965.
          Several relevant historiographic articles prepared by
      Soviet scholars and concerned with history, psychology,
      philosophy, and philosophy of science are included in this
      study. The article on psychology was prepared by S. L.
      Rubinstein.

D9   Mandelbaum, M. Concerning recent trends in the theory of
      historiography. *J. hist. Ideas,* 1955, *16,* 506-517.
          Mandelbaum discusses, in a relatively few pages, major
      aspects of historiography in connection with history as a
      a field, with particular attention to objectivity—more spe-
      cifically objectivity as a problem in historiography—the
      place of historiography in the economy of knowledge,
      what is the subject matter of history, and the importance
      of defining the subject matter, instead of accepting the de-
      featist position "history is what historians do."

D10   Meyerhoff, H. (Ed.), *The philosophy of history in our time.*
      Garden City, N.Y.: Doubleday, 1959.
          This collection of papers by modern philosophers and
      historians is in considerable measure devoted to the exam-
      ination of history as a field. The largest group of papers ap-
      pearing under the heading "Clio—Science or Muse?" deals
      with the subsidiary problem of the scope and the limits of
      contentual objectivity in history. Papers by Pirenne, Toyn-
      bee, Becker, Beard, Aron, Dewey, White, Nagal, and Walsh
      are included. The papers in the first group, however, are

more concerned with the speculative theories of history—
those of Dilthey, Croce, and Collingwood among others.
The general topic is that of the "Heritage of Historicism."
The last of the four sections is also relevant to the field
of history in that it concerns the meaning of history, with
the related issue of unity in history; the authors of the
papers are Bullock, Popper, Niebuhr, and Jaspers.

D11   Passmore, J. A. The objectivity of history. *Philosophy,*
1958, *33,* 97-111. Reprinted in W. H. Dray (Ed.), *Philosophical analysis in history,* pp. 75-94. (E5)
      The author considers various criteria of objectivity,
with the guiding principle that they depend on how high
one sets one's standards. In summing up, he concludes
that history can be considered a science in the sense that it
involves trying as exactly and as hard as possible to find
out what really happened, but not if by science we mean a
search for general theories.

D12   Smith, P. *The historian and history.* New York: Knopf,
1964.
      In the first half of the book Smith discusses the con-
cept of history throughout Western civilization in terms
that owe much to Collingwood and Croce, expounding not
only their views but also those of Burckhardt, Dilthey,
Hegel, Machiavelli, Niebuhr, Nietzsche, Spengler, Toynbee,
and Voltaire. A chapter on historians as professionals,
especially as they related to the social sciences, separates
the two halves, with Carl Becker and Charles Beard considered as the transmitters of ideas of social progress to American historians. The early phases of the historiography of
psychohistory are also sketched. The need is stressed
throughout for a plurality of historiographical approaches.

Stern, F. (Ed.), *The varieties of history.* (E35)

D13   Todd, W. *History as applied science: A philosophical study.*
Detroit, Mich.: Wayne State University Press, 1972.
      Two-thirds of the book is devoted to an examination
and differentiation of a wide variety of kinds of historical
work, some cast in familiar rubrics, such as social history
and the history of ideas, others not so familiar, particularly

what he refers to as "systematic" history, meaning by it attempts to establish in history uniformities of the sort that are basic to the natural sciences.

PSYCHOLOGY

Boring, E. G. *Psychologist at large.* (E1)

D14   Brozek, J. History of psychology: Diversity of approaches and uses. *Trans. N.Y. Acad. Sci.,* 1969, *31,* 115-127.
       Brozek argues convincingly for a pluralistic approach to the study of the history of psychology, in terms both of the approaches followed and the uses to which these results are put. Various examples are provided.

D15   Brozek, J. The psychology and physiology of behavior: Some recent Soviet writings on their history. *Hist. Sci.,* 1971, *10,* 56-87.
       This review covers the literature from 1960 to 1971 in a thoroughly informative manner.

D16   Brozek, J. Contemporary West European historiography of psychology. *Hist. Sci.,* 1975, *13,* 29-60.
       Brozek gives a detailed presentation, obtained not only from the written record but also by personal visitation. His account integrates many disparate trends that are just emerging in this burgeoning specialization.

D17   Brozek, J., Watson, R. I., & Ross, Barbara. A summer institute on the history of psychology. Part 1, 2. *J. Hist. behav. Sci.,* 1969, *5,* 307-319; 1970, *6,* 25-35.
       A detailed description of the goals and accomplishments of an NSF-sponsored institute for college teachers of history.

D18   Dunlap, K. The historical method in psychology. *J. gen. Psychol.,* 1941, *24,* 49-62.
       Perhaps the first modern call for greater attention to historical research in psychology, along with specific ar-

guments designed to show its importance for the psychologist.

D19 Gruhle, H. W. *Geschichtsschreibung und Psychologie*. Bonn: Bouvier, 1953.

A historical and methodological review of the relationship between history and psychology. The author presents the value of psychology in biographical and autobiographic studies and in art and literature.

D20 Gruber, H. *Darwin on man: A psychological study of scientific creativity*. New York: Dutton, 1974.

The fact that Jean Piaget's insights into the cognitive processes provided Gruber with the theoretical frame within which to analyze Darwin's creativity against the broader schema of general scientific development is the reason for the inclusion of this volume in this section. For source material to show Darwin's happy and productive life there is heavy and appropriate reliance upon the notebooks he kept. Gruber also expresses his criticisms of the psychoanalytic portrait that presents Darwin as the neurotic victim of a tyrannical father.

D21 Jaynes, J. The routes of science. *Amer. Scientist,* 1966, *54*, 94-102.

Although ostensibly a review of several books on the history of psychology, this article goes beyond this to capture some of the complexities both of psychology and of science, which must be taken in consideration when writing the history of psychology.

D22 Keller, F. S. *The history of psychology: A personalized system of instruction course*. Roanoke, Va.: Scholar's Press, 1973.

A description of the "Keller method" of modular teaching as applied to the history of psychology. "Factually correct" rote replies can presumably be brought forth—if one agrees with the source from which one is expected to draw the answer. Along with a companion book of *Selected Readings* the course culminates, to no one's surprise, in the work of Skinner.

D23   Keniston, K. Psychological development and historical change. *J. interdisc. Hist.*, 1971-1972, *2*, 329-345. Reprinted in R. J. Lifton, with E. Olson (Eds.), *Explorations in psychohistory: The Wellfleet Papers.* New York: Simon & Schuster, 1974, pp. 149-164.

           The author makes a plea that goes beyond the scope of psychohistory—that, in addition to the intertwined concepts of socialization, acculturation, and modal personality that have characterized the contributions of psychology to history so far, much more attention should be paid to the concepts of developmental psychology. He then proceeds to illustrate.

D24   Krantz, D. L. Toward a role for historical analysis: The case of psychology and physiology. *J. Hist. behav. Sci.*, 1965, *1*, 278-283.

           In addition to historical analysis serving its three traditional roles of producing awareness of heritage and of past successes and mistakes and of providing a source for research hypotheses, Krantz argues that it also performs another role—that of providing an increased awareness of the nature and operation of variables affecting him as a psychologist as he goes about his tasks. Generally these variables can be subsumed under the heading of *Zeitgeist.* He proceeds to illustrate, for example, by relating Skinner's elimination of physiological variables and Krech's insistence upon using them as both being rooted in the old and repressed mind-body issue.

D25   Little, L. K. Psychology in recent American historical thought. *J. Hist. behav. Sci.*, 1969, *5*, 152-172.

           Under the headings of biography, collective biography, myths and images, the field of education, and a more general closing section, Little presents illustrations of the way historians have used psychology as a tool of analysis.

D26   MacLeod, R. B. The teaching of psychology and the psychology we teach. *Amer. Psychologist*, 1965, *20*, 344-352.

           A prominent historian of psychology takes as his topic in this paper not the teaching of history, but teaching in general. A historical spirit pervades every page as he first considers how psychology meets four major objectives of teaching, such as the transmittal of culture and contributing to the growth of the individual. He then takes up four blocks to psychology's effectiveness, such as the danger of losing its identity as a subject and the confusion of the role of the psychologist with the reality of solving problems.

D27 Madden, E. H. Discussion: E. G. Boring's philosophy of science. *Phil. Sci.*, 1965, *32*, 194-201.

The point of departure for this discussion is the collection of Boring's papers, *History, Psychology, and Science* (E2).

D28 Mandelbaum, M. To what does the term 'psychology' refer? *Stud. Hist. phil. Sci.*, 1971-1972, *2*, 347-361.

The author argues that psychology refers to all fields of inquiry involved when one sets out to understand the behavior of organisms. In the course of the paper he criticizes extensively the Skinnerian view of psychology.

Manuel, F. *The use and abuse of psychology in history.* (D94)

Marx, M. H., & Hillix, W. A. *Systems and theories in psychology.* (B74)

D29 Raack, R. C. When plans fail: Small group behavior and decision-making in the conspiracy of 1808 in Germany. *Conflict Resolution,* 1970, *14,* 3-19.

This study has the unusual merit of using findings on the concepts of group dynamics in social psychology as a framework against which the author traces the historical evidence covering the particular conspiracy, which he labels a microstudy—and microstudies should come before consideration of the macrohistorical level, a bit of advice a considerable number of historians of psychology have chosen to ignore.

D30 Nance, R. D. Current practices in teaching history of psychology. *Amer. Psychologist,* 1962, *17,* 250-252.

A questionnaire survey with an unusually high rate of return found 89 percent of psychology programs had history courses. Details of their organization and teaching practices are supplied.

D31   Riedel, R. G. The current status of the history and systems
of psychology courses in American colleges and universities.
J. Hist. behav. Sci., 1974, *10,* 410-412.

A study giving details about the teaching of the history of psychology in various schools surveyed. In summary, 74 percent of the 393 schools involved did offer at
least one course in the history of psychology.

D32   Riegel, K. F., History as a nomothetic science: Some generalizations from theories and research in developmental
psychology. *Report Number 74: Development of language
functions; A research program-project,* The University of
Michigan, November 7, 1968.

The author considers the application of theories from
developmental psychology to the study of process and
causation in history. He describes five models based on
psychological processes and social interactions and directed
toward deterministic interpretations of growth.

D33   Sullivan, J. J. Prolegomena to a textbook of psychology.
In Mary Henle, et al. (Eds.), *Historical conceptions of psychology,* New York: Springer, 1972, pp. 29-46.

In histories of particular sciences, four taxonomic elements are to be found: a theory, model, or set of proposals;
a temporal sequence of events, i.e., the narrative; a person
with a set of cognitive predispositions and problems to solve
and, usually, with a sense of the direction in which an adequate solution is to be sought; and the presence of a person's reference group, be this a school, profession, or rational or cultural period. Combinations of two, three, or
all four elements may appear in a particular historical writing; these the author proceeds to illustrate.

D34   Watson, R. I. The history of psychology: A neglected area.
Amer. Psychologist, 1960, *15,* 251-255.

Evidence of the neglect of the history of psychology,
circa 1959, and a plea for greater attention to it.

D35   Watson, R. I. The role and use of history in the psychology
curriculum. *J. Hist. behav. Sci.,* 1966, *2,* 64-69.

The values for the student that may be found in

courses in the history of psychology is the theme of this paper.

D36   Watson, R. I. A note on the history of psychology as a specialization. *J. Hist. behav. Sci.,* 1967, *3*, 192-193.
       The various ways in which the training of historians of psychology has been carried out is a major theme of this note.

D37   Watson, R. I. Recent developments in the historiography of American psychology. *Isis,* 1968, *59*, 199-205.
       The period before 1960, considered as that of pre-specialization, is briefly characterized. Developments since then are sketched in terms of special interest groups, news-letters, a journal, archival matters, teaching, graduate train-ing programs, and institutes.

D38   Watson, R. I., Sr. The history of psychology as a speciality: A personal view of its first 15 years. *J. Hist. behav. Sci.,* 1975, *11*, 5-14.
       The history of changes that have taken place during the past 15 years both in terms of persons and organiza-tions is traced, using 1960 as a basis of comparison.

D39   Wettersten, J. R. The historiography of scientific psychol-ogy: A critical study. *J. Hist. behav. Sci.,* 1975, *11*, 157-171.
       A student of Agassi argues that, while the overwhelm-ing problem of the history of psychology is the develop-ment, conflict, and decline of the schools of psychology, typical specified historians of psychology use primarily either the conventionalist or the inductive theories of science, both methods that are inadequate to the task of depicting the history of the aforementioned central prob-lem.

D40   Woods, P. J. (Ed.), *Source book on the teaching of psychol-ogy.* Roanoke, Va.: Scholars Press, 1973.
       This volume is made up of course outlines and bibli-ographies for many course areas of psychology, including some outlines devoted to the history of psychology by

R. B. MacLeod and R. I. Watson; implicit in these is their own approach to the field in question.

BEHAVIORAL SCIENCE

D41   Bry, Ilse. Bibliographic foundations for an emergent history of the behavioral science. In G. Mora & Jeanne L. Brand (Eds.), *Psychiatry and its history: Methodological problems in research,* pp. 82-118. (C6)

Bry offers a review of the literature in a manner that conceives the behavioral sciences in the same spirit as does this *Guide.* This calls for psychiatry, her particular concern, to be considered in a different and wider perspective than when it is regarded as part of the parent discipline of medicine. Quite properly, her review ranges over the behavioral aspects of many disciplines.

D42   Campbell, D. T. Ethnocentrism of disciplines and the fish-scale model of omniscience. In M. Sherif & Carolyn W. Sherif (Eds.), *Interdisciplinary relationships in the social sciences.* Chicago: Aldine, 1969, pp. 328-348.

Campbell argues that the only hope for a unified behavioral science is through an overlap of multiple narrow specialties—the fish-scale model of the title. Each of the various disciplines, as it is now organized in academic departments, is a hodgepodge, that of psychology being "a hodgepodge of subjective biography, of brain operations, of school achievement testing. . . ." Ethnocentricism within subspecialties and within departments is vividly demarcated, still within the content of this model. He then discusses current efforts to provide alternative social organizations that will still permit viable interdisciplinary specialization.

D43   Carlson, E. T., & Watson, R. I. Editorial: The birth of a journal. *J. Hist. behav. Sci.,* 1965, *1,* 3-4.

An account of the founding of a journal directed toward the history of the behavioral sciences.

Kaplan, A. *The conduct of inquiry: Methodology for behavioral science.* (E11)

D44   Senn, P. R. What is "behavioral science?"—Notes toward a history. *J. Hist. behav. Sci.*, 1966, *2*, 107-122.

The paper is concerned with the various ways in which "behavioral science" has been conceived by different groups at different times.

D45 Watson, R. I., & Merrifield, Marilyn R. Characteristics of individuals eminent in psychology in temporal perspective: Art. 1. *J. Hist. behav. Sci.*, 1973, *9*, 339-359.

Knowledgeable psychologists had been asked to identify eminent contributors to the history of psychology, and they selected 538 individuals. In this analysis, 58 percent were judged to be primarily identified with disciplines other than psychology, and it was necessary to use 22 disciplinary categories to identify them properly. Eminent contributors to psychology continued to be drawn from these other fields even after the emergence of psychology as a distinct discipline. The history of psychology is more properly conceived as an aspect of the history of the behavioral sciences.

D46 Young, R. M. Scholarship and the history of the behavioral sciences. *Hist. Sci.*, 1966, *5*, 1-51.

A critical and pessimistic view of the state of scholarship in the history of the behavioral sciences in the mid-sixties. Most generally stated, the difficulty stems from naivete about professional work in history being carried on outside its own small circle. E. G. Boring and R. I. Watson bear the brunt of these criticisms.

SCIENCE AND THE PHILOSOPHY OF SCIENCE

D47 Agassi, J. *Towards an historiography of science.* The Hague: Mouton, 1963.

This is a provocative and important monograph, castigating what Agassi considers to be the two major approaches to the writing of the history of science. There is, he says, the inductivist approach, going back directly to Bacon, in which scientific theories are supposed to emerge from facts; this has the effect of dividing scientists into those who, according to present standards are "right" or "wrong," or "scientific" or "superstitious." There is also the conventionalist approach adopted when some historians revolted against this black-or-white categorizing with the proposal that scientific theories are neither true nor false in themselves, they are merely agreed-on pigeon holes into which to enter and store empirical information. To Agassi, both approaches are pernicious and stupid, and this he tries to demonstrate through illustrations drawing upon past generations of historians of science. Agassi suggests as an alternative to these inadequate solutions Popper's critical philosophy, in which scientific theories are conceived as explaining known facts and refutable by new facts. Duhem, Koyré, and Popper are the major figures examined.

D48   Bartley, W. W., III. Theory of language and philosophy of science as instruments of educational reform: Wittgenstein and Popper as Austrian schoolteachers. In R. S. Cohen & M. W. Wartofsky (Eds.), *Boston studies in the philosophy of science.* Vol. 14. *Methodological and historical essays in the natural and social sciences.* Dordrecht: Reidel, 1974, pp. 307-336.

This paper gives an interpretation of Popper's Viennese years that is at variance with Popper's own account (E16), stressing, as Bartley does, the influence of the psychologists, especially of Karl Bühler, who was openly hostile to the positivism of the Vienna Circle.

D49   Brodbeck, May. The nature and the function of the philosophy of science. In H. Feigl & May Brodbeck (Eds.), *Readings in the philosophy of science.* New York: Appleton-Century-Crofts, 1953, pp. 3-7.

A succinct and authoritative statement of what the philosophy of science is all about.

D50   Crombie, A. C., & Hoskin, M. A. A note on history of science as an academic discipline. (With discussion.) In A. C. Crombie (Ed.), *Scientific change*, pp. 757-794. (E3)

The article itself deals primarily with work in Britain, but discussants consider similar activity in United States, Scotland, Poland, and Russia.

D51   Elias, N. Theory of science and history of science: Comments on a recent discussion. *Econ. Soc.*, 1972, *1*, 117-133.

Some aspects of the task of the sociology of science are explicated by considering an exchange between a historian of science, Kuhn (E63), and a philosopher of science, Lakatos (E64). The author chides them for taking for granted that one can work out a theory of science by concentrating upon one science—in this particular case, theoretical physics. The article also serves as a portrayal of just what is the task of the sociologist of science vis à vis history and the philosophy of science. The distinction between internal history and external history is made central.

D52   Feigl, H., & Maxwell, G. (Eds.), *Minnesota studies in the philosophy of science.* Vol. 5. *Historical and philosophical perspectives of science.* Minneapolis, Minn.: University of Minnesota Press, 1970.

Four important papers on the relationship—or lack of it—between the history of science and the philosophy of science are to be found in this volume. They are by H. Feigl, "Beyond peaceful coexistence"; by E. McMullin, "The history and philosophy of science: A taxonomy"; by A. Thackray, "Science: Has its present past a future?" and by P. K. Feyerabend, "Philosophy of science: A subject with a great past." Succinct summarization is impossible. Many of the sources on which they draw are precontemporaneous, such as Mach, but there is sufficient discussion of Carnap, Feyerabend, Koyré, Kuhn, Lakatos, Merton, and Polånyi to warrant mention.

D53   Frank, P. Historical background. In *Modern science and its philosophy.* New York: Collier, 1961, pp. 13-61. (1941)

An autobiographical statement by one of the founders of Vienna Circle, which has been so important in the Unity of Science movement. Fully two-thirds of the account, however, concerns events before the emergence of the Vienna Circle as the major voice in the philosophy of science for a period of years.

D54   Giere, R. N. History and philosophy of science: Intimate relationship or marriage of convenience? *Brit. J. phil. Sci.,* 1973, *24,* 282-297.

The author gives a critical review of papers on the relation of the history of science and the philosophy of science by Feigl, Feyerabend, McMullan, and Thackray in the volume edited by Feigl and Maxwell (D52).

D55   Guerlac, H. Some historical assumptions of the history of science. In A. C. Crombie (Ed.), *Scientific Change,* pp. 797-812. (E3)

A survey of the evolution of history and of the history of science, with a plea that historical writing be both synthetic and analytic.

D56   Hahn, R. Reflections on the history of science. *J. hist. Phil.,* 1965, *3,* 235-242.

This paper must be read in conjunction with Agassi's monograph (D47) of which it is a devastating critique. In particular, the author calls attention to the historians of science on whom Agassi does *not* draw a critical bead. On a higher plane he makes it clear that Agassi was equating the history of science with the narrower history of ideas, that is, with the history of scientific thought.

D57   Hanson, N. R. The genetic fallacy revisited. *Amer. phil. Quart.,* 1967, *4,* 101-113.

In the setting of a discussion of the so-called genetic fallacy—the confusion between the temporal order of events and the logical order of events, to use but one definition—Hanson shows how the philosophy of science differs from the history of science, since representatives of both disciplines are in danger of committing the fallacy of mixing statements of fact and statements of analysis. And yet a judicious integration of the two fields is essential, since otherwise the philosophy may be transparently clear but factually insignificant; the history factually full but conceptually dark.

D58   Kuhn, T. S. The history of science. In D. L. Sills (Ed.), *International encyclopedia of the social sciences.* Vol. 14. New York: Crowell-Collier & Macmillan, 1968, pp. 74-83.

After briefly surveying its early history, the author finds it necessary to treat internal and external history as virtually separate enterprises. The contributions of Durkheim, Koyré, Tannery, and Merton are evaluated in some detail.

D59   Kuhn, T. S. Alexandre Koyré and the history of science. *Encounter,* 1970, *34*(1), 67-70.

D60   Kuhn, T. S. The relations between history and history of science. *Daedalus.* 1971, *100,* 271-304.

A thoughtful and detailed discussion of the personal reactions of a historian of science to his colleagues in history and of some of the reasons for the current separation of the fields and the consequent neglect of the history of science by other historians. This, in turn, is due to its own history and here the historian of science seems to be at fault. Until relatively recently there were only two main traditions in the history of science: the one typified by Sarton, whose view of scientific advance was to see it as the triumph of reason over superstition, and the efforts of practicing scientists to produce histories of their specialties in what only can be described as a blatantly presentist tradition. Both were repelling to the academic historian. Without the historian necessarily being aware of it, these views have given way to more sophisticated ones.

D61   Lauden, L. Theories of scientific method from Plato to Mach: A bibliographic review. *Hist. Sci.,* 1968, *7,* 1-63.

The most comprehensive and yet succinct statement available of theories of the scientific method through the nineteenth century. A very useful bibliography is provided both for the history of science and the history of the philosophy of science.

Losee, J. *A historical introduction to the philosophy of science.* (B91)

D62   Lowinger, A. *The methodology of Pierre Duhem.* New York: AMS Press, 1967, (1941)

D63   Magee, B. *Karl Popper.* New York: Viking Press, 1973.

The author presents an introductory exposition of Popper's point of view on philosophy, science, epistemology, and metaphysics and a critique of Marxism.

D64   Neurath, Marie & Cohen, R. S. (Eds.), *Otto Neurath: Empiricism and sociology. With a selection of biographical and autobiographical sketches.* Boston: Reidel, 1973.

This memorial volume for Neurath includes biographical material by friends, autobiographical excerpts, selections from his writings including those devoted to the history of science and social science, and a bibliography of his publications. The Vienna Circle and his education and social and political activities come over vividly.

Sarton, G. *Horus: A guide to the history of science.* (A11)

D65   Sarton, G. *The life of science: Essays in the history of civilization.* Intro. C. Zirkle. Bloomington, Ind.: Indiana University Press, 1960. (1948)

This book is difficult to classify. The history of science is its background, to be sure, but what comes through most clearly is Sarton, the civilized man, who was a historian of science: his ways of thinking, his ideals, and his dreams for the future of the history of science. In this sense, it is historiography.

Schilpp, P. A. (Ed.), *The philosophy of Karl Popper.* (E16)

D66   Stimson, Dorothy. The place of the history of science in a liberal arts curriculum. In M. Clagett (Ed.), *Critical problems in the history of science.* Madison, Wisc.: University of Wisconsin Press, 1959, pp. 223-234.

D67   Thackray, A., & Merton, R. K. On discipline building: The paradoxes of George Sarton. *Isis,* 1972, *63,* 473-495.

A critical evaluation of the activities and attitudes of Sarton, the founder of the modern discipline of the history of science. His achievements and plans are evaluated against the backdrop of his biography and then contemporary sociocultural events.

D68   Toulmin, S. Rediscovering history: New directions in the philosophy of science. *Encounter,* 1971, *36*(1), 53-64.

Since the 1960s the dominance of a static, ahistorical view in the philosophy of science has given way to an evolutionary-functional, adaptive view of science. The logical structure, the nature of hypothetic deduction, and the interpretation of probability calculus, the traditional concerns of the philosopher of science, have not been wholly abandoned, but they are seen in a new light. Logical models no longer dominate, the historical analysis of rational development is the most striking feature of contemporary philosophy of science. The central problem of conceptual change is expressed in the work of Kuhn (E60), Lakatos, and Musgrave (E66). His critiques of the "new" and the "old" Kuhn (as represented by the first and second editions) are particularly worthwhile.

D69   Various. Fiftieth anniversary celebration of the Society. *Isis*, 1975, *66*, 443-482.

The fiftieth anniversary celebration of the History of Science Society is the basis for several reminiscences. The volume is relevant in other respects, since *Isis*, the journal of the Society, and its founder-editor, George Sarton, figure prominently.

Wallace, A. C. *Causality and scientific explanation.* (B101)

D70   Zubov, V. P. Historiography of science in Russia. In A. C. Crombie (Ed.), *Scientific Change*, pp. 829-846. (E3)

PHILOSOPHY

D71   Gallie, W. B. *Philosophy and the historical understanding.* London: Chatto & Windus, 1964.

Understanding in history contrasted with understanding in science is the first theme of this volume. This serves as the background for the second theme, which is the relevance of historical consideration to politics in the practice of science and of philosophy. The essence of writing history consists of the construction of a narrative, a topic he develops.

D72   Itzkoff, S. W. *Ernst Cassirer: Scientific knowledge and the concept of man.* Notre Dame, Ind.: University of Notre Dame Press, 1971.

A philosopher whose absorption in history, particularly intellectual history, makes this evaluation relevant to this section.

D73   Klibansky, R. (Ed.), *Philosophy in mid-century: A survey.* (4 vols.) Florence: La Nuova Italia, 1958-1959.

This series of articles prepared by an array of international specialists deals with contemporary philosophical issues. The topics of each volume are as follows: Volume 1, logic and the philosophy of science (e.g., semantics, induction, scientific methodology, and probability); Volume 2, metaphysics and analysis (e.g., phenomenology, linguistic analysis, relating psychology and philosophy, epistemology); Volume 3, the philosophy of value, history, and religion (e.g., aesthetics, political thought); Volume 4, the history of philosophy (with special chapters on Leibniz, Kant, and Dewey) and a consideration of contemporary philosophy in eastern Europe and Asia.

D74   Kilbansky, R. (Ed.), *Contemporary philosophy: A survey.* (4 vols.) Florence: La Nuova Italia, 1968-1969.

A more contemporary version of the earlier series also edited by Klibansky (D73), with a focus on those problems that have been in the center of philosophical interest in recent years. The format is essentially the same as that of the earlier volumes, although logic and philosophy of science as well as the contributors from Eastern Europe are given greater coverage.

D75   Passmore, J. The idea of a history of philosophy. The historiography of the history of philosophy. *Hist. Theory,* 1964-1965, *4,* Suppl. 5, pp. 1-32.

Passmore classifies the historiography of the history of philosophy in terms of both polemics for and against a particular philosopher or system, and elucidatory, divided into doxographical, retrospective, and problematic. Hegel, Hume, and Kant, from the *Contributors,* receive major attention, while R. G. Collingwood, George Herman Randall, and Charles Renouvier, among others, are examined critically, with revealing side comments on many more individuals.

D76   Randall, J. H., Jr. *How philosophy uses its past.* New York: Columbia University Press, 1963.

The values to be found in the study of the history of philosophy, its cultural functions, the contributions of historical patterns within philosophy, and the way in which the study of philosophy's history brings understanding are the major themes of this volume. From among the *Con-*

tributors, Berkeley, Descartes, Dewey, Hegel, Hume, Kant, Leibniz, Locke, Newton, and Whitehead receive emphasis, as does Bertrand Russell.

PSYCHIATRY

D77   Brand, Jeanne L. The social historian and the history of psychiatry. In G. Mora & Jeanne L. Brand (Eds.), *Psychiatry and its history: Methodological problems in research,* pp. 56-81. (C6)

In this paper the author traces the historiography of social history, considers the social historian's use of psychology and psychiatry, and relates social history to the history of psychiatry.

D78   Carlson, E. T., & Simpson, Meribeth, M. Interdisciplinary approach to the history of American psychiatry. In G. Mora & Jeanne L. Brand (Eds.), *Psychiatry and its history: Methodological problems in research,* pp. 119-148. (C6)

An account is given of ways in which psychiatrists and historians collaborate in a particular medical school-hospital setting on problems of the history of psychiatry to remedy their respective deficiencies, thereby indicating something about the fields involved. They warn that non-psychiatrists writing psychiatric history must become familiar with the practical problems faced by psychiatrists.

D79   Marx, O. M. What is the history of psychiatry? *Amer. J. Orthopsychiat.,* 1970, *40,* 593-605.

To bring out the multiplicity of approaches essential for the history of psychiatry, the author discusses the limitations of some of them. The history of psychiatry is not merely an aspect of intellectual history, nor does its course follow the development of the traditional medical specialties, nor can it be approached only in a humanist vein.

D80   Mora, G. Historiographic and cultural trends in psychiatry: A survey. *Bull. hist. Med.,* 1961, *35,* 26-36.

A study of the diversity, uncertainty of direction, and other themes that make the historiography of psychiatry different from other aspects of medicine, with exemplification over time. The author argues that a comprehensive history of psychiatry should take into account the various psychiatric traditions in the light of cultural history.

D81   Mora, G. The historiography of psychiatry and its development: A reevaluation. *J. Hist. behav. Sci.,* 1965, *1,* 43-52.

In a few pages Mora gives a masterly survey with copious references. Interpretation is seen in terms of moving between two poles—the cultural and the individual. He advocates that all future accounts should focus on the delicate interplay between the individual psychotherapeutic relationship and the sociocultural context.

D82   Mora, G. The history of psychiatry: A cultural and bibliographic survey. *Int. J. Psychiat.,* 1966, *2,* 335-356. (Reprinted from *Psychoanal. Rev.,* 1965, *52,* 298-328.)

Psychiatry is now an accepted field of endeavor, with sufficient maturity to look at its past with serenity. In Mora's opinion this is reflected in a new orientation toward the history of psychiatry. Mora sees major historical work of the future as falling into the following areas: critical understanding of the classical texts, presentation of psychiatric concepts in their cultural background, and investigation of particular cultural topics and their psychiatric background. He discusses biases in history with respect to conventionalism and continuity in history, citing Agassi (D47) frequently in connection with these issues. A very extensive bibliography emerges in the course of his development of these themes.

D83   Mora, G. The history of psychiatry: Its relevance for the psychiatrist. *Amer. J. Psychiat.,* 1970, *126,* 957-967.

The author begins with the history of interest in the history of psychiatry within the American Psychiatric Association, examines the field in the context of the history of the behavioral sciences, reviews the history of scholarship in the field from the beginning of the nineteenth century, and considers recent trends, the outlook for the future, and the current new spirit with which the past is being examined.

D84   Nelson, B. Psychohistory and its histories: From tradition to take off. In G. Mora & Jeanne L. Brand (Eds.), *Psychia-*

try and its history: Methodological problems in research, pp. 229-259. (C6)

Nelson presents a variety of ways in which the history of psychiatry has been approached, with illustrations.

PSYCHOANALYSIS AND PSYCHOHISTORY

D85 Barzun, J. *Clio and the doctors: Psychohistory, quanto-history, and history.* Chicago: University of Chicago Press, 1974.

Barzun contends that history and psychohistory are essentially incompatible, and he proceeds to marshall a variety of arguments to support his view.

D86 Brown, N. O. *Life against death: The psychoanalytic meaning of history.* Middletown, Conn.: Wesleyan University Press, 1959.

Largely unaware of his desires, man unconsciously seeks his own destruction—this is a bald statement of the theoretical position that Brown defends. A one-sentence summarization cannot do justice either to the considerable evidence that he presents or to the subtle elaboration of this central point.

D87 Coles, R. *Erik H. Erikson: The growth of his work.* Boston: Little Brown, 1970.

An intellectual biography of the senior figure in psychohistory. Each of Erikson's major essays and books is summarized, evaluated, and related to that which went before. The author also considers Erikson's place within the Freudian and neo-Freudian traditions. It is both a strength and a weakness that if you have not read Erikson, this is a good place to start; it you have, the book may be a disappointment.

D88 Erikson, E. H. *Life history and the historical moment.* New York: Norton, 1975.

One could legitimately draw from the work of Erikson for half of the cited references devoted to psychohistory, so great is his influence. Instead, since his works such as *Childhood and Society, Ghandis' Truth* , and *Young Man Luther* are well known and easily accessible, citing this one volume will suffice. This chosen volume reprints his most succinct statement of psychohistorical methodology, "On the nature of psychohistorical evidence; In search of Ghandi." Other topical themes are the identity crisis, the nature of insight, nonviolence and violence in history, and the interrelation between "life history" of the psychotherapist and "history."

D89   Fromm, E. *Escape from freedom.* New York: Holt, Rinehart & Winston, 1941.

From a neo-Freudian standpoint, Fromm explores the problem that faced modern man who on more than one occasion has fled from freedom to fascism. This willingness to submit to totalitarian rule is traced from its medieval background, where every man had his place, through the loss of this place by the emergence of personal freedom in the period of the Reformation, to today, where the mechanisms of escape from freedom are conceived to be authoritarianism, destructiveness, and conformity. The psychology of Nazism and of democracy is then explored.

D90   Freud, S. Moses and monotheism: Three essays. (1939) Reprinted in *The standard edition of the complete psychological works of Sigmund Freud.* Vol. 23. Ed. by J. Strachey, et al. London: Hogarth Press, 1964, pp. 1-56.

These essays are the culmination of Freud's consideration of historical factors through the use of the analogy of the neurotic process (early trauma, defense, latency, outbreak of neuroses, partial return of the repressed) and of religious events at the time of Moses and the Exodus. The thesis that he defends is that one of the two religions founded by Moses was repressed by the other. He considers that the "Great Man" has a place in the network of causal factors. History, it would seem, is a projection of the individual psyche upon the environment.

Hughes, H. S. *History as art and as science.* (D7)

Hutten, E. H. *The origins of science.* (B89)

Keniston, K. Psychological development and historical change. (D23)

D91 Langer, W. L. The next assignment. *Amer. Hist. Rev.,* 1958, *43,* 283-304. Reprinted in B. Mazlish (Ed.), *Psychoanalysis and history,* pp. 87-107. (D96)

In 1957 a call came from the then president of the American Historical Association for the next assignment of the historian to be "the needed deepening of our historical understanding through exploitation . . ." of "psychoanalysis and its later developments and variations. . . ." Among other points made, he indicated that its most immediate application is in the field of biography. This is an important milestone in retrospect, in that the paper is often cited as one that encouraged the utilization of psychoanalysis in historical endeavors.

D92 Langer, W. L. *The mind of Adolf Hitler: The secret wartime report.* New York: Basic Books, 1972.

The psychoanalytic interpretation prepared at the instigation of the OSS is an excellent illustration of the role of the psychoanalytic interpretation of historical materials. Langer and his associates not only drew on available published information, but they also had access to classified information and carried on special interviews with individuals who had known Hitler. The report includes specific predictions about his personality, the psychopathology he manifested, and the courses of action he might be expected to take. Many of these turned out to be accurate on the basis of later recovered information, and hence the study is pertinent to biographical methodology.

D93 Lifton, R. J. On psychohistory. In R. J. Lifton with E. Olson (Eds.), *Exploration in psychohistory: The Wellfleet Papers.* New York: Simon & Schuster, 1974, pp. 21-41.

An idiosyncratic view of psychohistory by a psychiatrist who, while associated with Erikson, developed his own increasingly independent view, stressing cultural values, some would say at the expense of the significance of the individual personality as it affects history.

Madden, E. H. Explanation in psychoanalysis and history. (E95)

D94 Manuel, F. The use and abuse of psychology in history. *Daedalus,* 1971, *100,* 187-213. Reprinted in F. Gilbert &

S. R. Graubard (Eds.), *Historical studies today.* New York: Norton, 1972, pp. 211-237.

A sympathetic and yet critical paper. Historians since the time of the Greeks and Romans have always committed themselves to some theory of motivation and personality. Vico, Michelet, Dilthey, each in their own way, were interested in fusing psychology with history. Psychoanalysis as interpreted by Herbert Marcuse and Erik Erikson broadened and merged with history, resulting in the Marxian-Hegelian historical view in the former and in "psychohistory" in the latter. It is Erikson who is then examined in detail. The author concludes that a new orientation has been provided, which enables one to read old or neglected documents with a new and deepened orientation.

D95   Marcuse, H. *Eros and civilization: A philosophical inquiry into Freud.* New York: Vintage Books, 1955.

A socio-philosophical critique of the metapsychology of Freud and the neo-Freudians. It amounts to an interpretation of the origin, development, and implications of Freud's most salient concepts within Western culture, e.g., the development of the reality principle and the suppression of Eros within Western civilization. Freud is seen as maintaining that a society can be created in which man's instincts can be freely gratified.

D96   Mazlish, B. (Ed.), *Psychoanalysis and history.* (Rev. ed.) New York: Grosset & Dunlap, 1971. (1963)

This is a collection grouped under two topics. One is Freuds' theory of history, with papers by Rieff, Kroeber, Barron, Meyer, and, as the lone psychoanalyst, Roheim; the other is miscellaneous applications of psychoanalysis to history—a reprinting of Langer's "The next assignment" (D91), an episode in the life of Machiavelli, a review of a book about a psychoanalytic interpretation of Woodrow Wilson, a paper by Flugel on Henry VIII, two papers showing the influence of Erikson, a paper by Erikson himself on Ghandi and how Erikson became involved with him (D88). A selected bibliography is more valuable than its relative brevity would suggest.

D97   Mazlish, B. What is psychohistory? *Trans. roy. hist. Soc.,* 1971, *21* (5th ser.), 79-99.

A clear and comprehensive statement of the advantages and disadvantages to the various approaches psychohistorians have chosen. The individual and the group approaches are both essential, which suggests to the author that "psychosocial history" is the more accurate term for the field.

D98   Mazlish, B. Psychiatry and history. In S. Arieti (Ed.), *American handbook of psychiatry*. Vol. 1. *The foundations of psychiatry*, (2nd ed.) New York: Basic Books, 1974. pp. 1034-1045.

Similarities and differences are discussed between psychoanalysis and history, organized around the thinking of major theoretical contributors. Ways are shown in which the approaches of Freud, Jung, Adler, Sullivan, Fromm, Marcus, and Erikson have been or may be used in history.

D99   Meyerhoff, H. On psychoanalysis as history. *Psychoanalysis & Psychoanal. Rev.*, 1962, *49*(2), 3-20.

A statement of the comparative methodologies of history and psychoanalysis. Psychoanalysis uses a historical method of its own and *is* history in this sense, with its own philosophy of history in Freud's works, chiefly *Totem and Taboo* and *Moses and Monotheism* (D90). However, one should not confuse this with the problem of the use of psychoanalysis in history, a problem that is not discussed.

D100   McGuire, J. E. Newton and the demonic furies: Some current problems and approaches in history of science. *Hist. Sci.*, 1973, *11*, 21-48.

On the cover of the particular issue in which this article appeared, the editorial choice of the title was "Psychology in Historiography," which more precisely captures its contents. True, the ostensible intent is to discuss Manuel's *A portrait of Isaac Newton*, but the article goes far beyond this, specifically in a psychohistoric vein.

D101   Rieff, P. History, psychoanalysis and the social sciences. *Ethics*, 1952-1953, *63*, 107-120.

A critical examination of the basic theoretical constructs of Freudianism. The author discusses the analogy between the individual and the social, and between the psychological and the historical.

Saffady, W. Manuscripts and psychohistory. (A213a)

D102 Schmidl, F. Psychoanalysis and history. *Psychoanal. Quart.,*
1962, *31,* 532-548.
The author, then a practicing psychoanalyst who also
worked in the substantive history of psychoanalysis, takes
a wary view of psychoanalytic applications to history, because psychoanalysis requires the cooperation of a living
person. It can be hazarded that he reflects the view of
many psychoanalysts. He does suggest that historians
could gain a greater understanding of unconscious motivation by studying psychoanalysis.

Smith, P. *The historian and history.* (D12)

D103 Strout, C. Ego psychology and the historian. *Hist. Theory,*
1968, *7,* 281-297.
Strout calls upon the historian to come to terms with
psychoanalytic ego psychology and its relevancies to the
study of history, especially of intellectual history. As support for this contention he refers to his own psychohistorical work on William James, as well as strongly emphasizing the studies of Erik Erikson.

Weinstein, F., & Platt, G. M. *Psychoanalytic sociology.*
(D136)

D104 Wyatt, F. Notes on the scope of the psychohistorical approach. *Int. J. Psychiat.,* 1969, *5,* 488-492.
A thoughtful appraisal of an article by Erikson on
Ghandi, also published in this journal. But it is more than
this, since it is also a psychologist's reaction to what he
sees to be the limits of the psychohistorical approach in
general.

D105 Wyatt, F., & Willcox, W. B. Sir Henry Clinton: A psychological exploration in history. *William & Mary Quart.,*
1959, *16,* 3-26.
A collaborative effort between a psychologist with a
neo-Freudian orientation and a historian. They argue that
collaboration is the most appropriate way to proceed, since
otherwise they would go beyond their levels of professional
competence. The thread of consistency in the vacillating

behavior of General Clinton during the campaigns of the American Revolution they consider a conflict between a desire for authority and yet a fear of exercising it. For this and related points they marshall considerable evidence.

BIOLOGY, PHYSIOLOGY, AND MEDICINE

D106   Bell, W. J., Jr. Richard H. Shyrock: Life and work of a historian. *J. hist. Med.*, 1974, *29*, 15-31.

D107   Blake, J. B., (Ed.), *Education in the history of medicine.* New York: Hafner, 1968.
   Report of a conference sponsored by the Josiah Macy, Jr. Foundation with papers by L. G. Stevenson, G. Rosen, O. Temkin, D. G. Bates, and J. H. Cassedy.

D108   Brozek, J. Six recent additions to the history of physiology in the USSR. *J. hist. Biol.*, 1973, *6*, 317-334.
   This review of physiological publications, 1969 and thereafter, is of major interest because of Brozek's comments on the intricacies of the problem of understanding the significance of work in the Soviet Union, a problem created by particular terminological usage, the attitudes toward work outside the country, and bureaucratic complexities. In connection with most of the publications discussed, Pavlov dominates.

   Clarke, E. (Ed.), *Modern methods in the history of medicine.* (A4)

D109   Curti, M. The historical scholarship of Richard H. Shyrock. *J. hist. Med.*, 1974, *29*, 7-14.

D110   Miller, Genevieve, Lippard, V. W., & Cassedy, J. H. The status of medical history in the universities of North America and Europe. *Bull. hist. Med.*, 1969, *43*, 259-283.
   Visits to medical schools in the United States and Canada were an important source of the data reported on both undergraduates and graduate education by the first-named author. Cassedy described European centers—some visited, others learned about indirectly.

D111   Poynter, F. N. L. The history of medicine in 1960-61. *Hist. Sci.*, 1962, *1*, 44-56.

This article, even though it is confined to the two years mentioned, brings out clearly the considerable amount of work being done in the history of medicine.

D112   Rosen, G. People, disease, and emotion: Some newer problems for research in medical history. *Bull. hist. Med.*, 1967, *41*, 5-23.

The author describes the historiography of medicine in terms of a shift from the history of professional interests of physicians to viewing its problems within a societial context, with particular emphasis upon the consequences of the latter.

D113   Temkin, O. Scientific medicine and historical research. *Perspect. Biol. Med.*, 1959, *3*, 70-85.

Temkin gives his view of the nature of historical research in medicine.

Underwood, E. A. (Ed.), *Science, medicine and history* (B179)

D114   Veith, Ilza. The function and place of the history of medicine in medical education. *J. med. Educ.*, 1956, *31*, 303-309.

The values to be found in its study are explored.

SOCIOLOGY AND THE SOCIAL SCIENCES

D115   Antoni, C. *From history to sociology: The transition in German historical thinking.* (Trans. H. V. White, foreword B. Croce) Detroit: Wayne State University Press, 1959.

Essentially as a derivative from the thinking of Croce, Antoni examines the German historiographic tradition of Dilthey, Weber, and others, interpreting history as becoming sociology, to the detriment of history. This book is relevant also for its consideration of both speculative and nineteenth-century historiography and dynamics.

D116   Aronson, S. H. Obstacles to a rapprochement between history and sociology; A sociologist's view. In M. & Carolyn W. Sherif (Eds.), *Interdisciplinary relationships in the social sciences.* Chicago: Aldine, 1969, pp. 292-304.

As might be expected, the author finds numerous obstacles. One is the historian's suspiciousness of the emphasis on methodology, including quantification, which sociologists stress.

D117   Berkhofer, R. F. *A behavioral approach to historical analysis.* New York: Free Press, 1969.

The author, a historian, also did graduate work in anthropology and sociology. Concepts drawn from these fields, rather than from psychology, permeate the book. Typical chapters concern society and culture and systems analysis. It is not quantitative in the sense of presenting techniques, but a spirit of objectivity pervades it. Overall, it presents an approach to history that draws upon the social sciences with a defense of a pluralistic approach to human action. Explanation, the topic of the last two chapters, is the means whereby the material covered in the earlier chapters is synthesized.

D118   Cahnman, W. J., & Boskoff, A., Sociology and history: Reunion and rapprochment. Review and outlook. In W. J. Cahnman & A. Boskoff (Eds.), *Sociology and history: Theory and research.* New York: Free Press, 1964, pp. 1-18, 560-580.

As an introduction to this volume the authors examine some of the conceptual and methodological problems they consider to obscure the relationship between the two fields, and they take the opportunity to explain the principles on which the papers included in the rest of the volume were selected. To bring it to a close, they reflect upon the meaning of a sociological approach to historical materials and include in footnotes a considerable bibliography of related studies.

D119   Cohn, B. S. Ethnohistory. In D. L. Sills (Ed.), *International encyclopedia of the social sciences.* Vol. 6. New York: Macmillan, 1968, pp. 440-448.

By ethnohistory is meant the historical study of any non-European peoples. The sources and methods open to it are written documents, oral traditions, and field work.

D120   Hofstadter, R. History and the social sciences. In F. Stern
       (Ed.), *The varieties of history,* pp. 359-370. (E35)
           Hofstadter presents an autobiographical statement of
       how he, a historian, interacted with the social sciences,
       what he derived from this interaction, and what hazards he
       thinks the future will hold.

D121   Hofstadter, R. History and sociology in the United States.
       In S. M. Lipset & R. Hofstadter (Eds.), *Sociology and his-
       tory: Methods.* New York: Basic Books, 1968, pp. 3-19.
           A short but significant historiography of history that
       blends into a study of the relationship of the historian to
       sociologists to and to sociological findings.

D122   Hall, A. R. Merton revisited, or science and society in the
       seventeenth century. *Hist. Sci.,* 1963, *2,* 1-15.
           A statement criticizing the approach to the sociology
       of science expressed in the work of Merton and arguing
       for the history of science as a history of ideas.

D123   Hallowell, A. I. The history of anthropology as an anthro-
       pological problem. *J. Hist. behav. Sci.,* 1965, *1,* 24-38.
           Instead of being written in terms of the figures pre-
       sumed to have been great from the past of anthropology,
       its history itself is seen as an anthropological problem.
       The first stage is conceived to be the ideas and events that
       shaped the folk anthropology of early Western culture,
       which simultaneously laid the groundwork for observa-
       tions of a more reliable nature. Geographical and temporal
       perspectives gradually emerged. The appearance of special-
       ists and organized disciplines followed.

D124   Hughes, H. S. The historian and the social scientist. *Amer.
       hist. Rev.,* 1960, *66,* 20-46.
           An account by a well-known student of intellectual
       history of how he, a practicing historian, has found the
       social sciences, including psychology, useful—or not so use-
       ful—in his work.

D125   Landes, D. S., & Tilly, C. (Eds.), *History as social science.*
       Englewood Cliffs, N.J.: Prentice-Hall, 1971.
           A report of a survey of the historical profession spon-

sored by the National Academy of Sciences and by the Social Science Research Council. It captures the wide diversity of opinion expressed by historians about the nature of history, the position of quantification, the humanistic stance, the varieties of history, instructional needs, and research, domestic and foreign. Diversification, increased support, and cooperation are urged as final recommendations, which is a somewhat pedestrian close to this otherwise lively report.

D126   Lipset, S. M. History and sociology: Some methodological considerations. In S. M. Lipset & R. Hofstadter (Eds.), *Sociology and history: Methods.* New York: Basic Books, 1968, pp. 20-58.

A companion piece to Hofstadter (D121), this article sketches methodological considerations in the revival and nature of contemporary historical sociology and comparative history.

D127   Machlup, F. Are the social sciences really inferior? *South. Econ. J.,* 1961, *27*(3), 173-184. Reprinted in M. Natanson (Ed.), *The philosophy of the social sciences: A reader.* New York: Random House, 1963, pp. 158-180.

Nine grounds of comparison with the natural sciences (such as invariability of observations, objectivity, and predictability) were evaluated, with mixed conclusions about the inferiority of the social sciences.

Nagel, E. *Structure of science.* (E12)

D128   Oberschall, A.(Ed.), *The establishment of empirical sociology: Studies in continuity, discontinuity, and institutionalization.* New York: Harper & Row, 1972.

How empirical research in sociology was institutionalized in some countries and not in others is the central theme of this collection of essays, with Newton and Durkheim from the *Contributors* and Le Play as central figures. Other essays concern the institutionalization of American sociology and the failure of such institutionalization in nineteenth-century England.

D129   Ogburn, W. F., & Goldenweiser, A. (Eds.), *The social sci-*

ences and their interrelations. Boston: Houghton Mifflin, 1927.

This volume is concerned with the interrelation among anthropology, economics, history, political science, and sociology, in a permutation of combinations, each chapter written by a specialist. Emphasis was placed on conditions, problems, and methods as they existed circa 1927.

D130   Pargellis, S. Clio in a strait jacket. *American Quart.,* 1959, *11,* 225-231.

While history and the social sciences do have close interrelationships, an argument one might expect from the title is that the former should emphasize its autonomy.

Popper, K. R. *The poverty of historicism.* (E34)

D131   Saveth, E. N. (Ed.), *American history and the social sciences.* Glencoe, Ill.: Free Press, 1964.

The book is divided into five parts: Part I is Saveth's introduction; Part II contains seven articles by spokesmen of the social sciences commenting upon 'History and the Disciplines'; Part III, particulary important, is made up of 21 articles by historians around the theme of 'The Concepts' from the social sciences useful in history, such as motivation, type, class, role, and the like; Part IV contains three articles concerned with quantification and machine processing; and Part V is made up of four cautionary articles by historians.

D132   Saveth, E. N. American history and the social sciences: A trial balance. *Int. Soc. Sci. J.,* 1968, *20,* 319-330.

This is a survey of the historians' involvement in the use of social science concepts, particularly of those arising from psychology. The controversies over their use are put into an evolving historical context, with some emphasis upon the pros and cons of methodology.

D133   Schutz, A. Concept and theory formation in the social sciences. (1962) In M. Natanson (Ed.), *Collected papers: Vol. 1. The problem of phenomenology and social reality.* The Hague: Nijhoff, 1962, pp. 48-66.

Schutz accepts the position of Max Weber and his

school that social phenomena must be understood in terms of meaningful categories of human experience, not of the natural sciences, thus rendering the causal functional approach of the natural sciences inapplicable to social inquiry. He then proceeds to answer criticisms of Nagel and Hempel, who have argued against this view. He also defends and explains *Verstehen.*

D134　Social Science Research Council. *The social sciences in historical study: A report of the committee on historiography, Bulletin No. 64.* New York: Social Science Research Council, 1954.

In part, at least, this report was prepared because of a recognition of the need to examine the interrelationship between the social sciences and history. Hence chapters are devoted to a survey of the concepts of the specific social sciences and, in the last chapter, to an appraisal of social sciences and historical synthesis. Between these chapters the relation to the theme is not so apparent, since one is concerned with historical analysis, another with change and history, and still another with trends in methods in theory and practice. But in each instance the theme is examined against similar thematic material for the social sciences. See Aronson (D116) for some comments on its effect 15 years later.

D135　Weber, G. Science and society in nineteenth century anthropology. *Hist. Sci.,* 1974, *12,* 260-283.

The theme of the history of anthropology, seen as arising from the life sciences and serving as a bridge to the study of history, has been minimized by selective edition and exclusion, according to the author of this paper. This minimization Weber seeks to correct, along with an account of other interests and concepts that have influenced the development of anthropology.

D136　Weinstein, F., & Platt, G. M. *Psychoanalytic sociology: An essay on the interpretation of historical data and the phenomena of collective behavior.* Baltimore, Md.: Johns Hopkins University Press, 1973.

Contemporary psychoanalytic ego psychology, not in the sense of an Eriksonian study of individual, elite figures but more as a sociological model, is applied to the mass or group. This opens the way to an exploration of theoretical issues relating psychoanalysis, sociology, and history.

D137   Winch, P. *The idea of a social science and its relation to philosophy.* London: Routledge & Kegan Paul, 1958.

Winch attempts to demarcate social science as a unitary idea in relation not only to philosophy, his primary aim, but also to history and natural science as well. Causal explanation (including *Verstehen*) and generalization in social phenomena are related to this unitary idea.

EDUCATION

D138   Borrowman, M. L. History of education. In C. W. Harris (Ed.), *Encyclopedia of educational research.* (3rd ed.) New York: Macmillan, 1960, pp. 661-668.

The author considers its relation to history as a discipline and the way it is taught in schools of education.

Brickman, W. W. *Guide to research in educational history.* (A2)

INTELLECTUAL HISTORY

D139   Barzun, J. Cultural history as a synthesis. In F. Stern (Ed.), *The varieties of history,* pp. 387-402. (E35)

Barzun distinguishes his view of cultural history from what he considers to be the narrower intellectual history and from the "all-embracing" work of the cultural anthropologist. He stresses a middle course, with emphasis on the "style" shown by a particular period or school.

D140   Baumer, F. L. Intellectual history and its problems, *J. mod. Hist.,* 1948-1949, *20-21,* 191-203.

The author describes the origin of intellectual history and its major problems, and he considers the question of its value.

D141   Brinton, C. Intellectual history. In D. L. Sills (Ed.), *Inter-*

national encyclopedia of the social sciences. Vol. 6. New York: Macmillan, 1968, pp. 462-468.

Although several historians are mentioned in passing, this article serves as a general survey of types of intellectual history and the kinds of studies associated with them.

D142 Gilbert, F. Intellectual history: Its aims and methods. In F. Gilbert & S. R. Graubard (Eds.), *Historical studies today.* New York: Norton, 1972, pp. 141-158.

Emphasis is placed on intellectual history in terms of individuals, rather than on a summary of current developments.

D143 Higham, J. Intellectual history and its neighbors. *J. hist. Ideas,* 1954, *15,* 339-347.

As he conceives it, intellectual historians tend to see their task from either one of two perspectives: the relation of thought to external events, or the relation of behavior or thought to other contexts of thought. Hence, external and internal intellectual history are two different conceptions of the discipline.

D144 Horowitz, Maryanne C. Historiography of ideas. *J. hist. Phil.,* 1974, *12,* 506-509.

Major historical approaches to the phenomenon of ideas are divided by Horowitz into two major categories—*vertical* (extending over at least two historical periods) including the history of an idea, specific topic inferences, the history of a discipline, and social history; and *horizontal* (within one historical period), including intellectual history, *Zeitgeist,* cultural history, and the impact of ideas on events, life, and times.

D145 Lovejoy, A. O. Reflections on the history of ideas. *J. hist. Ideas,* 1940, *1,* 3-23.

The first article to be published in the *Journal* and designed to be a prefatory statement of its nature and aims—the study of the history of ideas.

D146 Mandelbaum, M. The history of ideas, intellectual history, and the history of philosophy. In J. Passmore (Ed.), The historiography of the history of philosophy. *Hist. Theory,* 1964-1965, *4,* Suppl. 5, pp. 33-66.

A. O. Lovejoy receives major attention.

D147   Skotheim, R. A. *American intellectual histories and his-torians.* Princeton, N.J.: Princeton University Press, 1966.

An analysis of the approaches of Robinson, Beard, Carl Becker, Parrington, Curti, Morison, and Miller and their influence upon intellectual history.

D148   Welter, R. The history of ideas in America: An essay in redefinition. *J. Amer. Hist.,* 1964-1965, *51,* 599-614.

Welter distinguishes the history of ideas from intellectual history on the basis that the former practices internal history and the latter external history. He goes on to discuss alternative interpretations, with heavy reliance upon the thinking of John Dewey.

D149   Wiener, P. Some problems and methods in the history of ideas. *J. hist. Ideas.,* 1961, *22,* 531-548.

Twenty years after the Lovejoy statement of purpose (D145), Wiener examines some of the problems this approach to history has encountered.

E. HISTORIOGRAPHIC THEORIES

The books and articles that follow present important and representative views of the theories that have been applied to the historical fields that deal with human beings. If a writer confused the history of physics with the history of science and did not at least come to grips with the existence of human sciences, the title was considered irrelevant. Retrospectively, it has turned out that there is more-or-less equal representation of works by historians of the behavioral sciences, historians of science, philosophers of science, and philosophers of history.

Despite its theoretical implications, the greater methodological import of *Verstehen,* objectivity in its methodological aspects, and the stance of historicism-presentism had led to placement of that relevant literature in Section C, which is concerned with the narrative. Also one should remember what was said in connection with Section D: "Historiographic Fields": that a view of an historical field may also be a statement of theory.

The more general contemporary theoretical statements are annotated in the section immediately following. Thereafter, more specific problems are grouped under the headings of "Speculative Theories of History and the Nineteenth- and Twentieth-Century Reactions from Historians," "Contemporary Pluralistic Emphasis on Dynamics of Historical Change," "Methodological Individualism-Holism and Psychologism as Problems in Dynamics," and "Explanation and Related Problems."

GENERAL THEORETICAL STATEMENTS

Since contemporary views were sought, it should be indicated that relevant annotations that concern earlier theories of the philosophy of science and philosophy of history are to be found in the primarily substantive historical annotations of Section B, and discussions of speculative theories of history and the nineteenth-century reaction to them in the section that follows immediately after this one. This reversal of temporal order is necessary, because some of the general theoretical books to be described consider speculative philosophy, but the reverse is not true; the other papers and books concerned with speculative philosophy do not consider the contemporary theoretical problems, except as a background for evaluating the earlier speculative views.

These general theoretical references take up a variety of more specific problems and are cited again in more specific sections.

E1   Boring, E. G. *Psychologist at large: An autobiography and selected essays.* New York: Basic Books, 1961.

As the very title indicates, these papers were selected to show the breadth of the work of E. G. Boring. Great men, *Zeitgeist*, determinism, freedom, and positivism are major relevant themes. His autobiography considers his thinking about the writing of history.

E2   Boring, E. G. *History, psychology, and science: Selected papers.* Ed. R. I. Watson & D. T. Campbell. New York: Wiley, 1963.

Papers grouped under several headings, with most of the pertinent papers falling into "The Zeitgeist and the psychology of science" category. Controversy, determinism, discovery, eponymy, Great Men, and *Zeitgeist* are leading themes. A paper in a later section, "The role of theory in experimental psychology," is his basic statement on this topic. Cast in a historical mold, Boring discusses various kinds of theories held in psychology—analytical, generalization as theory, systematic classification as theory, physiological theories, conceptual theories, physical models, mathematical theories, and several more.

E3   Crombie, A. C. (Ed.), *Scientific change: Historical studies in the intellectual, social and technical conditions for scientific discovery and technical invention, from antiquity to the present. Symposium on the History of Science, University of Oxford, 9-15 July 1961.* New York: Basic Books, 1963.

This Oxford symposium of 1961 is devoted to the intellectual, technical, and social conditions that encourage or discourage scientific discovery; hence it is concerned with the dynamics of historical change. Papers on ancient Chinese and medieval science that touch upon this theme are followed by a paper by Kuhn on dogma in scientific research and by two series of historical papers with a theme of discovery, one on problems in the physical sciences and the other on problems in biological, psychological, and medical sciences. There is then a section on the organization of science and technology in modern science. The remaining sections on the history of science as an academic discipline and on problems in historiographic fields of science, not strictly speaking called for by the theme of the Conference, close the volume. Throughout, detailed accounts of the discussion that followed presentation of each of the papers add considerably to its value.

E4   Danto, A. C. *Analytical philosophy of history*. Cambridge: Cambridge University Press, 1965.

Danto first distinguishes "substantive" (speculative) and analytical (critical) philosophy and proceeds to develop the latter in detail. This task is conceived to be application of philosophy to the conceptual problems of history. The major theoretical topic is that of explanation, which also involves cause, description, evidence, and general laws, but he also considers in a theoretically important way methodological individualism and socialism. He challenges the proposition that all statements in history are to be understood in terms of individual human behavior.

E5   Dray, W. H. (Ed.), *Philosophical analysis and history*. New York: Harper & Row, 1966.

This book of readings was selected so as to deal with four interrelated theoretical problems—the logical structure of historical explanation and the extent to which general laws are possible, the nature of causal analysis, the objectivity of historical conclusions, and the question of the individual as the fundamental unit of study in history. Some of the papers the author includes are cited, either collectively or individually, in connection with specific theoretical problems.

E6   Feigl, H. Empiricism at bay? Revisions and a new defense. In R. S. Cohen & M. W. Wartofsky (Eds.), *Boston studies in the philosophy of science.* Vol. 14. *Methodological and historical essays in the natural and social sciences.* Dordrecht: Reidel, 1974, pp. 1-20.

The question mark in the title should not be overlooked. Feigl offers a detailed and thoroughgoing defense of logical empiricism against what at least at one point he calls the "obscurantist stance of Polanyi, Kuhn and Feyerabend." He is hardly easier on Popper and Lakatos and naturally finds allies in Carnap, Nagel, and Reichenbach. Empiricism is still "a fruitful and adequate philosophy of science" and an adequate approach to its dynamics.

E7   Feyerabend, P. K. Problems of empiricism. In R. Colodny (Ed.), *Beyond the edge of certainty.* Englewood Cliffs, N.J.: Prentice-Hall, 1965, pp. 145-260.

The arguments supporting an empirical point of view are first examined, then a historical sketch is given of the three periods in the history of empiricism—the Aristotelian, the classic empiricism of the seventeenth, eighteenth, and nineteenth centuries, and then that of modern physics, which, he contends, is actually closer in spirit to the empiricism of Aristotle than to that of the immediately preceeding centuries. Contemporary radical empiricism is then examined in critical detail and found wanting in two major respects: through incompleteness and through the inclusion of undesirable assumptions, the first to be removed by regarding empiricism as a cosmological hypothesis and the second by a use of a theoretical pluralism.

E8   Feyerabend, P. K. An attempt at a realistic interpretation of experience. *Pro. Aristotelian Soc.,* 1957-1958, *58,* 143-170.

A contrast of positivistic and realistic interpretations of experience. Consequences of positivism that tend to support the realistic position are explored.

E9   Gustavson, C. G. *A preface to history.* New York: McGraw-Hill, 1955.

An introductory manual addressed to the college student to develop what the author calls "historical mindedness." In the present perspective this book is seen as an introductory pluralistic discussion of the theoretical dynamics of history; social factors, including the institutional, the individual, invention, and the role of ideas in history are chapter themes pointing in this direction.

E10   Harré, R. *The philosophies of science: An introductory survey.* London: Oxford University Press, 1972.

A one-page preface captures with admirably succinct lucidity the central issue involved—that problem is apparently "specific to science are actually species of wider philosophical issues." The "two opposed positions," ". . . in which a rational basis for science has been sought" (the positivist and the realist), "seem to coalesce" in his exposition. Lest it be inferred that his is a rather tepid compromise, it should be added that the author also reaches the conclusion that an unrelieved positivism is untenable, a position that he supports by offering a number of rather telling arguments. In the course of his discussion, a variety of specific problems is considered—causality, deductivism, inductivism, explanation, individualism, logic, and theories. Bridgman, Mach, J. B. Mill, and Popper are central figures in his exposition and criticism.

E11   Kaplan, A. *The conduct of inquiry: Methodology for behavioral science.* San Francisco, Calif.: Chandler, 1964.

The use of "methodology" in the subtitle may be misunderstood if it is not made clear at the onset that "techniques" are dismissed in a page, and by methodology the author means "the description, the explanation and the justification" of methods. Hence the book belongs in this section. After a short introduction there are nine major headings, including concepts, generalizations, laws, theories, and explanation, all obviously germane to theory in the behavioral sciences. But what of the sections not yet mentioned? "Experiment," while not within the province of the typical historian, is still something with which he should have some acquaintance, while "measurement," "statistics," "models," and "values" are also part of the theoretical armamentarium of the behavioral scientist and do have direct relevance to the activities of the historian. "Discovery" is given a brief exposition. While this book is cited primarily in connection with methodology, concepts, laws, and theories, Kaplan's organization of its contents leads to a summary of each particular problem as he conceives it to apply to the behavioral sciences. He thus may be said to be

offering a multifaceted definition of behavioral science,
and indirectly of its history.

E12   Nagel, E. *The structure of science: Problems in the logic of
       scientific explanation.* New York: Harcourt, Brace & World,
       1961.

An authoritative textbook in the philosophy of science,
which considers most of the specific issues relevant to
theory in history. Explanations, their deductive pattern,
the logical character of scientific laws, experimental laws,
and theories, and the cognitive status of theories are earlier
chapter headings. The explanation of individual events is a
topic within the discussion of the deductive pattern of
explanation. The author does not commit himself on the
issue of methodological individualism. Most of the chapters are devoted to theory in the natural sciences, to be
sure, but what is said is then related to history and the
social sciences in later chapters. The last three chapters are
devoted respectively to "Methodological problems of the
social sciences," "Explanation and understanding in the
social science," and "Problems in the logic of historical
inquiry," Nowhere does he come to grips with the question
of psychology as a science—indeed, the term psychology is
not in the index.

E13   Popper, K. R. *Conjectures and refutations: The growth of
       scientific knowledge.* New York: Basic Books, 1962.

This is a thematically rich book, but it is frustrating
to find the precise themes within it. What must one do
when it is found that the key words in the title, "conjectures" and "refutations," are not indexed? True, the papers
are grouped under one or another of these headings, but
this is of little help. I fall back on quoting from the preface.
"The way in which knowledge progresses, and especially
our scientific knowledge, is by unjustified (and unjustifi-
able) anticipations, by guesses, by tentative solutions to
our problems, by *conjectures.* These conjectures are con-
trolled by criticism; that is, by attempted *refutations,* which
include severely critical tests. They may survive these tests;
but they can never be positively justified: they can neither
be established as certainly true nor even as 'probable' (in
the sense of the probability calculus). Criticism of our
conjectures is of decisive importance: by bringing out our

mistakes it makes us understand the difficulties of the problem which we are trying to solve. This is how we become better acquainted with our problem, and able to propose more mature solutions: the very refutation of a theory —that is, of any serious tentative solution to our problem —is always a step forward that takes us nearer to the truth. And this is how we can learn from our mistakes." (p. vii) Change, confirmation, corroboration, testability, truth, and verification are the indexed themes most relevant to dynamics. Logic, explanation, deduction, and induction are also major themes. From among his contemporaries, the author cites Carnap, Einstein, Neurath, Schlick, Tarski, and Wittgenstein.

E14   Popper, K. R. *The logic of scientific discovery.* London: Hutchison, 1959. (1935) (Reprinted 1961)

Despite reference in the title to "discovery," Popper is not concerned with how a new idea came about but, rather, with examining logically what happens when we test a new idea to see whether it should be taken seriously. After an introductory section dealing with induction, deduction, and experience, he considers the structural components of the theory of experience, including the nature of theories, their empirical basis, falsifiability, testability, the place of probability, and, lastly, the central problem, corroboration, or how a theory stands up to test. It is this last chapter that gives the volume its most original and provocative note, which rests on the argument that one tests the *most improbable* of surviving theories and, after proving it to be false if this be the case, one turns to next most improbable, and so on.

E15   Popper, K. R. *Objective. knowledge: An evolutionary approach.* London: Oxford University Press, 1972.

This is a collection of papers, some previously published, which Popper sees as having the theme of presenting and defending "an objective theory of essentially conjectural knowledge." In view of the numerous other references by Popper, this volume is not cited in later sections.

E16   Schilpp, P. A. (Ed.), *The philosophy of Karl Popper.* (2 vols.) La Salle, Ill.: Open Court, 1974.

A critique and description by senior scholars of Pop-

per's views on science, philosophy, and history, 33 topics
in all, occupies three-quarters of the two volumes. To these,
Popper replies in a series of comments. It is a crucial volume, not only because of Popper's importance, but also
because it provides a forum for many other scholars to present their views against a Popperian background. Papers by
Agassi, Ayer, Bronowski, Campbell, Donagan, Eccles,
Feigl, Meehl, Kuhn, Lakatos, Suppes, Wisdom, and Winch
are representative.

The problem of dynamics is pervasive throughout.
The suggestion may be ventured that Popper's view is best
captured in a statement made while discussing Kuhn's paper,
when Popper looks at science in an evolutionary context
and conceives it to be the conscious and critical form of an
adaptive trial and error. This, it would seem, is why we learn
from our mistakes by the use of conjecture. Campbell's
paper in these volumes is seen by Popper as supporting this
view. An autobiography, which gives many details about
his "relation" with the Vienna Circle and other intellectual
currents, and a bibliography of Popper's writings are included.

E17   Suppe, F. (Ed.), *The structure of scientific theories*. Urbana,
      Ill.: University of Illinois Press, 1974.

The volume is introduced by a lengthy but clear and
balanced statement of contemporary positions on scientific
theory by the editor. He utilizes Putnam's term, the "Received View," for the position that conceived "scientific
theories as axiomatic calculi which are given a partial observational interpretation by means of correspondence
rules," and he traces its history as a product of logical
positivism and beyond. Thereafter, its present status and
criticisms and alternatives are examined. The influence
of Carnap, Hempel, Nagel, and Reichenbach on the development of the mainstream of the "Received View" is presented along with the alternative from Feyerabend, Hanson, Kuhn, Popper, and Toulmin. The analytical index under the name of each participant is especially worthwhile
in finding his point of view on various specific matters of
theory. Both the introductory statement contrasting the
received view and the newer radical alternatives proposed
by the editor and by several others are relevant to the

problem of dynamics. Explanations, laws, and predictions are also discussed by the various symposium participants.

E18   Toulmin, S. *Human understanding.* Vol. I. *General introduction* and *Part I. The collective use and evolution of concepts.* Princeton, N.J.: Princeton University Press, 1972.

The central thesis for a planned three-volume work is that preoccupation with logical systematicness in terms of the relationships between propositions has hampered historical understanding and philosophical criticism. Instead, the rationality of science is to be found within intellectual disciplines in describable patterns in historical evolution. This may be illustrated by his criticism of Hempel. Confirmation in scientific theory as envisaged by Hempel through an analysis based on twentieth-century formal logic is a view whose relevance still needs to be demonstrated and bears no relation to the actual work of scientists. Something of the range and complexity of the discussion is shown by the titles given to the three parts contemplated. Part I: The collective use and evolution of concepts (in this, the first volume); Part II: The individual grasp and development of concepts; Part III: The rational adequacy and appraisal of concepts. Some—but only some—of the questions on which Volume I focuses are what has here been called the dynamics of history—above all, conceptual change and its evolutionary character. The author argues that scientists demonstrated their rationality by their preparedness to meet new situations with open minds. The Kuhnian problem is significantly referred to as the "revolutionary illusion." Kuhn's position is illusory, not only in not accounting for scientific change, but also in not accounting for stability as well. Kuhn, he argues, accounts for change (revolutions) and stability (normal science) in quite different terms. The two key concepts, "revolution" and "paradigm," are separate and independent both in historical origins and in implications, which Toulmin then traces, going on to examine his views of revolutions through "five distinguishable phases." In his concluding chapter, Toulmin contrasts his view with those of Popper and Lakatos. They started from formal logic and extended rationality beyond its scope. Toulmin would invert the process and put formal structures to work in the service of the rational enterprise. Another theme related to dynamics is conceptual change within an intellectual discipline, which is the setting for his discussion of innovation, in which he uses historical examples. He criticizes the Great Man theory, since views of individuals in science give way and are supported by collective debate. An individual scientist submits his ideas to a collective judgment. Other problems considered are the externalist-internalist dichotomy, causality, the psychology and sociology of innovation (discovery), and the social relations of science. Collingwood, Hume, Kant, Koyré, Kuhn, Lakatos, Mach, and Popper receive considerable attention.

E19   Turner, M. B. *Philosophy and the science of behavior.* New York: Appleton-Century-Crofts, 1967.

After a historical introduction extending from the classical rationalists to the logical empiricists, theory in contemporary psychology is the major theme of this volume, with emphasis upon explanation, laws, generalization, and causation. Justification of induction-deduction, including hypothetico-deductivism, probability, and reductionism, are prominent topical concerns. The relationship of these topics to history in general and to dynamics in particular is not explicitly considered. Individuals associated with logical positivism are depended upon most heavily. The positions of Bergmann, Brodbeck, Carnap, Duhem, Feigl, Hanson, Hayek, Hempel, Nagel, Neurath, Popper, Reichenbach, Scriven, and Toulmin are discussed in some detail.

E19a   Walsh, W. H. *Philosophy of history: An introduction.* (Rev. ed.) New York: Harper, 1960. (1951)

This slim volume is an excellent introduction to the philosophy of history, in a clear style, free from jargon. The author considers both the critical and the speculative aspects, in that order, and the problems of the nature of the field, the relation of history to the sciences, explanation, truth, fact, and objectivity. He makes Collingwood's idealist theory central in historical explanation, and his description of the procedure of the "re-thinking of past thoughts" is important methodologically. Thereafter he offers criticisms of the procedure. As Walsh sees it, limits are imposed upon the goal of objectivity of history by moral and metaphysical "preconceptions" in a way not found in the sciences. Impartiality, to be sure, is demanded, but still interpretations may—and should—differ, since there are conflicting theories of historical interpretation. In the setting of a discussion of truth and fact in history, he considers the merits and difficulties of the correspondence and coherence theories of truth and argues for a synthesis or an intermediate position. He also considers the factors that make for lack of objectivity—personal bias, group prejudice, conflicting theories of historical interpretation, differing beliefs on morality, and differing views on the on the nature of man or of the nature of *Weltanschauungen*. He leads into the topic of dynamics directly from this. There are conflicting theories of historical interpretation due to underlying philosophical conflicts, so thereafter he discusses various reactions—historical skepticism, personal perspective, and an objective historical consciousness. He then moves on to consider speculative and dynamic philosophies of history as conceived by Kant, Herder, and Hegel.

SPECULATIVE THEORIES OF HISTORY AND THE NINETEENTH- AND TWENTIETH-CENTURY REACTIONS FROM HISTORIANS

Annotations in this section concern the speculative philosophies of history and the nineteenth- and twentieth-century reactions to them by professional historians and others.

History emerged from the matrix of philosophy, as did all specialized branches of knowledge. When history came to be differentiated from philosophy, philosophers could and did consider it among their taks to bring together the results of the various specialized fields of knowledge including history, to relate them to the rest of philosophy, and to reflect upon the whole of history. In recent times this task has come to be referred to as the speculative philosophy of history. Baldly put, it is an interpretation of history that, based on consideration of man's past, offers a dynamic concept or concepts as sufficient to explain the ultimate direction of historical change at every point in the historical process. Although not demanded by logic, since pluralistic theories were conceivable, the great majority of speculative philosophers of history were monistic in an almost exclusive espousal of a single dynamic factor. These philosophers wished to account for the dy-

namics of history—how and why events in history take place. Accepting the law or principle as paramount, then, meant that historical inevitability—that events *must* occur as they do—was a con-
sequence.

Since modern philosophies of history are often referred to as
"analytical" or "critical," an invidious inference may be drawn.
The so-called speculative philosophies were neither more nor less
speculative in the sense of being uncritical than the then current
philosophical views on other topics.

There are several excellent readers containing selections from
the speculative philosophers in history. Those edited by Gardiner
(E24), Nash (E31), and Tillinghast (E36) supply a convenient,
relatively expeditious way to start to find one's path in this enormous literature. These readings are excerpts from the classical historical statements. Since they make access easy to the volumes
from which they were drawn, no detailed citation and annotation
are provided to these sources. Another category of annotations is
that of considerations by nineteenth- and early-twentieth-century
historians of the earlier speculative theories and their modern
counterparts.

Papers from Meyerhoff (D10) examine "The Heritage of Historicism," from the period after speculative philosophy had been
on the wane but still had its effect; so too do some of those in
Gardiner (E24) from the same temporal period, under the heading
"The Nature of Historical Knowledge." Still later reactions, primarily from the thirties, forties, and fifties, are also included.

This section is distinguished from the others by the fact that
it is retrospective, that is, it looks back upon earlier historiography.
The section that precedes and those that follow it, while they may
refer to earlier work, attempt to present contemporary views.

Antoni, C. *From history to sociology*. (D115)

E20   Berlin, I. *Historical inevitability*. London: Oxford Uni-
       versity Press, 1954.
              A critique of historical inevitability as the basis for
       the dynamics of history as espoused in various ways by
       Hegel, Marx, Spengler, and Toynbee. Historical inevitability
       is fallacious, not because determinism is a fallacy, which it
       is not, but because its application in history is impossible.

E21   Berlin, I. *The hedgehog and the fox: An essay on Tolstoy's
       views of history*. New York: Simon & Schuster, 1957.

Boas, G. D. *Dominant themes of modern philosophy.* (B104)

E22   Bober, M. M. *Karl Marx's interpretation of history.* (2nd ed.) New York: Norton, 1965. (1927)
 A critical but not unsympathetic treatment by a non-Marxian.

E23   Collingwood, R. G. *The idea of history.* New York: Oxford University Press, 1946.
 To show how the idea of history developed, the author considers Bacon, Bergson, Croce, Dilthey, Fichte, Hegel, Herder, Kant, Marx, Vico, and Voltaire against the perspective of his particular approach to history, which is an emphasis upon the task of understanding through imagination and reenactment in order to write the narrative properly. While history is concerned with mind and the science of thought, he takes the rather idiosyncratic position that psychology is not the base from which to work, because as a field it is a science of feeling, not of thought.

Danto, A. C. *Analytical philosophy of history.* (E4)

Freud, S. Moses and Monotheism. (D90)

E24   Gardiner, P. (Ed.), *Theories of history.* Glencoe, Ill.: Free Press, 1959.
 The grand design of history is represented by excerpts from the writings of Vico, Kant, Herder, Hegel, Comte, Marx, Plekhanov, Tolstoy, Spengler, and Toynbee. These are followed by a section devoted to exploration of the "nature of historical knowledge" through papers by Dilthey, Croce, Mannheim, and Collingwood. The third section is given over to recent critiques of classical theories of history, with papers by Popper, Russell, Walsh, Berlin, and Blake, and with a debate between Geyle and Toynbee. Still another major topic in this volume is the diversity of interpretation of explanation, causal theories, and laws, with papers by Hempel, "The function of general laws in history,"—also included in his cited book (E93)—another by Morton White, "Historical explanation," and still others by J. W. N. Watkins, E. Nagel, W. B. Gallie, W. Dray, C. Frankl, A. Donagan, and M. Scriven (E101).

Gottschalk, L. *Understanding history.* (C5)

E25   Hook, S. *The hero in history: A study in limitation and possibility.* Boston: Beacon Press, 1955. (1943)

E26   Hook, S. *From Hegel to Marx: Studies in the intellectual development of Karl Marx.* Ann Arbor, Mich.: University of Michigan Press, 1962. (1936)

E27   James, W. *The will to believe and other essays in popular philosophy.* New York: Longmans, Green, 1897. (Reprinted 1956)

As might be expected, William James was on the side of the individual. His two essays on great men are reprinted in this volume.

E28   Mandelbaum, M. *The problem of historical knowledge: An answer to relativism.* New York: Liveright, 1938.

The author contrasts the relativistic views of history expressed by Croce, Dilthey, and Mannheim with the counterrelativist views of Simmel, Rickert, Scheler, and Troeltsch and, since the views of the latter are considered inadequate, develops his own position with a general methodological analysis of the materials of historical understanding. His thesis is that the presuppositions of the relativism of Croce, Dilthey, and Mannheim can and are countered by a more objective view of history found in the correspondence theory of truth. He also offers an important critique of the speculative philosophies of history and devotes two chapters to problems of explanation.

E29   Manuel, F. E. *Shapes of philosophical history.* Stanford, Calif.: Stanford University Press, 1965.

Manuel sees two modes of historical perception—the cyclical and the progressive. He proceeds in three lectures to take soundings of these intertwining views through the Ancient and patristic periods and the Renaissance, before arriving at four lectures concerned with the modern period where, of the *Contributors,* Comte, Condorcet, Hegel, Herder, Kant, Lessing, and Marx receive major attention. Other individuals made central are Christopher Dawson, Reinhold Niebuhr, Pitirim Sorokin, Henri de Saint-Simon, Oswald Spengler, and Arnold Toynbee.

E30   Mazlish, B. *The riddle of history: The great speculators from Vico to Freud.* New York: Harper & Row, 1966.

      An account of the systems of history from today's perspective for a number of philosophers whose lives fell in the interval between the time of Vico and that of Freud. He also considers Voltaire, Condorcet, Kant, Hegel, Comte, Marx, Spengler, and Toynbee. Relatively consistent themes, such as progress, religion, and scientific method, are considered for each.

Meyerhoff, H. (Ed.), *The philosophy of history in our time.* (D10)

E31   Nash, R. H. *Ideas of history.* (2 vols.) New York: Dutton, 1969.

      The first volume includes excerpts from St. Augustine, Vico, Kant, Herder, Hegel, Marx and Engels, Spengler, Toynbee, and Niebuhr. The author concludes with two papers critical of the speculative philosophies by Mandelbaum and D'Arcy. The second volume includes selections from the nineteenth and early twentieth century, with reactions to earlier speculative views represented by papers by Dilthey, Croce, and Collingwood. Other papers are admirably selected to bring out the difference between positivism as represented by papers by Comte, Buckle, and Mill, and idealism as represented by papers by Dilthey, Croce, and Collingwood. Several papers on explanation are reprinted, including ones by Hempel, Dray, and Mandelbaum.

E32   Nisbet, R. A. *Social change and history: Aspects of the Western theory of development.* New York: Oxford University Press, 1969.

      Social change expressed throughout historic times in the metaphor of organic growth is used by Nisbet as a sociologist's view of the "dynamics" of change, closing with a chapter devoted to the issues, abuses, and irrelevances of the metaphor, these last indicated by its degree of abstractness. The more concrete and behavioral the subject matter, the less the applicability of the metaphor. From the Greek period Aristotle dominates the discussion, for the Patristic it is Augustine, and for the modern, from among the *Contributors,* Comte, Condorcet, Darwin, Durkheim, Hegel, Hume, Kant, Leibniz, Marx, Smith, Spencer, Tylor, and Max Weber, and for others only Fontenelle, Lowie, Niebuhr, Spengler, Teggart, and Toynbee receive comparable attention.

E33   Popper, K. R. *The open society and its enemies.* (4th ed.) Vol. 2. *The high tide of prophecy: Hegel, Marx and the aftermath.* New York: Harper & Row, 1963. (1945)
         In Popper's sense of the term, historicism is a view that conceives the history of human society as predetermined and inevitable. If this proposition be accepted, then it follows that prophecy is possible. The fallacy of prophecy is the enemy against which the author arrays his scholarly armamentarium. Hegel and Marx are the principle individual targets, along with Toynbee more or less incidentally. In the course of this argument he faces the issues of methodological individualism, which he accepts, but he argues that this is not also psychologism, because psychological explanation cannot account for unintended consequences of the individual.

E34   Popper, K. R. *The poverty of historicism.* (3rd ed.) London: Routledge & Kegan Paul, 1961. (1957) (Reprinted 1964)
         This essay is directed primarily against the fallacious use of history for the sake of prophecy, i.e., telling of events we cannot prevent from occurring while accepting prediction in the sense that one can arrive at the steps to achieve a result. The author disagrees with the theories of Marx and others that history is prophetic in the sense that what happens is inevitable. The role of explanation as related to prediction and to prophecy is distinguished. He does not agree that history and the social sciences are qualitatively different from the natural sciences and argues that they, too, are subject to methodological naturalism, i.e., the scientific method.

E35   Stern, F. (Ed.), *The varieties of history: From Voltaire to the present.* New York: Meridian Books, 1956.
         This is the best of the "readers" surveying the literature on historians of the nineteenth and early twentieth century. While there is some overlap with speculative philosophy, in the main it covers the period when the pro-

fessional historians reacted against the speculative philosophies. Von Ranke, Macaulay, Michelet, Buckle, Mommsen, Turner, and Bury, to name but a few whose works are represented, restated the nature and aims of history. There are also papers by historians writing after the turn of the century, when history had come into its own as an academic subject in the United States—Lord Acton in England, Robinson and Beard in the United States, and Meinecke in Germany, along with the still younger Hofstadter and Barzun.

E36 Tillinghast, P. E. (Ed.), *Approaches to history: Selections in philosophy of history from the Greeks to Hegel.* Englewood Cliffs, N.J.: Prentice-Hall, 1963.

Tillinghast confines himself to selections from speculative writings—works from the Greeks, the Bible, St. Augustine, Bodin, Vico, Herder, and Hegel. With the exception of the last two or three, they are not typically represented in books of readings.

Walsh, W. H. *Philosophy of history.* (E19a)

CONTEMPORARY PLURALISTIC EMPHASES ON THE DYNAMICS OF HISTORICAL CHANGE

That which makes for change in history characterizes the papers and books in this section. There is the issue not only of the general nature of the dynamics of change, but also such related problems as whether change is evolutionary or revolutionary (also expressed as continuity/discontinuity); the issue of conceptual versus ideational change; the influence of paradigms, theories, and attitudes in relation to change; the importance of objectivity in relation to change; social and individual influences upon change (also expressed as the *Zeitgeist* and "Great Man" theories); the relation of the tradition of the "Received Opinion" traceable both to logical positivism and to these newer views; conditions encouraging or discouraging scientific discovery and change, including controversy and dogma; and the application of various points of view to fields other than that originally proposed, for example, Kuhnian conceptions applied to psychology and the social sciences.

One indication that dynamics is a central problem of historiography is the relatively large number of citations that follow. Another is the extent to which the problem of dynamics permeates other sections of the *Guide*. The two earlier sections devoted to theory are pertinent. It has already been indicated that each of the speculative theories of history lifted a source of progression and change to the level of *the* dynamic factor. Now pluralistic approaches predominate. By and large, contemporary emphasis is not upon something thought of as *the* dynamic factor. A theoretician may argue that one particular dynamic factor far outweighs all others. He may even argue that one can minimize, and even, under certain circumstances, ignore these other factors, but he does not deny their existence.

The last section, "Explanation and Related Problems," is pertinent to the question of dynamics. These papers, however, concern the logic and psychology of dynamics without necessarily singling out just what it is that is dynamic, while in the present section substantive events of history are specified as dynamic. But this by no means exhausts the problem categories of this *Guide*, which bear an intimate relation to the topic of dynamics. The very field of intellectual history is dedicated to the proposition that ideas are dynamic. It is characteristic of the literature of the fields of psychoanalysis and psychohistory that it is simultaneously an account of the dynamics supposed to be involved. The literature on methodological individualism bears obvious relation to the plea for the importance of the individual as dynamic in history. Some of the references from these sections of the *Guide* are cited again here; many others are not.

Agassi, J. Towards an historiography of science. (D47)

E37   Agassi, J. Continuity and discontinuity in the history of science. *J. hist. Ideas,* 1973, *34,* 609-626.

Whether historical change proceeds gradually by small steps or abruptly by turning points (revolutions) is the paper's theme. As might be expected from their chronologically earlier considerations of the topic, Duhem, Koyré, and Kuhn are the crucial theorists.

E38   Barber, B. *Science and the social order.* Glencoe, Ill.: Free Press, 1952.

This volume on the sociology of science includes a chapter on social influences on the history of science and several chapters on the scientist in American society and on the role of the individual and society in social discovery.

E39 Barbu, Z. *Problems of historical psychology.* New York: Grove Press, 1960.

The interaction of the individual with social events at particular historical periods is the theme. The author objects to views that would regard personality as fixed for all men in all societies at all times and argues, for example, that the perceptual field of the individual is different at different historical periods. He takes exemplifying soundings in Ancient Greece and in the origins of English character from the sixteenth century onward. His intellectual debt to L. Febvre, among historians, is acknowledged and profound.

Berkhofer, R. F. *A behavioral approach to historical analysis.* (D117)

E40 Bloor, D. Two paradigms for scientific knowledge. *Sci. Stud.,* 1971, *1,* 101-115.

A critique of Lakatos and Musgrave's *Criticism and the Growth of Knowledge* (E66), organized successively around the themes of a confrontation between the Popperian and Kuhnian positions, objections to Kuhn's views, Lakatos and the charge of irrationality, Kuhn's reply to his critics, and science and the irrational.

Boring, E. G. *Psychologist at large.* (E1)

Boring, E. G. *History, psychology and science.* (E2)

E41 Boring, E. G. Discussion. *Int. J. Psychiat.,* 1966, *2,* 357-361.

E42 Buchdahl, G. A revolution in historiography of science. *Hist. Sci.,* 1965, *4,* 55-69.

In this review of Kuhn's *Structure* (E60) and Agassi's *Historiography* (D47) Buchdahl captures very well, among others, the point that the authors of both volumes argue that it is impossible to isolate opinions concerning scientific knowledge from the question of validity of ideas. Although his criticisms are sharp and will create a sympa-

thetic resonance in many readers, he agrees with the two
of them that the history of science needs a "total re-evalu-
ation"—"a revolution in the history of science."

E43   Burgess, I. S. Psychology and Kuhn's concept of paradigm.
       J. behav. Sci., 1972, *1,* 193-200.
           Burgess reviews some of the literature concerning the
       application to psychology of Kuhn's concept of paradigm.
       On several occasions it has been used inappropriately, as
       he illustrates. He suggests that Masterman's modification
       in the form of the concept of the multiple paradigm is rele-
       vant for psychology.

E44   Chalmers, A. F. On learning from our mistakes. *Brit. J.
       phil. Sci.,* 1973, *24,* 164-173.
           The question at issue is whether or not the use of
       "bold" as opposed to "cautious" conjectures, as advocated
       by Popper, is effective when applied to actual historical
       events. In the historical events chosen as his illustrations,
       bold conjectures were not found to be particularly infor-
       mative.

E45   Cohen, L. J. Is the progress of science evolutionary? (Re-
       view) *Brit. J. phil. Sci.,* 1973, *24,* 41-61.
           Cohen's essay review is devoted to the first volume of
       Toulmin's trilogy (E18). He argues that there are several
       "severe flaws" in it, which he proceeds to spell out.

       Crombie, A. C. *Scientific change.* (E3)

       Curti, M. *Human nature in American historical thought.*
       (D4)

       Feigl, H. Empiricism at bay? (E6)

       Feyerabend, P. K. Problems of empiricism. (E7)

E46   Fuchs, A. H., & Kawash, G. F. Prescriptive dimensions for
       five schools of psychology. *J. Hist. behav. Sci.,* 1974, *10,*
       352-366.
           In this research study an inquiry was made into the
       patterns of Watsonian prescriptions (E75) held by various
       schools of psychology. A seven-point rating scale of degrees

of adherence was rated by knowledgeable psychologists for each school, and average ratings found. The pattern of ratings for psychoanalysis showed unique positive adherence to developmentalism, dynamicism, idiographicism, irrationalism, and unconscious mentalism, while sharing with some of the other schools positive emphasis on centralism, contentual subjectivism, and determinism. Each school showed relatively consistent adherence, rejection, and indifference or neutrality toward certain prescriptive attitudes that could be said to characterize the school.

Gottschalk, L. *Understanding history.* (C5)

E47   Greene, J. C. The Kuhnian paradigm and the Darwinian revolution in natural history. In D. H. D. Roller (Ed.), *Perspectives in the history of science and technology.* Norman, Okla.: University of Oklahoma Press, 1972, pp. 3-25.

    Greene attempts to apply Kuhnian theory to natural history and particularly to evolutionary theory. His excursion, he concludes, shows that the Kuhnian paradigm of paradigms can be made to fit certain aspects, but its overall adequacy is doubtful.

Gustavson, C. S. *A preface to history.* (E9)

E48   Hempel, C. G. On the 'standard conception' of scientific theories. In M. Radner & S. Winokur (Eds.), *Minnesota studies in the philosophy of science.* Vol. IV. Minneapolis, Minn.: University of Minnesota Press, 1970, pp. 142-163.

    A response by one of the stalwarts of the "Received Opinion" or, as he prefers to call it, the "standard conception," taking into account recent criticisms. A summary-abstract of this paper is contained in Suppe (E17).

E49   Henle, Mary. On controversy and its resolution. In Mary Henle, et al. (Eds.), *Historical conceptions of psychology.* New York: Springer, 1973, pp. 47-59.

    Typically, conflicts are not resolved, they are, instead, superseded. This thesis is illustrated by a variety of historical examples drawn from psychology.

E50   Hollinger, D. A. T. S. Kuhn's theory of science and its implications for history. *Amer. hist. Rev.,* 1973, *78,* 370-393.

This is a wide-ranging review of Kuhnian theory, with probably the best selected and yet general bibliography extant because of the wide scope of this topic—history. Moreover, Hollinger wishes to report and evaluate the literature and not use the topic as a convenient entree for presenting his own views.

E51   Holton, G. *Thematic origins of scientific thought: Kepler to Einstein.* Cambridge: Harvard University Press, 1973.

Holton distinguishes three uses of the concept of "thematic," but for the sake of brevity we mention here only *methodological thematic tendencies,* or the preferences that guide the scientist in matters such as seeking constancies or seeking extremes in stating laws of physics, and *thematic propositions,* or the thematic component of hypotheses, including symmetry, simplicity, mechanism, quantification, and order. Sometimes the latter are expressed as dyads, e.g., activity-passivity. The historical examples Holton uses most often draw upon the work of Einstein and almost completely depend upon the history of physics, so, for this *Guide,* the volume is unsuitable as a historical account. For the historian of the behavioral sciences, it may be valuable because of the possible extension of Holton's approach to dynamics to his particular area of interest.

E52   Hook, S. Dialectic in society and history. (1951) In H. Feigl & May Brodbeck (Eds.), *Readings in the philosophy of science.* New York: Appleton-Century-Crofts, 1953, pp. 701-713.

A clear summarization is offered as to why dialectic is so infected with ambiguity as to be useless as a concept either for a pattern of change or as a method of approach.

E53   Hull, D. L. A populational approach to scientific change. *Science,* 1973, *182,* 1121-1124.

This is an essay review of Toulmin's *Human Understanding* (E18), with an emphasis on his interpretation of scientific change.

E54   Kamenka, E. Marxism and the history of philosophy. In J. Passmore (Ed.), The historiography of the history of

philosophy. *Hist. Theory,* 1964-1965, *4,* Suppl. 5, pp. 83-104.
A summary of relatively recent work.

E55   Kawash, G., & Fuchs, A. H. A factor analysis of ratings of five schools of psychology on prescriptive dimensions. *J. Hist. behav. Sci.,* 1974, *10,* 426-437.
Commonalities and uniqueness of ratings of schools of psychology in an earlier study (E46), which applied Watson's prescriptive attitudes to characterize the schools, suggested that a factor analysis would be fruitful. When carried out, seven factors emerged. Factor scores were then used to compare the schools. Characterizations by factor were not only shown to be similar to those obtained by ratings but also to permit a more parsimonious explanation. Psychoanalysis, the illustration used for the earlier study, again showed a strong emphasis on dynamics and a commitment to understanding the individual (idiographician), but the factor analysis also brought out a commitment to dualism that was not apparent before.

Keniston, K. Psychological development and historical change. (D23)

E56   Knorr, Karen D., et al. (Eds.), *Determinants and controls of scientific development.* Dordrecht: Reidel, 1975.
This volume eventuates from an international conference held on the topic of the title and participated in by sociologists of science, philosophers, psychologists, and others. The three major groups of papers are titled "After the Kuhnian Revolution: New Trends in Metascience," "Cognition and Communication in Science Development," and "Societal Components in Scientific Development." The question of the presuppositions involved in the growth and development of science and the debate on external-internal determinants of change are considered to be two major problems by the editors. It is especially recommended as a many-faceted statement of the reactions of sociologists of science to the problem of dynamics in scientific development. Especially pertinent to the dynamics of history are the articles by Böhme, Capaldi, Harré, Knorr, Machan, Mullins, Silverman, Watson (E76), and Whitly. The think-

ing of Feyerabend, Harré, Kuhn, Merton, Popper, and Toulmin receive considerable attention.

E57   Koht, H. *Driving forces in history*. Trans. E. Haugen. Cambridge: Harvard University Press, 1964. (1959)

After a discussion of what it is that changes in history and of the nature of causes in history, the author considers social forces as exhibited in historical settings or, more specifically, religious cooperation, economic class consciousness, revolt, war, science, and internationalism.

Koyré, A. *From the closed world to the infinite universe*. (B90)

E58   Koyré, A. *Metaphysics and measurement: Essays in the scientific revolution*. Trans. R. E. W. Maddison. Cambridge: Harvard University Press, 1968.

These six papers include consideration of the scientific work of Galileo, Gassendi, Mersenne, Pascal, and others, and the volume was, therefore, appropriate for inclusion among titles devoted to the history of science. However, the emphasis on the influence of the metaphysical presuppositions of the scientist such that they dominated over the experimental component makes it even more appropriate for inclusion among titles devoted to theory, with a re-citation in substantive history.

E59   Kracauer, S. Time and history. In M. Horkheimer (Ed.), *Zeugnisse Theodor W. Adorno zum sechzigsten Geburtstag*. Frankfurt: Europaischer Verlag, 1963, pp. 50-64.

A critique of the *Zeitgeist* point of view.

Krantz, D. L. Toward a role for historical analysis. (D24)

E60   Kuhn, T. H. *The structure of scientific revolutions*. (2nd ed. enlarged) Chicago: University of Chicago Press, 1970. (1962)

With verve and abundant illustrations drawn particularly from the early history of physics, Kuhn sketches the history of the stages of scientific change. Under the guidance of a more-or-less commonly accepted set of assumptions, scientists go about the task of filling out details by solving the detailed problems called for by the paradigm, until some anomaly is found that cannot be made to fit with that paradigm. A revolution takes place in that a new paradigm emerges, e.g., the Copernican paradigm replaces the Ptolemaic. There are, then, two kinds of change, normal and revolutionary. This is the second edition, with the original text unchanged but with a postscript added in which changes in his thinking are outlined, particularly the assignment of a considerable role to the notion of a scientific community, as distinguished from the concept of paradigm. Kuhn's modifications and retrenchments in his "Postscript" have considerably weakened the element of conceptual change. It may be necessary to start referring to Kuhn by a system of subscripts—Kuhn_1, Kuhn_2.

E61   Kuhn, T. S. The function of dogma in scientific research. In A. C. Crombie (Ed.), *Scientific change,* pp. 347-369. (E3)

A prevailing paradigm, which serves as the author's dogma, tells the scientist with what problems he is dealing and how to deal with them procedurally. He strives to bring the paradigm in closer agreement with nature. Since he has confidence in it, he works within it on the smaller puzzles still remaining. He is told where to look for research, and since he knows what to expect from his research he is alerted to discriminate essential anomaly from mere failure. His paper is followed by critical discussions by A. R. Hall, M. Polanyi, B. Glass, S. E. Toulmin, and E. F. Caldin with a reply by Kuhn.

E62   Kuhn, T. S. Second thoughts on paradigms. In F. Suppe (Ed.), *The structure of scientific theories,* pp. 459-482. (E17)

A statement made in 1969 and related to his other responses to comment and criticism, with special emphasis upon the chapter's titular topic.

E63   Kuhn, T. S. Notes on Lakatos. In R. C. Buck & R. S. Cohen (Eds.), *Boston studies in the philosophy of science.* Vol. 8. Dordrecht: Reidel, 1970, pp. 136-146.

In his comments on the paper by Lakatos (E64), Kuhn remarks that he is pleasantly surprised to find it in many ways showing parallels with his own thinking. He agrees that scientists operate with preconceptions and that, instead of a choice between theories, there is a choice, as Lakatos puts it, between scientific research programs and comments on the similarity of Lakatos' "degenerating state" and his "crisis." On Lakatos' charge of his alleged irrationality he disagrees, as he does on Lakatos' version of the internal-external and his over-all conception of the history of science.

E64   Lakatos, I. History of science and its rational reconstruction. In R. C. Buck & R. S. Cohen (Eds.), *Boston studies in the philosophy of science.* Vol. 8. Dordrecht: Reidel, 1970, pp. 91-136.

The gist of the author's position is that the philosophies of science provide normative methodologies through which historians can reconstruct the "internal" history of science, which, it follows, is rational, that competing methodology can be equated with a normatively interpreted history, and that this rational reconstruction needs to be supplemented by an empirical external history. In the course of developing these themes, he discusses matters such as deductivism, conventionalism, and methodological falsification. Popper, Kuhn, and Durkheim are the principal sources of comparison and contrast with his views.

E65   Lakatos, I. The role of crucial experiments in science. *Stud. Hist. phil. Sci.,* 1973, *4,* 309-325.

Lakatos differentiates three solutions to the generalized demarcation problem—an attempt to offer a universal demarcation criterion, as do the falsificationists and probabilists, or by methodology of research programs, a position that he associates with Leibniz, Carnap, Popper, and himself; an admission that there is no universal criterion, although one may agree that one anomaly is more conclusive than another by virtue of the authority making the claim, the view of Polanyi and Kuhn; or the view that there are only competing beliefs, none epistemically superior one to another, the recent Feyerabend view.

E66   Lakatos, I., & Musgrave, A. (Eds.), *Criticism and the growth of knowledge.* London: Cambridge University Press, 1970.

This is a very important contemporary collection of essays directed to a contrast between the Kuhnian and Popperian theories of the dynamics of the history of science. Kuhn presents a comparison of his point of view concerning the philosophy of science to that of Popper, contrasting the logic of discovery with the psychology of research. Masterman, in an important paper, examines the nature of a paradigm, finding 22 different uses, and includes a section pertinent to the behavioral scientist on nonparadigmatic science. Watkins and Feyerabend, too, respond primarily to Kuhn, among other points attacking his idea of normal science. Popper, himself, reiterates his theory of conjectures and refutations, and Lakatos elaborates Popper's philosophy of science. Toulmin presents his evolutionary theory of scientific development, in which scientific "revolution" would no longer be an explanatory concept but merely a descriptive label.

E67   McEvoy, J. G. A 'revolutionary' philosophy of science: Feyerabend and the degeneration of critical rationalism into sceptical fallibilism. *Phil. Sci.,* 1975, *42,* 49-66.

In common with Hanson and Kuhn, Feyerabend is seen as reacting against positivism in the direction of defending the position that in scientific investigation pervasive presuppositions are fundamental. The intent of the paper is to trace how Feyerabend moved from the empiricism of critical rationalism of his earlier Popperian phase to the subjective relativism of sceptical fallibilism. A bibliography of Feyerabend's work is provided.

E68   Merton, R. K. Priorities in scientific discovery: A chapter in the sociology of science. *Amer. Soc. Rev.,* 1957, *22,* 635-659. Reprinted in B. Barber & W. Hirsch (Eds.), *The sociology of science.* New York: Free Press, 1962, pp. 447-485.

Conflicts over priority in science occur because science in our society places a high value on originality. Deviant behavior, self-assertive behavior, secretiveness, plagiarism, charges of plagiarism, and the like arise because of the enormous discrepancy between this emphasis and the problems encountered by scientists in achieving originality.

Mora, G. The history of psychiatry: A cultural and bibliographic survey. (D82)

E69   Musgrave, A. E. Kuhn's second thoughts. *Brit. J. phil. Sci.*,
1971, *22*, 287-297.

This paper reviews the 36-page "Postscript" added to
Kuhn's original 1962 text in the 1970 second edition (E60)
and centers on the two issues of paradigms as the basis of
scientific research and of scientific communities as the unit
responsible for paradigm-based research. In Musgrave's view,
the concept of the community does much to clear up some
of the challenging (and innovative) interpretations that have
arisen, but it leaves him a little disappointed that the "more
real Kuhn who emerges in it is but a pale reflection of the
old, revolutionary Kuhn."

Nevins, A. *The gateway to history.* (C7)

Popper, K. R. *Conjectures and refutations.* (E13)

Popper, K. R. *The logic of scientific discovery.* (E14)

Reigel, K. F. *History as nomothetic science.* (D32)

E70   Scheffler, I. *Science and subjectivity.* Indianapolis, Ind.:
Bobbs-Merrill, 1967.

Objectivity, as the author points out, is relevant to
all statements that appeal to evidence. Science is the field
that institutionalized objectivity in the most systematic
and explicit manner, and he wishes to examine in detail
the threat he sees as existing in current subjectivism. It is
his consideration of change that makes this book most directly relevant to the question of dynamics. Objectivity
does not demand fixed, immutable descriptions. As he
points out, there may be changes in category systems, in
laws, in meaning, in theories, and in paradigm shifts. Kuhn
is considered in connection with the latter, while Neurath's
appeal to protocol sentences and the rejection of subjectivity in all forms is central to the discussion of the epistemology of objectivity.

Schilpp, P. A. (Ed.), *The philosophy of Karl Popper.* (E16)

E71   Shapere, D. The structure of scientific revolutions. *Phil.
Rev.*, 1964, *73*, 383-394.

This is an important critique of Kuhn's position, especially of his concept of the paradigm.

Suppe, F. (Ed.), *The structure of scientific theories.* (E17)

E72   Taylor, C. *Explanation of behavior.* London: Routledge & Kegan Paul, 1964.
Taking the unusual step of combining the approaches of the philosopher of mind with an examination of the evidence of the psychologist, Taylor examines explanation by purpose and the relation of relevant theory and fact in learning and motivation. He concludes by favoring an explanation in terms of purpose.

E73   Toulmin, S. E. The evolutionary development of natural science. *Amer. Scientist,* 1967, *55,* 456-471.
Since this is an article organized around the theme of the title, it presents in short compass Toulmin's position concerning scientific development—that the ideas transmitted from one historical cross section to the next are neither a revolution nor a replication, they are evolutionary similarities from the past modified by selected novelties.

E74   Toulmin, S. Conceptual revolutions in science. *Synthese,* 1967, *17,* 75-91   Reprinted in R. S. Cohen & M. W. Wartofsky (Eds.), *Boston studies in the philosophy of science.* Vol. 3. New York: Humanities Press, 1967, pp. 331-347.
A statement of the author's view that conceptual choices in science have a dynamic role, with the thinking of Collingwood and of Kuhn to place his view in perspective.

Toulmin, S. *Human understanding.* Vol. 1. (E18)

Walsh, W. H. *Philosophy of history.* (E19a)

E75   Watson, R. I. Psychology: A prescriptive science. *Amer. Psychologist,* 1967, *22,* 435-443.
This is a pioneer paper on the part of a psychologist reacting to Kuhn. He accepted one of his definitions of a paradigm—a universally accepted contentual model that

guides practitioners of a science. Since psychology does not have this model, shown by lack of agreement about fundamentals and pronounced national differences, he argues that, as a preparadigmatic science, psychology was guided by a complex of attitudes that carry out some of the functions of a paradigm, although differing patterns exist at different temporal points. Illustrative of the ways in which these prescriptions are utilized conceptually on the contemporary scene in psychology, nomotheticism is seen as dominant, idiographicism as viable and counter-dominant, monism as once very explicit but now implicit.

E76   Watson, R. I., Sr., Prescriptive theory and the social sciences. In Karen D. Knorr, et al. (Eds.), *Determinants and controls of scientific development,* pp. 11-35. (E56)

It is maintained that the social sciences lack para-digms, and that it would be worthwhile to consider whether the guidance of specified prescriptive attitudes does not serve a preparadigmatic guidance function for them, as he has already attempted to demonstrate is the case in psy-chology. Prescriptions are units of change and a cause of change and in this sense they are motivational. To place attitudes in a context of role theory is an additional step taken. This theme is developed and its implications ex-plained with exemplification from the social sciences. Part paradigms, embracing limited areas of a preparadigmatic science, are acknowledged. Three other papers on prescrip-tive theory, other than (E75), are to be found in the references.

E77   Weimer, W. B. The history of psychology and its retrieval from historiography. I. The problematic nature of history. II. Some lessons for the methodology of scientific research. *Sci. Stud.,* 1974, *4,* 235-258, 367-396.

In the pages of this journal, since its inaugural year of 1971, a number of articles have made their appearance, concerned with whether psychology is paradigmatic, pre-paradigmatic, or nonparadigmatic, in one or another of the Kuhnian senses. The first footnote in these particular papers cites the four most important, those by Briskman (1972), Palmero (1971), Warren (1971), and Weimer and Palermo (1973). The present paper goes beyond this some-what limited Kuhnian focus and considers psychology in the light, not only of Kuhn's contentions, but also of those of Lakatos, Polanyi, Popper, Boring, and Blumenthal.

E78   Zollschan, G. K., & Hirsch, W. (Eds.), *Explorations in social change*. New York: Houghton Mifflin, 1964.

The exposition of the theory of social change (as differentiated from social structure) in a variety of forms gives consistency to this volume. Unfamiliar as the historian is apt to be with this burgeoning problem of sociology, this volume supplies him with a starting point in understanding how the sociologist views the dynamics of change. There are sections of papers on social change, on the theory of institutionalization, on social system, and on psychosocial models of change, historical perspective change, cultural contact and social movements, and special areas (e.g., innovation, trade union, American society). From among the *Contributors* only Comte, Durkheim, Freud, Marx, Smith, Spencer, and M. Weber receive more than passing mention.

METHODOLOGICAL INDIVIDUALISM-HOLISM AND PSYCHOLOGISM AS PROBLEMS IN DYNAMICS

The significance of the individual for the dynamics of history may be seen as falling along a continuum: from one extreme that considers all social behavior, including history, to be reducible without remainder to the behavior of individuals, to the position of Durkheim that, if a social explanation is offered in terms of the individual, you can be certain that it is wrong. A middle position on methodological individualism calls for reduction but with a remainder attributable to social factors. Positions toward the social extreme are variously referred to as methodological holism, collectivism, or communism.

Methodological individualism is closely related to psychologism, a narrower form of the same doctrine. The claim of the latter, stated baldly, is that the phenomena and laws of social science are ultimately reducible to *psychological* principles. Most often this point of view is rejected in the social sciences, even by those who hold to methodological individualism, since, to use Popper's term, institutional individualism is possible.

That there is a historical relation between the "Great Man" theories and methodological individualism, and between *Zeitgeist* theories and methodological holism, should be obvious, but contemporary views do not necessarily commit one to either of them.

Type theory, used in exploring the collective characteristics of individuals, is also represented by references in this section.

E79   Agassi, J. Methodological individualism. *British J. Sociol.*, 1960, *11*, 244-270.

The author summarizes his position—individualism need not be psychologistic—in his first sentence and then proceeds to defend Popper's institutionalistic individualism.

E80   Brodbeck, May. Methodological individualisms: Definition and reduction. *Phil. Sci.*, 1958, *25*, 1-22. Reprinted in W. H. Dray, (Ed.), *Philosophical analysis and history*, pp. 297-329. (E5)

As Brodbeck sees it, there are two intertwined issues in the controversy—one, the nature of the terms or concepts in social science or the issue of meaning, and the other, the nature of its laws or theories or the issue of reduction. She considers psychology, if not psychologism, in her account of the reduction process. In the course of her argument, she replies to Watkins (E88).

E81   Brodbeck, May. On the philosophy of the social sciences. *Phil. Sci.*, 1954, *21*, 140-156.

A critique of the positive position of Hayek on methodological individualism.

Danto, A. C. *Analytical philosophy of history.* (E4)

Garraty, J. A. The interrelations of psychology and biography. (C10)

Garraty, J. A. *The nature of biography.* (C11)

E82   Goldstein, L. J. The inadequacy of the principle of methodological individualism. *J. Phil.*, 1956, *53*, 801-813.

Problems in the social sciences, which require solution not amenable to individualistic analysis, are given, after spelling out a theory of methodological collectivism set in an anthropological framework.

E83   Hayek, F. A. *The counter-revolution of science.* Glencoe,
       Ill.: Free Press, 1952.
           Hayek combines a spirited defence of methodological
       individualism and a rejection of holism with a subjectivist
       view of the nature of psychology, although the term itself
       is avoided. The social sciences deal not with collective
       wholes but constitute these wholes by constructing models.

       Hempel, C. G. *Aspects of scientific explanation.* (E93)

E84   Lukes, S. Methodological individualism reconsidered. *Brit.
       J. Sociol.,* 1968, *19,* 119-129.
           A closely reasoned critique of the various guises
       under which methodological individualism has been pre-
       sented and an attempt at clarification.

E85   Mandelbaum, M. Societal facts. (1955). Reprinted in P.
       Gardiner (Ed.), *Theories of history,* pp. 476-488. (E24)
           The author defends the thesis that societal facts are
       not reducible without remainder to the thoughts and
       actions of individuals. However, he also admits that the
       latter class of facts exists and the two classes may interact.

E86   Mandelbaum, M. Societal laws. (1957) Reprinted in W. H.
       Dray (Ed.),*Philosophical analysis and history,* pp. 330-336.
       (E5)
           While rejecting methodological individualism, the
       author wishes to think that this does not automatically
       commit one to methodological holism, a relation Popper
       and Hayak have tended to infer. One can still accept
       societal laws as well as psychological laws.

       Nagel, E. *The structure of science.* (E12)

       Popper, K. R. *The open society and its enemies.* (E33)

E87   Watkins, J. W. N. Methodological individualism: A reply.
       Phil. Sci., 1955, *22,* 58-62.
           A reply to Brodbeck (E80), in which the author
       argues that her position is that of metaphysical holism.

E88   Watkins, J. W. N. Ideal types and historical explanation.

(1952) Reprinted in H. Feigl & May Brodbeck (Eds.), *Readings in the philosophy of science.* New York: Appleton-Century-Crofts, 1953, pp. 723-743.
A radical defense of methodological individualism.

EXPLANATION AND RELATED PROBLEMS

The nature of explanation in history is central to the annotations that follow. This topic brings with it a host of other issues—what Meyerhoff has described as a syndrome—laws, generalization, causation, to mention but three major interrelated themes, with other, somewhat narrower questions arising from interrelations among them. For example, the very statement about a syndrome just made does not meet with universal agreement. Some would argue that cause must be sharply distinguished from explanation. Many other issues are discussed: the question of whether there are general laws in history, uniqueness of historical events as a bar to explanation, the relation of explanation to understanding, the so-called covering law, and explanation analysis in relation to explanation prediction and/or prophecy in explanation in history and functional explanation.

Many references appeal to logic, inductive or deductive or both, in discussing explanation in history. Now logic can and perhaps should be divorced from substantive history. Analysis of the procedures and the logic of explanation are of major concern to some accounts, not substantive explanation of facts, which is the task of the historian, the scientist, or the social scientist *per se.*

True to the aim of contemporary philosophy to leave aside substantive matters as not of concern to philosophers, these intertwined concepts are supposedly treated at the level of logic. Presumably, the interrelation of, say, cause and explanation would be expected to hold no matter what causal event or explanatory situation were substituted for the abstract terms, provided they meet the limiting dimension put upon the discussion for example, cause and explanation in the social sciences, or in history, or in whatever substantive area forms the base from which one is talking. But not all theorists who appeal to logic in history are "logical" about this issue. They cheerfully turn to substantive issues of history in their discussions, as many of the reference attest. Witness the discussion of the genetic fallacy—the confusion of historical order with logical order. Both kinds, then, are included here.

Barzun, J., & Graff, H. F. *The modern researcher.* (C1)

Berkhofer, R. F., Jr. *A behavioral approach to historical analysis.* (D117)

E89 Brodbeck, May. Explanations, predictions, and "imperfect" knowledge. In H. Feigl & G. Maxwell (Eds.), *Minnesota studies on the philosophy of science.* Vol. 3. *Scientific explanation, space, and time.* Minneapolis, Minn.: University of Minnesota Press, 1962, pp. 231-272.

The author takes the position that there is no unique historical explanation, but, rather, that there is scientific explanation of historical events. She does this in a setting of the defense of the covering law model, originally derived from the deductive model that Hempel is given credit for popularizing. Among the views she criticizes are those of Donagan and Dray.

Danto, A. C. *Analytical philosophy of history.* (E4)

E90 Donagan, A. Historical explanation: The Popper-Hempel theory reconsidered. *Hist. Theory*, 1964, *4*, 3-26. Reprinted in W. H. Dray (Ed.), *Philosophical analysis and history*, pp. 127-159. (E5)

A clear review of historical explanation as promulgated by Popper, Hempel's first statement, and Hempel's later modification (which divided explanation into deductive-nomological and inductive-probabilistic). The author then considers the various ways in which the deductive thesis was defended and the logical relation between it and the general law thesis, takes up the grounds for a strict covering law thesis in natural science, and then proceeds to argue that explanations do not satisfy the covering law thesis and offers other criticisms of their views.

Fischer, D. H. *Historians' fallacies.* (C3)

E91 Gardiner, P. L. *The nature of historical explanation.* London: Oxford University Press, 1952.

After examining "explanation" in science and common sense, Gardiner describes history as a subject matter and turns to casual connectionism in history through a discussion of ways historians explain mental causation and other aspects of explanation. In a few trenchant pages he takes much of the mystery out of the so-called uniqueness of historical events by showing that to call an event "unique" "logically presupposes prior classification," against which he is comparing the event. Unique events do not bar the historian from classifying or generalizing but call for it before judging something as unique. Croce and Popper are frequently cited.

Gardiner, P. (Ed.), *Theories of history.* (E24)

Harré, R. *The philosophies of science.* (E10)

E92   Harré, R. *The principles of scientific thinking.* Chicago: University of Chicago Press, 1970.
        After a detailed critique of Hume's philosophy of science, Harré concludes by finding it wanting since, as he sees it, the problems of induction and lawful generalities are in principle insoluble, since any solution demands more than the premises allow. He "turns Hume right side up" and states that instead of laws being explanatory, generative "mechanisms," "powers," or "dispositions" are needed to explain the laws. Hence, he supplies an unabashed metaphysics of nature.

E93   Hempel, C. G. *Aspects of scientific explanation: And other essays in the philosophy of science.* New York: Free Press, 1965.
        The title essay considers explanation as related to cause, deduction and induction, prediction and law, and especially, so far as historians are concerned, covering law and incomplete explanations, as well as law in psychoanalysis. Another essay is directed specifically to the historian, "The function of general laws in history," in which field he considers there are laws quite analogous to those in the natural sciences. Incomplete laws are again considered, and the concept of explanation sketch is depended upon heavily. Confirmation, not discovery, is the setting for the discussion.

E94   Joynt, C. G., & Rescher, N. The problem of uniqueness in history. *History & Theory,* 1961, *1*, 150-162. Reprinted in

G. H. Nadel (Ed.), *Studies in the philosophy of history: Selected essays from history and theory*. New York: Harper, 1965, pp. 3-15.

It is argued that uniqueness, *per se*, is not a bar to a mode of explanation similar to that of the social and natural sciences.

Kaplan, A. *The conduct of inquiry*. (E11)

E95   Madden, E. H. Explanation in psychoanalysis and history. *Phil. Sci.*, 1966, *33*, 278-286.

Madden considers the differences and similarities among science, history, and psychoanalysis, with a particular emphasis on various sorts of explanation used, and then advances his own view as to the nature of psychoanalytic propositions.

Mandelbaum, M. *The problem of historical knowledge*. (E28)

Nagel, E. *The structure of science*. (E12)

Nash, R. H. *Ideas of history*. Vol. 2. (E31)

E96   Newman, F. D. *Explanation by description: An essay in historical methodology*. The Hague: Mouton, 1968.

A critique of Hempel's covering-law analysis of explanation in history. The modification he suggests would retain the validity of the deductive model even if there were no historical laws.

E97   Nowell-Smith, P. H. Historical explanation. In H. E. Kiefer & M. K. Munitz (Eds.), *Mind, science and history*. Albany, N.Y.: State University of New York Press, 1970, pp. 213-233.

A challenge is offered in this paper to Hempel's covering law as exposited in his *The Function of General Laws in History*. The author then compares it to Geyl's use of explanatory narrative.

E98   Oakeshott, M. Historical continuity and causal analysis. (1933) Reprinted in W. H. Dray (Ed.), *Philosophical analysis and history*, pp. 193-212 . (E5)

The author rejects, as inadequate in history, a variety

of meanings of cause, including that found in Bury's theory of contingent events. His affirmative proposal is that change in history carries with it its own explanation—the account of the events may be so complete that no external cause is necessary. The historian presents in such sufficient detail, in what he calls the principle of unity or continuity, that anything else in the way of cause is superfluous.

E99   Passmore, J. Explanation in everyday life, in science and in history. *Hist. Theory,* 1962, *2,* 105-123. Reprinted in G. H. Nadel (Ed.), *Studies in the philosophy of history.* New York: Harper & Row, 1965, pp. 16-34.

     To understand explanation in everyday life makes it easier to understand explanation in science and in history. Kinds of explanation are developed through illustration. Then the criteria of intelligibility, adequacy, and correctness are applied to explanation in everyday life, for science and for history.

Popper, K. R. *Conjectures and refutations.* (E13)

Popper, K. R. *The logic of scientific discovery.* (E14)

Popper K. R. *The poverty of historicism.* (E34)

Schilpp, P.A. (Ed.), *The philosophy of Karl Popper.* (E16)

E100   Scriven, M. Causes, connections and conditions in history. In W. H. Dray (Ed.), *Philosophical analysis and history,* pp. 238-264 (E5)

     The author begins with an analysis of the terminology used in history to refer to cause, reminding us how frequently words other than "cause" are used. How then are we to analyze the concept of cause itself? He does so by a nonreductionist classification of types. His account of causal explanation includes criticism of Nagel and other covering-law theorists. He also indicates that empathists and *Verstehen* theorists are right in recognizing the particular adroitness of the human instrument in diagnosing human behavior.

E101   Scriven, M. Truisms as ground for historical explanation.

In P. Gardiner (Ed.), *Theories of history*, pp. 443-475. (E24)

Scriven objects to the deductive model of historical explanation advanced by Hempel, which demands laws of history arguing that historical explanations need not appeal to laws when they are based on "extremely reliable knowledge of behavior despite its being usually too well known to be worth mentioning and too complex to permit any precise formulation." Scientific laws are neither more accurate nor more useful in historical explanations than these truisms.

Suppe, F. (Ed.) *The structure of scientific theories.* (E17)

Turner, M. B. *Philosophy and the science of behavior.* (E19)

Wallace, W. A. *Causality and scientific explanation.* (B101)

E102 Weber, M. *The methodology of the social sciences.* Trans. & ed. E. A. Shils & H. A. Finch. Glencoe, Ill.: Free Press, 1949. (1904-1917)

A collection of essays written between 1903 and 1917 and concerned with a variety of problems very much relevant to present considerations. The problems of causation and explanation in the methodology of the social sciences are central themes. Defense of objectivity in one's approach is persuasively presented.

Winch, P. *The idea of a social science.* (D137)

E103 Wright, G. H. v. *Explanation and understanding.* Ithaca, N.Y.: Cornell University Press, 1971.

The distinction between understanding and explanation is clarified.